D0955716

Catastrophic
Care

Catastrophic
Care

How American Health Care
Killed My Father—
and How We Can Fix It

DAVID GOLDHILL

ALFRED A. KNOPF   New York   2013

THIS IS A BORZOI BOOK
PUBLISHED BY ALFRED A. KNOPF

www.aaknopf.com

Knopf, Borzoi Books, and the colophon are registered trademarks of Random House, Inc.

Grateful acknowledgment is made to Chris Rock for permission to reprint an excerpt from *Chris Rock: Never Scared* (HBO Films, 2004). Reprinted by permission of the artist.

Library of Congress Cataloging-in-Publication Data
Goldhill, David.
    Catastrophic care : how American health care killed my father—and how we can fix it / David Goldhill.
        pages   cm
      ISBN 978-0-307-96154-9 (hardback)
    1. Medical care, Cost of—United States.   2. Health insurance—United States.   3. Health services accessibility—United States.   4. Medical errors—United States.   I. Title.
RA410.53.G655 2013   362.1′042580681—dc23   2012028745

Jacket photograph: Alamy Creativity/Alamy
Jacket design by Chip Kidd

Manufactured in the United States of America
First Edition

In memory of my father, the doctor

Contents

Catastrophic Care

Introduction

How American Health Care
Killed My Father

B ecky is a twenty-six-year-old who's worked in my company's marketing department for three years. It's her
first job out of school, and she's done very well. She's smart,
ambitious, and poised, and her future is promising.

Becky describes herself as a "bit hypochondriacal," so she
sees two primary care physicians a year. But she's generally
healthy and has no major health care needs. With the insurance plan she's chosen, she can see any doctor she wants,
but the annual deductible doubles, from $250 to $500, when
she goes out of network. Most of the treatments she uses
count as preventive care, which now has no cost sharing. So
with her share of the company's insurance premiums and
her out-of-pocket expenses, health care will cost Becky just
about $2,500 a year. That may be a bit more than she would
like, but all things considered, it's not terrible for someone
just starting out, right?

Wrong.

Becky will actually contribute over $10,000 to America's health care system this year—most of it through payments she's not aware of. That's right: health care will consume just under a quarter of Becky's true compensation, not the 7 percent she believes. I'll be providing a detailed breakdown of these additional—I call them deliberately disguised—costs in chapter 2. For now, what you urgently need to understand is that beginning on the first day of her working career, the cost of health care will be the major constraint on Becky's standard of living matching—much less, surpassing—that of her parents.

And it will only get worse for Becky as she settles down and starts a family. Because, as I'll show you, even if we somehow eliminate the explosive growth in health care costs—literally reduce growth to zero—our current system already ensures that Becky will pay well more than $1.2 million into it over her lifetime. If Becky's hoping the new Affordable Care Act will somehow reduce her cost, then she's unaware that the administration's own projections show per capita health costs rising by 5 percent per year over the next ten years (which would mean her lifetime contribution to the system will be $1.8 million, even assuming that after those ten years health costs don't grow at all). All this assumes she never has a major illness, in which case she will almost certainly pay much more.

None of this is on Becky's radar screen today. Although she's probably spending more this year on health care than on anything else (except maybe big-city apartment rent), and while she describes herself as a "true bargain shopper," Becky has no awareness at all of what health care is really costing her. She thinks about her health care benefits, not about her health care costs.

Becky hopes to be successful, perhaps someday earning "several hundred thousand" a year. That would put her in the top 1 percent of earners in America. When I ask her how much she would need over her lifetime to pay for health care, she mentions the possibility of dealing with cancer or other major issues and says "millions." There is "no way" she could afford to pay for her care on her own. But then I ask her how a society can afford health care for anyone if even people in the top 1 percent don't have the resources to cover their care. Where would the money come from? She's a bit embarrassed: "I'm sorry, that doesn't make any sense. I haven't really given this any thought." I assure her there's no reason to be embarrassed: almost no one seems to have given this much thought.*

I started thinking about health care because of a personal tragedy: almost five years ago, my father died from a hospital-borne infection he acquired in the intensive care unit of a well-regarded New York hospital. Dad had just turned eighty-three and had a variety of the ailments common to men of his age. But he was still working the day he walked into the hospital with pneumonia. Within thirty-six hours, he had developed sepsis. Over the next five weeks in the ICU, a wave of secondary infections, all contracted in the hospital, overwhelmed his defenses and caused him great suffering. But although his death was a deeply personal and unique tragedy for me and my family, my dad was

---

* Becky is a real person; I have changed her name, as I have with every personal story in this book. Rather than use her exact pay for my calculations, I used a typical entry-level salary at my company of $35,000 a year.

merely one of a hundred thousand Americans who died that year as a result of infections picked up in hospitals.

One hundred thousand preventable deaths! That's more than double the annual number of people killed in car crashes, five times the number murdered, twenty 9/11s. Each and every year!

A few weeks after my father's death, *The New Yorker* ran an article by Atul Gawande profiling the efforts of Dr. Peter Pronovost to reduce the incidence of fatal hospital-borne infections. Pronovost's solution? A simple checklist of ICU protocols for physicians and nurses governing hand washing and other basic sterilization procedures. Hospitals implementing Pronovost's checklist achieved almost instantaneous success, reducing deaths from hospital infections by more than half. But many physicians rejected the checklist as an unnecessary and belittling intrusion, and many hospital administrators were reluctant to push this simple improvement on them. Gawande's article chronicled Pronovost's travels around the country as he struggled to persuade hospitals to embrace his reforms.

It was a heroic story, but it was also deeply unsettling. Why did Pronovost need to beg hospitals to adopt an essentially cost-free idea that saved so many lives? In an industry that loudly protests the high cost of liability insurance and the injustice of our tort system, why did a simple and effective technique require such extensive lobbying?

And what about us—the patients? Our nation is quick on the draw to close down an imperfectly assembled theme park ride or a business serving an *E. coli*–infused hamburger. Why do we tolerate the carnage inflicted by our hospitals? The hundred thousand deaths from infections are compounded by a litany of routine mistakes that create preventable blood clots, drug dosage and prescription errors, and any number of other oversights. All this adds up to an estimated two hundred thousand Americans killed each year by medical mistakes. A single fatal accident at a school or even a nightclub will make headlines in your hometown newspaper. How did Americans learn to accept hundreds of thousands of deaths from avoidable medical mistakes as an inevitability of the system?

Keeping Dad company in the hospital for five weeks was an eye-opening experience. While the facility's diagnostic equipment was state of the art, the technology used to record that diagnostic information and track the patient was less sophisticated than the desktop computer at my local Jiffy Lube. And although we heard much about the hospital's efforts to maintain sterility, the patients' trash was picked up only once a day, and often only after overflowing onto the floor. Doctors and nurses discuss the importance of a patient's mind-set to the recovery process, and yet we saw little to no effort to make the hospital room cheerful or even moderately comfortable. And whose needs are served by the bizarre and unpredictable scheduling of hospital shifts, assigning an endless string of new personnel to care for a patient? Why had this supposedly high-quality hospital missed out on the revolution in quality control and customer service that has swept over every other industry in the past two generations?

I'm a businessman and I've never worked in the health care industry. But like the rest of us, I'm also often a patient, and so I can't help noticing that the industry of health care simply doesn't measure up to the standards of other industries in our economy.

Many of us believe that health care is fundamentally different and that applying experiences and standards from the rest of the economy makes no sense in matters of life and death. But health care is an industry. And the persistence of bad practices seems beyond all normal industrial logic. There must be a business reason that this industry, year in and year out, is able to get away with poor customer service, unaffordable prices, and uneven results—and even a business reason that my father and so many others are unnecessarily killed.

Like every grieving family member, I looked for that reason. I wanted some person or some institution to blame for my father's death. But my dad's doctors weren't incompetent—on the contrary, his hospital physicians were smart, thoughtful, and hardworking. Nor is he dead because of indifference on the part of the nursing staff—without exception, his nurses were dedicated and compassionate. There were no financial reasons limiting my father's quality of care; he was a Medicare patient, and the issue of expense never came up. No greedy pharmaceutical companies, evil health insurers, mindless hospital bureaucrats, or other popular villains populated his particular tragedy. So how is it possible that my father's death was an avoidable accident with no one to blame?

Since Dad's death, I've been looking at our health care system for an answer to this very troubling question. I've read as much as I could get my hands on, talked to doctors and patients, asked a lot of questions, and listened much more carefully to my friends' stories of medical care dysfunction. All of this exploration has transformed my thinking about what we can and should expect from our nation's health care system.

I'm a Democrat and once held views about health care

common in my party. But the more I've looked at our system, the more I've come to believe that the obsessions of our political debate—universal access, health insurance regulation, cost control—are irrelevant to the real problems that have created our mess. Despite the partisan screaming, I suspect all Americans have the same goal: high-quality, safe health care that is affordable for all. And yet the frustrating reality is that despite more than sixty years of government efforts—representing the work of both political parties—we are moving further and further away from what we want. Prices are higher, more people are excluded from needed care, more excess treatments are performed, and more people die from preventable errors. Why?

Life on the Island

Over time, I've come to believe that health care is indeed different from other industries, but primarily because we insist on treating it as different. Everything about health care—how we pay for it, how we regulate it, how we judge its effectiveness, how we're willing to accept low standards from it, even how we talk about it—exists on a separate island from the mainland of every other service or product in our economy. Forget the rhetoric: our health care system isn't an example of "socialism" or "profit-driven medicine." In fact, it is such a strange beast that I'm not even sure we have an appropriate label for it. The best analogy might be the Galápagos Islands, set so far offshore from the mainland of industrial evolution and economic laws that it has produced odd, anomalous creatures of policy and regulation. Though these products of convoluted laws and rules manage to thrive on the Island of Health Care, they would not survive on the Mainland, where all other industries are forced to compete for their customers.

Every business would like to get away with high prices, poor quality, and miserable service, but this behavior carries an unacceptable cost: lost customers, lost revenue, lost profits. In health care, bad behavior doesn't produce these bad results; bad behavior is often rewarded with additional revenue, and efficiency is penalized with less. All of the actors in health care want to serve patients well, but understandably most respond rationally to the backward economic incentives baked into the system.

At the heart of these perverse incentives is insurance. Unlike with anything else in the economy, we rely on insurance as the sole means of paying for everything in health care—from the most routine to the most urgent. Even our government health programs take the form of insurance. But not only is insurance the costliest way of financing our spending, it is the most distortive; the insurance model requires that we turn over our role as consumers to what I call the Surrogates: private insurers, Medicare, and Medicaid. As I'll show, their actions—and our own absence as a disciplinary force in the health care marketplace—create many of the incentives for bad behavior.

We are all patients

I first raised these ideas in "How American Health Care Killed My Father," the cover story of the September 2009 issue of *The Atlantic*. At the time, Congress was just beginning its debate on health care reform. In the months that followed, I received countless invitations to do interviews, speak at public events, engage in debates. At industry gatherings, at business groups, even at Harvard Medical School, I found myself publicly jousting with traditional experts— economists and public policy analysts who had spent their careers studying all angles of our complex health policy mess. Although my arguments received a broadly favorable reception, the most accurate description of the article came when it was called "widely praised and completely ignored." Everyone could find something to like. Traditional liberals appreciated my call for true national insurance. Traditional conservatives agreed that sensible economic incentives needed to be the centerpiece of any reform and that Medicare and Medicaid were unsustainable. But the whole of my argument—that we needed to rethink our entire approach, that this emperor had no clothes—had no supporting army in the gathering political war over health care reform.

Among the hundreds of e-mails, letters, and phone calls I received was one from a woman who had also lost her father to a hospital infection: "The hardest thing for me was the indignities this proud and humble man suffered, and the helplessness we felt through it all. When I talk to other families who have had a similar experience, they can still recount each hour in stark detail." Each of the many notes like hers confirmed what my father's death had already seared in me—fixing our health care system is about much more than money and politics. A call for true health care overhaul may have no natural constituency among the interests fighting over health care policy, but it should have an ally in the largest and ultimately the most important interest group: patients. And that includes every single one of us.

Health care is not an abstract policy issue for me, and I suspect it isn't for most families. I worry to the verge of panic when my mother or another relative needs to enter a hospital, even for a routine test. I watch more and more of my employees' compensation eaten up by health expenses and see my middle-aged friends making their professional decisions on the basis of health coverage. I listen to doctors complain that they are becoming glorified insurance clerks.

While the debate has focused on the vulnerability of the uninsured and uncovered, this book will show that our current health care system is also a disaster for the *insured*. It places ever growing burdens on young people and the middle class and impedes our ability to advance our standard of living and to create jobs. Our massive and failing Medicare and Medicaid programs are already unsustainable and unfixable. If you or your loved ones rely on either program for health or financial security, then you're already at risk.

The Affordable Care Act (aka Obamacare)

For all its promise of major reform, the final structure of the Patient Protection and Affordable Care Act of 2010 legislation (which, for simplicity's sake, I'll refer to as the ACA) turned out to be remarkably similar to all the other previously enacted bills: its central thrust is for ever more insurance to pay for health care. As before, additional government aid and rules to expand coverage are accompanied by a raft of complex restrictions, regulations, and pilot programs intended to mitigate the incremental cost. Despite the good intentions of its authors, the ACA is less a reform of our health care system than an extension of its current principles to their logical end.

With the costs of health insurance already a massive, if hidden, burden on American families, the ACA loads more cost onto private insurance. Medicare faces $36 trillion of unfunded liabilities, and yet the ACA has no specific plan for managing this impossible burden. And though spending for Medicaid already consumes a bankrupting 22 percent of state government budgets (just over 14 percent after federal contributions are excluded), the ACA promises a massive expansion of the program. In a system burdened by complexity, bureaucratic explosion, and lack of innovation, the ACA paves the way for even more rules, many of which are merely mandates for future rules and ever more committees and commissions. The problem with the ACA isn't that it represents "government takeover of health care" or "socialism" or even the famous but nonexistent "death panels." The problem with the ACA is that it's so old-fashioned.

Should you ever have the time to read the roughly nine-hundred-page bill, you'll be struck by how sensible it is. The ACA is health reform by technocrats, by those experts who believe that any problem can be fixed by an intelligent rule, a commission, or a subsidy. They have made a truly valiant effort, mandating prospective solutions to an extraordinary range of health care dysfunctions. But though I admire their intentions and ambitions, I contend that they have missed the big picture: the underlying insurance-based structure of our health care system drives excess treatment, cost inflation, and medical errors. It is this structure that needs to be changed. As I will discuss, I suspect that the unintended consequences of the ACA will only further exacerbate these perverse incentives, raising the overall cost of care, reducing access to essential treatment, and undermining the efforts of dedicated professionals to practice effective medicine.*

---

* As I was writing this introduction, my friend Jules woke up one morning with severe chest pain. Conscious of a family history of early and sometimes fatal heart attacks, Jules rushed to the hospital. Within ten minutes, the staff cardiologist

Changing the conversation

If we, the patients, are on the receiving end of such poor care, why do we continue to support only slight variations of the status quo? Fear. Afraid of losing access to health insurance, we continue to support expansion of insurance coverage. Worried about denial of reimbursement for needed procedures, we continue to endorse additional mandates. Concerned about our parents, we continue to oppose any limits on Medicare. Angry about high prices, we continue to favor limits on payments to providers and drug companies and on their spending for "unnecessary" expenses. Terrified of medical errors, we continue to demand ever greater rules constricting the profession. The basic policy approaches still rest on our broad popular approval: this is what we, the people, want.

And yet each and every one of us has at least one health

---

could compare the results of an echocardiogram with previous EKGs transmitted electronically from Jules's regular doctor. Within thirty minutes, the blockage in his right coronary artery had been cleared through angioplasty and a stent put in place to keep the artery open. Numbed only by local anesthesia, he watched the entire procedure—as the surgeons performed it—on a video monitor. Jules felt instantly better the moment he could see blood resume rushing through his artery. Though Jules was kept overnight as a precaution, his severe pain—and the threat to his life—had been effectively eradicated in that brief half hour.

American health care killed my father, but it also saved my friend's life. American health care is full of such achievements, of lives saved or transformed by great doctors and nurses, by innovative devices and drugs, by excellent clinics and hospitals. Our health care industries are heavily populated by altruists, heroes, and even near saints. We are fortunate to have access to superb hospitals dedicated to safety and patient experience, to truly lifesaving drugs and medical devices, to government agencies desperately trying to serve growing caseloads of needy and sick Americans.

But all this good work and these good intentions are undermined by economic incentives, regulatory restrictions, and institutional realities—in other words, by impersonal factors. To say that American health care is damaging to our economy and our health is not to imply that our doctors and nurses or our insurers and hospitals or our pharmaceutical and medical device manufacturers are villains. They are all marooned with us far from the Mainland.

care horror story: interminable waits, incomprehensible bill-ing, inexplicable mistakes, disorganization, lost test results, nonexistent follow-up, even utter incompetence. Many of us are angry about our experiences with health care, but we see the problems as inescapable side effects of an advanced and complex system. Health care is too complicated to get the little things (like us patients) right.

I disagree. We're surrounded by complex things made simple. I don't really understand how this laptop I'm writing on works. Or how a GPS knows where I am when I drive. Or how an ATM handles cash deposits. Or how I can instantly change TV channels beamed to me from a satellite. In each of these examples, some company profited by taking some-thing complex and making it simple for me to use. In health care, no one—including our politicians—profits by making it easier for us.

This book is written from the perspective of patients, or—as we're called off the Island—consumers. I think we can learn a lot about our health care problems by contrast-ing what we see in health care with what we see at Wal-Mart or Starbucks, by comparing health insurance with home-owners' insurance, by keeping in mind our experience with the corner auto mechanic while evaluating a hospital.

Some readers may feel these comparisons trivialize health care, which, after all, deals with matters of life and death, not toothpaste, coffee, or oil changes. But I remind these readers that our current approach frequently fails at these very matters of life and death. As I write this, Medicare has just announced the most recent results of its effort to reduce hospital errors through regulation and financial penalties. The frequency of major errors increased during these years; roughly a quarter of Medicare hospital patients are now victims of a major error. So I ask you to keep an open mind. How can health care benefit from lessons learned in other services?

A better approach

Over the past forty-five years, our health care system has transformed an essential service into what I call the Beast—a creature that has destroyed jobs, reduced incomes, threatened financial security, and diverted massive resources away from other worthwhile endeavors.* The Beast also tolerates—even encourages—excess and careless medicine, causing great physical harm. And despite all the spending, many Americans still have inadequate access to needed care or receive substandard care. On the Island, it is considered normal to quote health care waste estimates of $600 billion a year, or 25 percent of spending. Think of the good that could come from spending that wasted $600 billion on almost anything other than health care.

I believe that my father's death and the health care expense mountain that Becky must climb have the same fundamental underlying cause: the use of the insurance model to fund all health care expenses. This view is at odds with much conventional thinking in health care—that we must expand insurance to deal with high care costs, that only insurers have enough market power to discipline rising prices, that insurers' vested interest in our health can drive

---

* One could argue that the transformation of our health care system into its current form began when employer-provided insurance was afforded the tax advantages that allowed it to crowd out other forms of funding, but for simplicity throughout the book I'll be referring to our current system as forty-five years old, a slight rounding down of the time since 1966, when Medicare and Medicaid first took effect.

greater safety and quality. In the following chapters, I will show not only why this conventional wisdom is wrong but how, like with Becky's hidden health care charges, it prevents us from seeing what is really going on in health care.

Blaming incentives is far less dramatic than discovering a villain, but thinking in systemic terms is the only way to understand—and fix—an industry as multifaceted and complex as our nation's health care. And I believe this is exactly what we need: a full-scale intervention. We must dismantle the perverse incentives embedded in every layer of our system and force health care off its Island and back to the Mainland. Until we do, clever fixes and passionate political debates will offer only superficial solutions, the equivalent of rearranging deck chairs on our own health care *Titanic.*

This book will approach the issue from a very different perspective from those of the experts who guide much of our health care policy. On the Island, health care (as opposed to health, something quite different) is a good above all others, and providing as much of it as possible is the ultimate objective of public policy. On the Island, the problems of health care are complex because, well, health care itself is and must be complex. And most strangely, on the Island, our society needs ever more money to spend on health care because we are somehow getting sicker (despite all evidence to the contrary) or older (despite this in itself being a measure of improved health) or more dependent on technology (despite technology's cost savings in all other sectors).*

---

* What's more, Island residents often fail to acknowledge that the original construction of our health care system was predicated on assumptions that are no longer true. Certainly, there remains a need to protect all families from the burden of medical catastrophe. But our need for care is no longer only rare, urgent, and the result of bad luck. Health care is a constant presence in our lives, beginning

I believe this is nonsense. We've spent five decades under-mining all proper economic functioning in health care and are now at a loss for what to do about our dysfunctional health care system. We need to require of health care what we do of any consumer industry, but to achieve these goals, we have to stop believing that health care is so special that the normal economic rules don't apply.

I believe that true solutions to the problem are at hand. Liberals have long argued for comprehensive national health insurance, with conservatives pushing for more market-oriented approaches to health care. I believe we need *both* if we are ever going to address today's extreme dysfunc-tion. Society does demand a health care safety net—and it's certainly reasonable, considering that massive health care costs can be imposed on any unlucky individual from birth. But as I'll show, insuring everyone isn't the same as insur-ing everything. We should have a national cradle-to-grave safety net, but one that covers only truly insurable events: health crises that are major, rare, and unpredictable.

At the same time, we need to recognize that the health care system won't function properly—indeed, will continue to be downright dangerous—unless it is accountable to actual consumers. And the only way to increase consumers' role is to shift many of the enormous resources now pass-

---

with our highly medicalized process of birth and leading all the way up to our even more medicalized process of death. Our weight is a medical issue. Our daily physical activity is a medical issue. Our moods are a medical issue. And as the technology of care advances, care itself becomes ever more individual and more complex. My heart condition is truly different from your heart condition. Yet for the purpose of health care policy, our assumptions remain embedded in the reali-ties of the last century, with a centralized, highly bureaucratic, one-size-fits-all straitjacket around the most dynamic, individual, and now most widely used ser-vice in our economy.

ing through insurance and government programs back to us. We will need to confine insurance to what it does efficiently (protect us against catastrophe) and remove it from what it does disastrously (serve as the payment system for all care). Only then will we align health care incentives with our interests.

The government, too, should be radically recast in a new role—not necessarily bigger or smaller, but truly different. I believe a sustainable health care system requires a simplified but expanded role for government in protecting all Americans from health catastrophe. So this book calls for a national health insurance program that covers all Americans from cradle to grave, but one that is limited to true health catastrophes. Then we need to get the government out of the business of directly purchasing care so it can be an unconflicted advocate for patient-consumers: promoting transparency and competition, driving the collection and dissemination of data, and punishing (rather than funding) those who practice unsafe care.

Over the past forty-five years, Americans have been made utterly dependent on the current system, so it may require a generation to complete health care's transition to a more sensible and sustainable economic structure. But as I'll demonstrate in the following chapters, we can today make fundamental changes that will have large and immediate impacts in changing the performance of our system. With all the focus on politics and public policy, some of the necessary changes are in fact already occurring at the fringes of our system—as the burden of our current system forces consumers, employers, and providers to explore new treatment and business models. Achieving a truly reformed health care system will be hard—maybe even politically impossible today—but at some point soon it will be inevitable. Inevitable because of the system's unsustainable cost to Becky. And inevitable because of what happened to my father and threatens so many of us.

CHAPTER 1

Island-Speak

Eleven strange things we all believe
about health care

1. "Cost" instead of "price"

In the spring of 2008, gasoline prices shot up, increasing
from a national average of $2.95 a gallon to $4.05 in just five
months. Consumers were up in arms; polls showed that
71 percent of Americans believed high gas prices were causing them financial hardship. And no wonder: higher prices
meant the average American household would spend $1,200
more that year on gasoline.

In the same year, health care costs grew by roughly the
same amount: $1,110 per American household. In fact, health
care costs per household had grown by similar amounts in
the two previous years: $940 in 2007 and $990 in 2006.

Why do we get so incensed over increases in gas prices
yet remain so accepting of even greater increases in health
care costs?

One explanation can be found in the language we use to discuss health care. Notice how we always talk about gas "prices" but health care "costs"? How often do you hear someone talk about health care "prices"? I suspect the reason for this is that with gasoline—as with every other product and service—we believe there's an actual someone setting an actual price. We blame OPEC, or the major oil companies, or even our local service station, posting its prices on a big sign.

But in health care, our language reflects a different understanding of reality. We seem to accept what we pay as an inevitability, as something somehow generated outside the business decisions that drive health care. Health care seems too complex to have prices in the sense that other industries do. Interestingly, only in pharmaceuticals— where the large drug companies are visible actors—do we talk about "prices."

Our language also reflects wishful thinking. For many of us, it feels somehow inappropriate for health care to come at a "price." It's uncomfortable to think of our beloved family doctor setting a price for her services or of the local hospital charging a price for emergency care. Much more comforting to think of health care "costs" somehow imposed on these trusted servants by the system itself.

But of course, all health care costs are merely prices. Every bill for every appointment, test, and procedure ulti- mately reflects the price of someone's labor (salary, wages, etc.) or of someone's capital (interest, dividends, etc.). As with every other human activity, there are no costs indepen- dent of these prices.

The distinction isn't just a linguistic one—with "cost" serving as a polite synonym for "price." Calling costs "prices" would recognize that they are in fact the industry's active and calculated responses to incentives created by us.

On the Mainland, prices are signals that drive the allocation of resources, encourage innovation and competition, and force efficiency. But because we don't acknowledge their existence in health care, prices have a hard time doing their job. On the Island, no one refers to health care costs as invaluable market signals; instead, costs are cited as problems in need of regulation and better management.

So language does matter. Island-speak—like confusing "cost" and "price"—is what prevents us from seeing the health care mess clearly and from considering solutions that will bring the health care system back to the Mainland.

2. Health care isn't health

"Money is honey," my grandmother used to tell me, "but health is wealth." She said "health," not "health care." When we listen to debates over health care reform, it is often difficult to remember that there is a difference.*

Health care is merely one component of our overall health. There's no question medical advances have extended life spans and improved quality of life. But nutrition, exercise, education, emotional security, our environment, and public safety are now—and have always been—more important than care in determining the length and quality of our lives. Over the past thirty years, our spending on health care

---

* A recent column by the economist Alan Blinder exemplifies this confusion between health and health care. He writes: "Beyond the economics, our country was founded on the idea that the rights to life, liberty and the pursuit of happiness are inalienable. Access to affordable health care is surely essential to two of these three rights, maybe to all three" ("Life, Liberty and the Pursuit of Insurance," *Wall Street Journal*, April 19, 2012).

has grown from 6 percent to almost 18 percent of our gross domestic product. The average life span during this time has increased by roughly five years. It's impossible to directly measure how much of this increase can be attributed to more spending on health care, but many studies suggest it's not much. The Centers for Disease Control and Prevention shows death rates consistently declining over the past seventy-five years, by 60 percent in age-adjusted terms. In the past half century, the single greatest contributor to the increased longevity of Americans has been a decline in early cardiovascular deaths. A 2007 study published in *The New England Journal of Medicine* estimated that approximately half of the recent decrease in deaths related to coronary vascular disease was attributable to lifestyle changes (reduced smoking, better diet, more exercise) and that expensive treatments like angioplasty and heart bypasses accounted for only 7 percent of lives saved. Almost half of all deaths in the United States each year are caused by heart disease, diabetes, lung cancer, homicide, suicide, and accidents—all of which are influenced as much by environment and lifestyle choices as by health care.

Health is about probabilities, not certainties; health care, at its best, is about efforts to influence those probabilities to our benefit. We've all heard of that two-pack-a-day smoker still going strong in her nineties and that fitness fanatic who suddenly dropped dead at forty. But exercise is far more likely to increase your life span, and smoking to reduce it. And both are far more likely to determine your health than health care.

Imagine two neighboring counties. One fights an increasing number of fires by hiring more firemen, buying more trucks, and installing more hydrants. The other county also has a fire department but spends more of its resources on enforcing the fire-safety provisions of building codes, installing sprinklers, retrofitting with flame-retardant materials, guarding against gas leaks, and clearing brush regularly. The first county's approach is to maximize its response once fires have been detected. The second has a strategy to reduce the number of fires that actually occur. When you look at the $2.5 trillion we now spend on health care—and the smaller amounts we spend on all the other things that could proactively improve our health rather than treat diseases after their onset—which county does the United States most resemble?

There are many unknowns in health care, but if we better appreciated its real limitations, would we still be willing to spend $2.5 trillion a year on it? By what mechanism does society determine that an extra, say, $100 billion for health care will make us healthier than would $10 billion for cleaner air or water, or $25 billion for better nutrition, or $5 billion for parks, or $10 billion for recreation, or $50 billion in additional vacation time—or all of those alternatives combined?

The answer: by no mechanism at all. The factors that most predict your health are your wealth, education, and lifestyle—not your access to health care.* These personal

---

* A recent study by the University of Wisconsin's Population Health Institute found a growing link between college education and longevity. A lack of a college education was found to explain almost 35 percent of the variation in premature deaths (*County Health Rankings and Roadmaps*, 2012).

and societal investments are the real "preventive" care, yet they are buried under our growing demand for tests and procedures.

Many of us would consider our own health and that of our loved ones to be our most precious possession, to be protected at any cost; this very human commitment has driven our society's willingness to expand resources devoted to care. But as we increasingly talk about health care and health as interchangeable concepts, we risk making health care more important than health itself.

3. Health insurance isn't health care

How often have you heard a politician say that 15 percent of Americans "have no health care," when what she means is that they have no health insurance? How has a method of financing health care become synonymous with health care itself?

The notion of comprehensive health insurance is so ingrained in our cultural conversation that we forget it's a relatively recent concept. Private group insurance was introduced in 1929, and employer-based insurance began to blossom only during World War II, when wage freezes prompted employers to introduce other benefits as a way of attracting workers.

As late as 1954, only a minority of Americans had health insurance. That's when Congress codified tax rulings that employer contributions to employee health plans were tax deductible without the resulting benefits being taxable to employees. Not only did this seemingly minor tax benefit encourage the spread of traditional catastrophic insurance, it had the unintentional effect of making employer-funded health insurance the lowest-cost way of financing any type of health care. Over time, employer-based comprehensive insurance crowded out alternative methods of paying for health care expenses until it became the default mechanism for most employed Americans. In 1965, when the government was designing Medicare and Medicaid, it essentially replicated this same comprehensive-insurance model for its own spending, spreading the insurance net to an additional 15 percent of the population. In short, a minor tax benefit passed more than half a century ago is the source of all of our cultural assumptions surrounding health care.

Of course, the United States is not alone. Germany enacted the first national health insurance program in 1883, and for decades insurance remained a sensible model for paying for health care. When these early programs were designed, health care resembled other insurable occurrences. Most families saw a doctor only in cases of extreme emergency. Even as late as 1965, roughly a third of Americans did not see a doctor each year.

We've become so accustomed to our setup that we no longer recognize how unusual it is. On the Mainland, we would never attempt to pay for tune-ups with our auto insurance policy or for a paint job with our homeowners' insurance. But on the Island, we all assume that our regular checkups and dental cleanings will be covered at least partially by insurance. Most pregnancies are planned, and deliveries are predictable many months in advance, yet they're financed the same way we finance fixing a car after a wreck—through an insurance claim. For all of life's other necessities—shelter, food, clothing, and education—we accept that a variety of funding mechanisms are appropriate. Not with health care.

Anything we spend out of our own pockets is considered an inadequacy of our insurance plan.

Although health care began to be conceived as an insurable risk more than a hundred years ago, the conflating of health care and health insurance is a more recent trend. To many on the Island, being insured equals having access to essential health care; being uninsured means having no access to care at all. Both these views are inaccurate, yet they drove the recent health care reform debate. The ACA is fundamentally a health insurance bill, not a real piece of health care reform legislation, focusing as it does on the wrapper of insurance rather than on the complex and dysfunctional system inside.

And again, language matters. Equating health insurance with health care removes from consideration the most radical concept in real reform—the idea that the broad variety of health care goods and services shouldn't be funded by a single mechanism over our entire lives. This idea sentences all of us to the highest possible cost of funding our health care, and the weakest control over quality and safety.

4. *Health insurance isn't really insurance*

We call it health insurance and think of it as a type of insurance, but in reality health insurance has little in common with traditional insurance and provides few of its benefits.

Remember what insurance is supposed to do—spread the cost of a loss among a group of people who each face a risk of that loss. Let's look at a simplified example: say there are a hundred of us who each own a house, and there's a one-in-a-hundred chance that a fire would destroy one of our houses. Let's say each house is worth $50,000. We could all go without insurance, letting the unfortunate person whose house actually burned down bear the whole $50,000 cost. But none of us want to take that chance—none of us want to be the person who loses $50,000. So Enterprising Company forms an insurance pool of the hundred of us. Each of us pays a premium of roughly $500 (the $50,000 loss multiplied by the 1 percent chance of a fire), and whoever has the house that burns down will get reimbursed by said Enterprising Company. For $500, we each avoid ever having to lose $50,000 on a fire.

Now, of course, we would each pay a bit more than $500 in premiums to cover the cost of organizing the insurance pool, signing everyone up, and making sure that other pool members were telling the truth when filing claims. And Enterprising Company will want some profit for its effort. All of that adds up to a little extra expense to share the risk. But even if the premium is $525 or $550, most of us would still rather pay it than risk being out $50,000.

This type of insurance offers an important form of risk sharing for almost every economic activity. But with health insurance today, the idea of bearing a small premium and a little extra expense to avoid the possibility of a major loss is turned upside down. In our current health insurance model, we all pay a large premium and bear a lot of extra expense to fund the *certainty* of a major loss.

Health insurance doesn't really pool risk efficiently because using the health care system isn't a risk—it's an inevitability for all of us. (Try to imagine what the market for homeowners' insurance would look like if all of the hundred people in the risk pool will have their homes burn down.) The most we can say about the risk-sharing aspect of health insurance is that it shifts resources based on timing.* Those of us not having major health problems this year fund care for those who are. For reasons I will discuss later in the book, insurance is a terrible mechanism for accomplishing even this limited goal.

What about life insurance? Doesn't that—like health insurance—also insure against certainty? Not really: life insurance protects against the possibility of dying early, not of dying at all. Since every policyholder is going to die, life insurance policies pay out a fixed amount—a "defined benefit" that exceeds an insured's contributions only if he dies prematurely. This also means that, unlike health care, a claim doesn't involve expensive review or adjustment—essential to keeping costs down when every policyholder will be a claimant.

If health insurance isn't real insurance, then what is it? Fundamentally, it's the payment mechanism for health care. Health insurers are essentially giant intermediaries between consumers and the health care system, negotiating charges, checking bills, assuring payment—basically shifting money

---

* Of course, having health insurance is essential for handling the truly catastrophic, but this role pales in health relative to other insured activities. A recent article described the tragic history of Scott Crawford, who died in 2009 after a series of devastating health problems. Medicare spent $2.1 million on Mr. Crawford's care in 2009, making him one of their five costliest patients in the country. That amount—$2.1 million—is certainly a lot of money, well beyond the means of any but a few Americans. Mr. Crawford's situation was a clear example of the need for catastrophic insurance. But remember Becky will put $1.2 million into our system over her lifetime, almost all of it in the form of premiums for private insurance or government insurance programs. What kind of insurance system needs $1.2 million in contributions from everyone when the most catastrophic imaginable risk costs $2.1 million? One that spends most of its money on managing noncatastrophic claims and associated administrative expenses (Janet Adamy and Tom McGinty, "The Crushing Cost of Care," *Wall Street Journal,* July 6, 2012).

around from consumers and taxpayers to providers. They perform this function at an almost inconceivable level of complexity and expense.

U.S. health insurance companies employ over half a million workers. That's one worker for every two doctors. The administrative cost of managing our system of health care payments alone is almost $1,000 a year per American household.* So for most Americans, their annual share of this administrative cost exceeds the amount of actual health care they use in a typical year.

These numbers don't include all the time, effort, and money spent by patients, doctors, human resources departments, and others on health insurance's paperwork requirements. It is this administrative cost—not any actual risk sharing—that fundamentally characterizes health insurance. Yet our very use of the word "insurance" prevents us from seeing this system for what it really is.

5. Procedures aren't necessarily good care

If one broader implication of the insurance model is the complex and costly system of paying for care, another is far more important to our health—what is often called treatment bias. Health insurance is designed to pay for tangible

---

* For 2010, the data on national health expenditures from the Centers for Medicare and Medicaid Services shows administrative costs of $170 billion for the insurance system; over $100 billion of this was for private insurance (roughly $1,000 per covered person), and Medicare and Medicaid accounted for approximately $30 billion each. This figure does not include all the expenses borne by providers in managing their side of the payment arrangements with insurers. A study by Dante Morra and others published in *Health Affairs* in August 2011 estimated this cost at $82,975 per physician per year (or roughly $40 billion). In his 2012 book *Inside National Health Reform,* John McDonough quotes an estimate of 14 percent of a practice's revenue going to the claims-management process.

products and services such as tests, procedures, pills, and surgeries; it hates paying for time. So as insurance has taken over the payment of health care, those providers in the business of selling quality time with patients (general practitioners, pediatricians, geriatricians) have lost out to those who are in the business of selling procedures (specialists, surgeons, device manufacturers, pharmaceutical companies). The whole health care system has a bias toward performing procedures, which I'll discuss later at greater length. And performing procedures is not necessarily the same thing as providing care.

We're tempted to believe that this shift was inevitable, a result of technological improvements in medicine. But it's really about language—we've come to equate health care with these treatments and procedures. At the end of the day, the family doctor who has the time to recommend a broad range of lifestyle changes and medical approaches to address your risk of heart disease—and has the time to oversee your progress—is practicing more sophisticated medicine than the one who merely prescribes you drugs. But our priorities become clear when you look at what we're willing to pay for. Although we'll happily reimburse both doctors for the EKGs they perform and the pills they prescribe, we won't reimburse the first doctor for the extra ten minutes he spends with you, the phone calls he makes to follow up, or his responses to your e-mails.

If you've been to a doctor in the past decade, you know something our politicians apparently don't: the explosion in spending on health care has not necessarily led to an improvement in health care. It's led to an explosion in treatments, in billable procedures. Somehow, we're buying a lot more care, yet we're receiving ever less quality time with physicians. Not surprisingly, we're facing shortages of generalist doctors (as chapter 7 will cover in greater detail); medical students long ago learned that the best economic model was to practice a procedure-based specialty.

We patients have mostly bought into this model, demanding useless antibiotics for viral infections, tests to rule out improbable diagnoses, surgical solutions to lifestyle issues. As I'll discuss in chapter 5, perhaps the greatest victims of treatment bias are our seniors. Many of the conditions of senior years—loss of energy, declining motor skills, memory impairment, depression—are related. Yet Medicare is set up to pay for specific procedures aimed at a specific diagnosis. So seniors get an extraordinary number of treatments from specialists working independently of one another. Meanwhile, the number of geriatricians—doctors who are trained to deal with these interrelated problems of old age—has now declined to only seventy-two hundred for the whole country! That's one geriatrician for every fifty-four hundred seniors. All this is a direct result of the way our system prioritizes health procedures over health care, which is itself a result of our use of insurance to pay for everything.*

6. *Technology: The well-known "inflator"*

Today, I withdrew cash at an ATM and paid bills online, saving myself considerable time by not having to stand in line at the bank, as well as the expense of envelopes, stamps, and gas to get to the post office. I called my wife, who was

---

* Perhaps it isn't inevitable that an insurance-based approach preferences procedures over physician time, but a reform that allows doctors to charge based on the time they believe they should spend with individual patients would almost certainly encourage abuse and significantly increase the cost of claims oversight (see the discussion of moral hazard in chapter 3).

visiting her parents in rural Russia, for five cents a minute. I used a free application on my phone to find a good Italian restaurant, reserve a table, and provide me with a map and directions to get there. At work, I participated in a four-city video conference (the total cost for the hour was $50—significantly cheaper than flying everyone to one location). I microwaved some leftovers in an oven that cost less than a tank of gas. I watched a movie on my $49 DVD player and a baseball game in high definition on a large-screen TV that I bought this year for a third of what I paid for one of the same size five years ago. I finished my day sitting down to write this chapter on a $1,200 laptop that has two thousand times the processing power of the first desktop computer I bought—for three times the price—in 1989.

I did something else today: I read yet another article explaining that technology is driving up the cost of health care and will continue to do so for a long time.

What?

How is it possible that technology has made easier and cheaper almost every aspect of our everyday lives, yet on the Island, we all simply accept the conventional wisdom that high-tech medicine is driving high prices?

Almost ten years ago, my wife needed a brain MRI. At the time, we lacked insurance, so we were charged $1,200. Incredible: $1,200 for fifteen minutes' use of a technology that was already twenty years old and required only a little electricity and a little labor from a single technician!

By contrast, consider LASIK surgery. It is seldom covered by insurance and exists in the competitive economy more typical of the Mainland. So people who get LASIK surgery—or, for that matter, most cosmetic surgeries, den-

tal procedures, or other typically uninsured treatments—
act like consumers. If you do an Internet search, you can
find LASIK procedures quoted as low as $299 per eye—a
price decline of roughly 90 percent since the procedure was
first commercialized in the early 1990s. You'll also find sites
where doctors advertise their own higher-priced surgeries
(which usually cost about $1,500 per eye) and warn of the
dangers of discount LASIK. Many ads publicize the quality
of equipment being used, as well as the performance record
of the doctor, in addition to price. In other words, from
day one we've had an active, competitive market for LASIK
surgery of the sort we're used to seeing for other goods and
services.

The history of LASIK surgery fits well with the pattern
of all capital-intensive services outside the health insurance
economy. If you're one of the first ophthalmologists in your
community to perform the procedure, you can charge a
high price. But once you've acquired the machine, the actual
cost of performing a single procedure (to economists, the
marginal cost) is relatively low. So as additional ophthalmologists in the area invest in LASIK equipment, you, the
first provider, are forced to meet the new competition by
cutting your price. In a fully competitive marketplace, the
price of the procedure will decline toward that low marginal
cost; the declining price of the service will in turn pressure
equipment manufacturers to lower their price tags.

Keep in mind that no business likes to compete solely
on price, so most technology providers seek to add features
and performance improvements to new generations of a
machine—anything to keep their product from becoming
a mere commodity. In most consumer industries, we can
see this in action: observe how DVD players have gone, in

a matter of only a few years, from high-priced luxuries to disposable boxes sold in every discount store. At this point, the DVD player market is mature, and manufacturers have run out of new features for which customers will pay premium prices. Even those products that are continuously being updated—such as PCs—still suffer price declines. New features can only slow, not stop, the natural tendency of competition to drive down technology prices. That now seems to be finally happening to MRIs, too. After a long run of high and stable prices, you can now find ads for discount MRIs.

Because of the peculiar way we pay for health care, this downward price pressure on technology operates less vigorously on the Island. But technology itself isn't to blame for rising costs in health care. Instead, as I'll discuss in a later chapter, the cause is the unusual lack of consumer price discipline in our system, which allows the manufacturers of high-tech medical equipment—and the medical institutions that charge us for these services—to avoid the normal competitive pressures on technology prices.

7. "Nonprofit" hospitals

For some people, the very idea of making a profit in health care seems wrong. In their view, the search for profit distorts decisions that should be made in the best interests of patients. Even those of us comfortable with the profit motive are often squeamish about a life-and-death decision being influenced by profit considerations.

But in practice what would eliminating profits mean? In addition to converting all hospitals to nonprofits, would we regulate the profits—also known as incomes—of doctors, nurses, and hospital administrators; control the profits of drug companies and device manufacturers; regulate the prices of outside clinics providing diagnostic services? How far should we go with this approach? Do you regulate the prices of vendors who provide paper goods to a hospital, pick up its trash, or prepare its food?

Today, there are 2,923 nonprofit hospitals in the United States, accounting for 68 percent of all hospital beds. The very existence of nonprofits in an industry is unusual: outside of education, health care is one of the few industries in which nonprofits and for-profits provide similar services, often in competition with one another.

There's little evidence that the absence of a profit motive leads nonprofit hospitals to behave any differently from their for-profit counterparts. An IRS survey of some three hundred nonprofit hospitals showed that almost 60 percent provided charity care equal to less than 5 percent of their total revenue, and about 20 percent provided less than 2 percent. The fifty largest nonprofit hospitals or hospital systems made a combined net income (that is, profit) of $4.27 billion in 2006, eight times their profits five years earlier.

Almost all the components of nonprofit hospitals are identical to those of for-profits. Both pay the same for the services of their doctors and nurses and compete for their other employees in the same local wage markets. Nonprofits generally get no discounts on equipment, supplies, or utilities. If a nonprofit maintains adequate financial reserves (comparable to the shareholders' equity of for-profits), it can borrow at similar interest rates to expand or to purchase or upgrade equipment. Nonprofits need similar administrative resources to deal with insurers and the Medicare and Medicaid bureaucracies. They even engage in mergers and acquisitions, just like for-profits.*

In other words, the nonprofit motive is producing identical results to the profit motive; the real problem is that the profit motive isn't succeeding in driving good results in health care, because it is responding to administered incentives, not market imperatives. Understand that the social function of profit is not to make people rich; it is to send signals to the marketplace—signals as to shortages, surpluses, and the need for innovation. In other industries, we rely on the profit motive to regulate supply, improve quality, and drive down costs and prices. Those objectives are certainly not achieved in our health care system today, and for-profits and nonprofits are failing equally to achieve them. Again, it's health care's distorted incentives that explain why the profit motive—and for that matter, the nonprofit motive—is producing bad results.

8. *"This is not a bill"*

As every service business knows, the bill is a crucial tool for retaining customers. At its most basic, a bill demonstrates that a service has been completed and that payment is due. But it also provides a way to make known to customers key characteristics of your business: your professionalism and reliability, your attention to the needs of customers, even

* And they pay their CEOs like for-profits. A September 29, 2011, story from Kaiser Health News reported that three CEOs of nonprofit children's hospitals earned more than $5 million each in 2009, and it quoted a report by a nonprofit hospital advocacy group warning that when it came to CEO compensation, "many nonprofit organizations have been pressing their luck by imitating patterns in the for-profit sector."

your fairness and affordability. In some cases, a bill communicates friendliness or a personal touch (as when a waiter adds a thank-you). Even my plumber's handwritten bill on notebook paper conveys an important message: "I'm not a big business, but just a guy working on his own."

Recently, one of my relatives got the following from an insurer for a five-day hospital stay:

 **Empire** BlueCross BlueShield

Explanation of Benefits
THIS IS NOT A BILL
RETAIN THIS COPY FOR YOUR ▉▉▉▉▉

 PPO

Services provided by Empire HealthChoice Assurance, Inc.,
a licensee of the Blue Cross and Blue Shield Association,
an association of independent Blue Cross and Blue Shield Plans.

Page 1 of 4

Statement Date: 10/21/10	Have Questions? Visit *www.empireblue.com* or call Member Services at **(800) 433-9592** Monday – Friday, 8:30 a.m. – 5:00 p.m.
Member Name: ▉▉▉▉	
Member ID Number: ▉▉▉▉	Empire HealthChoice Assurance, Inc.
Total Number of Claims: 01	PO Box 1407 Church Street Station
Claim Number(s): 02949222680	New York, NY 10008-1407

Patient: ▉▉▉▉	Provider Name: ▉▉▉▉
Claim Number: 02949222680	Provider Address: ▉▉▉▉
Date Claim Received: 10/21/10	NEW YORK NY 10087
	212-434-2000

DATES OF SERVICE	SERVICE	AMOUNT CHARGED BY PROVIDER	DISCOUNT AMOUNT	YOUR RESPONSIBILITY				PAYABLE BY EMPIRE	NOTES
				CHARGES NOT COVERED	DEDUCT-IBLE	COINSUR-ANCE	COPAY-MENT		
09/22/10-09/23/10	SEMI-PRIVATE ROOM	5,161.40	0.00	4,061.40	300.00	0.00	0.00	800.00	1, 2
09/24/10-09/25/10	SEMI-PRIVATE ROOM	23,180.00	0.00	23,180.00	0.00	0.00	0.00	0.00	2
09/26/10-09/27/10	INTENSIVE CARE	23,180.00	0.00	23,180.00	0.00	0.00	0.00	0.00	2
09/22/10-09/22/10	OPERATING ROOM SERV	7,370.06	0.00	7,370.06	0.00	0.00	0.00	0.00	2
09/22/10-09/22/10	EMERGENCY ROOM	1,357.00	0.00	1,357.00	0.00	0.00	0.00	0.00	2

Claim Number 02949222680 is continued on the following page.

Payment for the claim(s) in this Explanation of Benefits, if any, has been sent to your provider(s).

Si necesita ayuda en espanol para entender este documento, puede solicitarla sin costo adicional, llamando al numero de servicio al cliente que aparece al dorso de su tarjeta de indentificacion o en el folleto de inscripcion.

Details of Claim(s):

Member Name: ▮▮▮▮▮▮▮   Member ID #: ▮▮▮▮▮▮▮

Have Questions?
Visit our web site at
www.empireblue.com
or call (800) 433-9592.

Patient: Provider Name: ▮▮▮▮▮▮▮

Claim Number: 02949222680   Provider Address: ▮▮▮▮▮▮▮

Date Claim Received: 10/21/10   NEW YORK NY ▮▮▮

Claim Number 02949222680 continued from previous page.

DATES OF SERVICE	SERVICE	AMOUNT CHARGED BY PROVIDER	DISCOUNT AMOUNT	CHARGES NOT COVERED	DEDUCT-IBLE	COINSUR-ANCE	COPAY-MENT	PAYABLE BY EMPIRE	NOTES
09/22/10-09/22/10	RECOVERY ROOM	4,433.52	0.00	4,433.52	0.00	0.00	0.00	0.00	2
09/22/10-09/27/10	CT SCAN	4,320.00	0.00	4,320.00	0.00	0.00	0.00	0.00	2
09/22/10-09/27/10	ANESTHESIA	1,847.98	0.00	1,847.98	0.00	0.00	0.00	0.00	2
09/22/10-09/27/10	INHALATION SERVICE	492.28	0.00	492.28	0.00	0.00	0.00	0.00	2
09/22/10-09/27/10	RADIOLOGY	1,139.16	0.00	1,139.16	0.00	0.00	0.00	0.00	2
09/22/10-09/27/10	LABORATORY	121.14	0.00	121.14	0.00	0.00	0.00	0.00	2
09/22/10-09/27/10	LABORATORY	4,253.46	0.00	4,253.46	0.00	0.00	0.00	0.00	2
09/22/10-09/27/10	LABORATORY	788.20	0.00	788.20	0.00	0.00	0.00	0.00	2
09/22/10-09/27/10	LABORATORY	1,248.00	0.00	1,248.00	0.00	0.00	0.00	0.00	2
09/22/10-09/27/10	LABORATORY	804.10	0.00	804.10	0.00	0.00	0.00	0.00	2
09/22/10-09/27/10	LABORATORY	32.80	0.00	32.80	0.00	0.00	0.00	0.00	2
09/22/10-09/27/10	PATHOLOGY	130.67	0.00	130.67	0.00	0.00	0.00	0.00	2
09/22/10-09/27/10	ELECTROCARDIOGRAM	672.00	0.00	672.00	0.00	0.00	0.00	0.00	2
09/22/10-09/27/10	PHYSICAL THERAPY	461.83	0.00	461.83	0.00	0.00	0.00	0.00	2
09/22/10-09/27/10	SUPPLIES GENERAL	4,363.76	0.00	4,363.76	0.00	0.00	0.00	0.00	2
09/22/10-09/27/10	DRUGS-GENERAL	19,517.33	0.00	19,517.33	0.00	0.00	0.00	0.00	2
09/22/10-09/27/10	DRUGS IV SOLUTIONS	77.50	0.00	77.50	0.00	0.00	0.00	0.00	2
	Total:	**$104,952.19**	**$0.00**	**103,852.19**	**300.00**	**0.00**	**0.00**	**$800.00**	

Your Responsibility:	$104,152.19
Less Other Insurance Payment:*	($103,852.19)
Your Total Responsibility To Your Provider	**$300.00**

Claim Number 02949222680 is continued on the following page.

I have only a slight idea what any of this means (and I used to be a chief financial officer). Is she supposed to pay something, and if so, to whom? The charges seem to be detailed but really have little meaning: there are seven separate charges for "LABORATORY." And look at the numbers: "Your Responsibility" is $104,152.19, but "Your Total Responsibility To Your Provider" is a more manageable $300. And as we all know, this is a statement, not a bill, which really means that more charges related to the same hospital stay, but perhaps generated by providers billing separately, can always come at a later time. The only message being communicated is that my relative is very lucky to be insured, because otherwise the cost would be astronomical (even though the insurer itself has only $800 payable, plus an intentionally vague $103,852.19 "other insurance payment") and too complicated for her to understand.

This incomprehensibility is consistent across health care, from my mother's Medicare and Medicare Plus statements to the form outlining the services rendered during your regular doctor's appointment. Even the late notices seeking overdue payment are unreadable, often using unrecognizable technical terms to refer to the procedures performed.

The health care economy is too big and too rich for all of this to be an accident, so what can we conclude from the incomprehensible language of billing? I believe that the notices and bills sent to us are unreadable because we are not their intended readers. The health care system does not consider us its real customers, which means we can't command the customer service that underlies billing in all other industries.*

---

* The Obama administration is trying to address incomprehensibility. In March 2012, the Centers for Medicare and Medicaid Services introduced a new format for Medicare statements, designed to be more consumer friendly. A pro-

So who are the customers? For your doctor and the other providers you use (hospitals, clinics, testing facilities, etc.), the real customer is your insurer, Medicare, or Medicaid. Everything about the billing process is set up to address their needs, and your role is merely to pay whatever they won't. For insurers, your employer—not you—is the primary customer.

As for us, we are all patients, not customers. We aren't expected to ask questions, negotiate, complain, or even have a viewpoint as to what is and is not reasonable or transparent. As patients, we're expected to pay—just pay.

9. "Effective health care"

To control costs, our policies assume that our Surrogates—insurers, Medicare, and Medicaid—will pay only for "effective" care. Yet the system is widely regarded as having a massive amount of waste and excess. Part of the problem is, again, Island-speak. In one sense, all health care—even that regarded as waste—is effective. In another sense, no health care—even that regarded as essential—is effective. How is this possible? The answer lies in our understanding of the word "effective."

The power of patient psychology and the placebo effect in health care has been well documented, but its impact on our view of health care policy is minimal. Underlying much of our demand for health care is the strange reality that we

posed Department of Health and Human Services rule requires that insurers provide a clear summary of benefits and costs. To ensure that such summaries are comparable, the proposal mandates that the summary must be no longer than four double-sided pages in 12-point type. Unfortunately, such microregulation addresses only the symptom; the underlying reason that insurers provide unreadable statements is not changed by requiring them to provide readable ones.

all feel at least a little better for treatment—any treatment. Of course, an inert drug will not cure a lethal illness, but for some period of time it will make the sufferer feel better. When your child starts sneezing, taking him to the doctor's office and being reassured that it is, in fact, just a cold somehow makes everyone healthier. This beneficial feeling of being cared for—not necessarily being cured—is one of medicine's great contributions to our life and well-being. It's also a major reason we seek so much health care.

But when our politicians talk about "effective" care, they have a different kind of medicine in mind. They visualize health care as providing solutions—either outright cures for illnesses or correct responses to injuries. But although almost all health care is effective in the sense of making us feel cared for, very little of it is effective in the way, say, a repair to your car's engine is effective. With few exceptions, most health care treatments deliver probabilities of being successful; they're likely to cure some of us, improve the condition somewhat for more of us, and be completely ineffective for many, perhaps even most, of us.

Why does this matter? Look at the example of Avastin. In a controversial decision, the Food and Drug Administration recently ruled that the drug was not approved for treatment of advanced (metastatic) breast cancer. Critics of the decision complained that the FDA was looking at the high cost of Avastin—roughly $88,000 for a typical course of treatment—in making its determination. The FDA noted that the median increase in life expectancy was only one month and that such a small increase in survivorship was not worth the drug's extreme side effects: hypertension, hemorrhaging, and bowel perforations. Christi Turnage of Madison, Mississippi, a breast cancer survivor, told the

Associated Press: "It's a miracle drug for me and for several of my friends, and to deny it to women being diagnosed with metastatic disease is wrong." And Fred Upton, a Republican congressman from Michigan, noted that "the FDA is withdrawing its approval of a drug that helps prolong the lives of thousands of women living with aggressive breast cancer."

On the surface, Avastin is a perfect illustration of what seems like one of the most impossible conundrums in health care. Who doesn't think an extra month with their loved one is worth $88,000? On the other hand, how can society ever afford health care if we value each month of everyone's life at $88,000?

But the real problem here isn't one of economics or fairness; it's of language. Like essentially all drugs, Avastin both works and doesn't work. Within that "one month of median survival" statistic is a far more complicated story. A few women may well benefit from Avastin; many don't. And some of those who do benefit don't benefit much. And many of those who don't benefit suffer additionally because of taking the drug. To make matters even more complicated, we don't know why it works for some and not for others. We don't even know if Ms. Turnage benefited from Avastin. She survived, it's true, but a certain percentage of cancer sufferers survive without any treatment at all.

The only honest approach to questions about the effectiveness of Avastin is to try to measure—and communicate—its probabilities of working for a given patient. But honesty is not enough for our system. We demand a simple yes or no— is Avastin effective or not effective? Why do we require a yes-or-no answer about something that is inherently unanswerable? For reimbursement. Our insurance-based system needs to decide if insurers and Medicare should reimburse for the use of Avastin for advanced breast cancer. It's a false choice, yet such a choice lies at the center of almost all health care policy.

Island residents have a lot of confidence in centralized authorities to make these up-or-down, one-size-fits-all determinations. But the issue is too complicated for that approach. If a drug completely cures one patient in a million of a late-stage cancer but leaves the other 999,999 extremely nauseated—and uncured—should it be reimbursed? What if it only costs a dollar a dose? Or $10,000 a dose? What about a drug that increases the life of 10 percent of patients but shortens the life of 10 percent by an equal amount? It may all seem absurd; yet underlying so much of the thinking of our health care policy is that there is a right answer, that we can centrally determine what should be paid for and what shouldn't.

Not only do we each have different physical and psychological reactions to disease and treatment, we also have different preferences as to our personal trade-offs between, for example, pain and increased odds of survival. If we were given more information on the probability of a particular treatment working for a specific disease, as well as on its risks, side effects, and the time required for treatment, we as individuals would almost certainly each make a different and very personal choice. Perhaps society's resources would be better used to uncover, update, and communicate the probabilities that underlie alternative treatments. But our insurance and Medicare structures rest on the faulty assumption that there is a single best choice—that somehow a group of wise men and women can determine what should be paid for and what shouldn't.

The search for those single right (i.e., reimbursable) choices is illusory and restrictive. It prevents us from understanding that—at least at our current level of medical practice—many of the key decisions in health care, from how aggressively to treat cancer to what type of end-of-life care to provide, are fundamentally a matter of personal preference. And it's very hard to manage an insurance-based system around personal preference.

10. Our sacred duty

Two years ago, I sat on a panel moderated by William Cutter, a rabbi who edited a book about the powerful place of health care in Jewish tradition as a form of duty to both God and the community. There is a special place for health care in many ancient religions and cultures, and to this day (remarkably good-looking) heroic doctors and nurses remain a staple of television dramas. We feel an almost visceral obligation to care for the sick among us, to try to save the lives of those desperately ill. Even my most doctrinaire libertarian friends admit they don't want to live in a society that "lets people die in the street."

Our feelings about health care will never—indeed, should never—meet a test of rationality. They are an emotional expression of our concerns for our own mortal selves, for our loved ones, and even for perfect strangers. We honor the healer and feel noble when we care for others. We will never be "rational" consumers of care for ourselves (in fact, we're not rational consumers of anything, but that's been a subject of many other books), nor do we expect others to be. In the section above, I referred to debates over how much an extra month of life is worth. Who can be comfortable making that determination for a stranger with a name and a face, much less for a loved one?

But while our very humanistic commitment to healing may be founded on deep emotions, as a society we must have some balance. Let's remember that truly effective modern medicine is barely a century old. Our cultural—even biblical—reverence of healing dates back to a time when health care couldn't accomplish much of anything. We revered the miraculous. Is this same degree of reverence justified or sensible in an era when health care tries to do everything?

Our attachment to the special value of health care is deep, visceral, emotional, and tied up with complicated feelings about our mortality and that of our loved ones. It underpins our important commitment to provide for the well-being of all in society. But in the age of the Beast, it may also prove to be the undoing of our system of health care. We may speak of health care as a sacred duty, but it cannot actually be one without limits and qualifications, or it will undermine our other treasured values.

11. Health care "benefits"

I just finished reading a very good scholarly analysis of the effects of the ACA by the Harvard professor Joseph New-house. He looks at four groups that together include most Americans and concludes:

> For those who are now in Medicaid or who are unin-sured, the reform will be a major gain. For those who obtain health insurance in the individual and small-group markets, reform should bring improvements.

For those who have health insurance from mid-size and large-group insurers, reform will bring little change. Finally, for Medicare beneficiaries, reform promises to bring positive change. However, financing future health spending overall, and Medicare spending in particular, poses a formidable challenge.

The paper is well done and thoughtful, but it's a striking example of Island thinking. To determine whether a particular group of people is better off, Newhouse has confined his analysis to only the direct costs and benefits of health insurance. But look at his last sentence; the elephant in the room—how to pay for it all—is assigned to no one. In judging the law's benefit to each group, he has ignored its more general costs, as well as its likely enormous effects on wages, taxes, and job creation.* It's unfair to single out the always

---

* Supporters of the ACA don't necessarily agree that it will negatively impact wages and job creation. Before the bill's drafting, some argued that its effectiveness at curbing costs would enable U.S. employers to improve their competitiveness, although you rarely hear that argument now that projections show growth in health costs and insurance premiums outpacing GDP growth for at least the next decade.

At the very least, shoveling ever more money into health care causes a shift in job creation, to health care jobs from everything-else jobs. To the extent these jobs achieve slower gains in productivity, national income will grow more slowly. More important, to the extent health care jobs offer less utility—less improvement in our lives—than other uses of the same labor, our quality of life will decline, whatever the statistics say (and haven't we seen some of that over the past decade as the growth of health care has outpaced everything else?).

Our policy to have employers provide most health insurance is distortive. It saddles companies with a significant administrative burden, which is more affordable by larger employers than smaller ones. If the ACA mandate is effective, it will spread this job tax to employers not currently bearing it—especially companies in low-wage and low-margin industries. ACA's proponents see this as "leveling the playing field," but making both IBM and a small janitorial company pay for health insurance doesn't make the labor market more fair: it simply means fewer janitorial jobs.

Finally, no matter what politicians say, health care is a form of current consumption. As more of our national income goes into health care consumption, there is less available for investment, reducing our future incomes. There is no

insightful Newhouse, though; treating the visible parts of health care's costs and benefits as the whole story, while ignoring the broader—and usually larger—effects, is standard in health care policy analysis.

Just before the vote on the ACA, I posted an article titled "A Democrat's Case for No," in which I asked if the new bill would be good for the uninsured. For most of my fellow Democrats, it was a silly question. Of course the bill was good for the uninsured: it gave them health insurance. But the uninsured are not like an ethnic group; most are uninsured only for short periods of their lives (more on this later). Many are unemployed or low-income or both. It is estimated that over the next decade the ACA will cost the government at least $1 trillion and the uninsured themselves at least the same amount. So my question was whether the additional short-term security of guaranteed health insurance would be worth the longer-term cost in lower rates of job creation, wage growth, and after-tax income. Simply put, would those whom the bill intended to help actually benefit when *all* of the legislation's effects on their lives were considered? I don't know the answer to the question, but I can't find any evidence that it was ever even asked by the bill's proponents.

If a salesman offered you a new car for a mere dollar plus some unspecified payments in a different form and at some later time, would you consider it a good deal? Before deciding, wouldn't you insist on knowing exactly what those future payments would be? Without that knowledge, how could you know if you had a good deal? And yet this is

---

better illustration of this than looking at the ever shrinking ratio of government's infrastructure spending to health care consumption.

how we think and talk on the Island of Health Care every day—as if the fine print, not to mention the future, couldn't possibly matter.

This unique way of thinking and talking about health care persists because we as consumers are disengaged from our own health care costs. Our system has taken away our traditional role as customers and assigned it to big intermediaries—insurers, Medicare, and Medicaid. I discuss this fundamental disconnect in detail in chapter 3, but first let me show you how these intermediaries make health care much more expensive than most of us realize.

CHAPTER 2

The Hidden Beast

The myth of affordable care

In 2010, Congress passed the Dodd-Frank Wall Street Reform and Consumer Protection Act. Among its other provisions, it created a new agency to protect consumers from deceptive mortgage lending practices by financial institutions—practices that create the illusion of immediate affordability while sticking borrowers with very large future obligations.

Merely four months before, that same Congress passed the ACA, further expanding our insurance-based system. Yet the practices of "affordable" health care are virtually the same practices now outlawed in mortgage lending: we all make our health care decisions with their financial implications intentionally hidden from us.

How can politicians call for "affordable" health care while at the same time embracing provisions certain to drive up prices? I could never understand this seeming contradiction until I was a guest on National Public Radio's *Planet*

Money alongside Richard Kirsch. He has been a tireless advocate for single-payer national health insurance and, as head of Health Care for America Now, a leading supporter of the Obama administration's health care policy. Kirsch explained to me that the point of affordable care is not necessarily low prices but a low payment made by the consumer-patient at the time of delivery of care. The concept is that no consumer should have to forgo needed treatment because his payment at the moment of getting treatment is too high.

Like so much on the Island of Health Care, this is one of those ideas that seems logical when applied to a single situation—your own, let's say—but prove disastrous when applied to a whole population. Kirsch isn't saying that the consumer wouldn't ultimately bear the full cost of care; rather, because the consumer would bear this cost later and in another form—such as increased insurance premiums, higher income taxes, bigger Medicare payments—it wouldn't affect his decision to seek treatment. In other words, just like with the deceptive financial practices prohibited by Dodd-Frank, consumers would purchase services precisely because they wouldn't understand what those services would really cost them.

There are all sorts of ways that businesses encourage you to believe their goods are more affordable than they really are. That $800 plasma TV feels much more affordable when you charge it to a credit card and pay nothing at the point of purchase. And that new razor seems like a good deal because the high-priced cartridges aren't included. Psychological manipulation of the consumer is common practice in business, but health care takes it to a new level. It's a credit card with massive monthly bills that aren't itemized so you can never tie your payments to your own spending.*

Do you think health care is affordable because you don't know what it costs you? Or because you assume someone else out there is really paying the bills? Who else do you think could afford it? Imagine confiscating all the profits of all the famously greedy health insurance companies. That would pay for four days of health care for all Americans. Now add in the profits of the ten biggest "rapacious" drug companies. Another thirteen days. Indeed, confiscating all the profits of all American companies, in every industry, would cover only seven months of our health care expenses (and we'd then have no economy left for next year's health costs). As long as health care is expensive, its cost to each of us will be high; no matter how we chop it up—insurance premiums, taxes, co-pays—expensive health care can't be affordable.

If McDonald's offered cheeseburgers for twenty-five cents, you may well consider that a "Super Value." But if McDonald's charged your employer a $1,000 membership fee before letting you in, used taxpayer funds to pay their workers, grazed their cattle on your front lawn, and sent you a bill to cover their air-conditioning costs, that twenty-five-cent cheeseburger might seem a little less affordable.

---

* So much of our reluctance to pursue true health care reform reflects our fear of being unable to afford urgent care when we need it. Shortly after my *Atlantic* article was published, my company's general counsel—one of the smartest people I know—told me that while he agreed with most of what I had written, he couldn't help thinking of a friend whose child had needed an appendectomy. Without insurance, how could this family have afforded the unexpected $10,000 bill? I reminded him that his friend's family coverage was costing him and his employer roughly $15,000 a year; if that money had instead been paid out to his friend, he could easily afford an appendectomy *annually*, with plenty of money left over for other health care.

The personal financial position of my employee Becky is a good illustration of the true cost of affordable health care. To appreciate how big these disguised costs are, let's take a deep look into her paycheck.

Becky's mountain

Since Becky's single without dependents, my company will pay $5,679 this year for her health insurance; she'll pay $2,112. Or so she thinks. In reality, Becky is paying all $7,791 of her insurance premium. How is it that employees are actually paying for the "benefit" of having their employer provide health insurance?

To understand this seeming paradox, put yourself in my company's position when we originally decide whether to create that job for Becky. We weigh two factors: the value of Becky's work to our company and the cost to us of hiring Becky. Notice the issue is "cost to us," not wages or salary, because an employee always costs an employer more than just her wages.

What are these additional costs above wages? Some are business related, such as space for Becky to work. But the bulk of the additional expenses are "benefits": some required by law (Social Security, unemployment insurance), others not (a retirement plan, health care—at least before the ACA). Of these, health care is by far the largest cost a company will bear for an employee.

Let's say Becky's work would be worth around $40,000 a year to us; if we can hire her for $40,000 or less, we'll do it. What does hiring her cost? For simplicity, forget about all other benefits and costs for a moment and just focus on health care. Paying our share of Becky's health insurance premiums will cost us about $5,000 a year. So the maximum salary our company will pay Becky is actually $35,000—the $40,000 her job is worth to us minus the $5,000 cost to us of her premiums. The more health insurance costs us, the less our company can afford to pay out to Becky or to any employee as salary or wages. Of course, all Becky knows is that her salary is $35,000.

I admit I've simplified here for purposes of illustration. Companies don't really calculate individual employees' pay after subtracting their individual health care costs on an ongoing basis. Most of us compute an average premium cost for all employees and apply that to individual hiring decisions. But the end result is the same: paying for your health insurance is just another way your employer compensates you for your work. Which means that over time, the money your company spends on your premiums really comes out of your own pocket—where else would it come from?

Now, I suspect most people have a hard time believing this; after all, what company that drops health insurance turns around and gives employees raises covering its savings? But over time—and over the whole economy—the effect is accepted by economists of all ideologies: the more companies shell out for health care, the less they pay in salaries and wages.

With health care expenses increasing faster than inflation over the past forty-five years—and faster than overall economic growth for many of those years—we've clearly seen the impact of higher health insurance premiums in slower wage growth.*

* In the decade before the recession—1998 to 2008—the American economy grew by 25 percent and corporate profits grew by 54 percent. Yet average wages grew by only 13 percent. Cast your mind back to those good old pre-recession days. Liberals

In our recent recession, most companies have tried to hold the line on compensation costs. Yet employer health insurance premiums continue to grow—up by 4.7 percent in 2008, 5.5 percent in 2009, and 3 percent in 2010. So what are companies doing to compensate? Many are cutting back on their benefits packages and increasing deductibles, co-pays, or employee shares of premiums. In other words, to avoid cutting pay, they are passing on more costs to their employees.

I saw a stark illustration of this recently in my own company. After almost eighteen months of salary freezes, we set aside in our 2010 budget $1 million for wage increases. Yet shortly after enacting the budget, we were hit by a 22 percent rise—almost $500,000—in health insurance premiums. What did we do? We turned to the co-pays on our health plans. For employees who use our most expensive plan, we increased their share of premiums from 15 to 20 percent. We then created financial incentives to encourage more employees to take less expensive plan options, retaining the premium share rate of 15 percent only for high-deductible plans. (The number of enrollees in these plans jumped from two to thirty-four.) But even these changes saved us only $150,000 of the premium increase; so what about the excess balance of $350,000? We thought about reducing the planned raises by that amount but decided to accept them as a short-term

---

and conservatives argued furiously as to why the American worker seemed to be doing so poorly. Was it because of tax cuts, declining unionization, deregulation, or globalization? But while the data are difficult to measure precisely, President Obama's Council of Economic Advisors suggested an alternative leading cause: the explosion of employer health insurance costs. In its 2009 "Economic Case for Health Reform," the CEA includes a chart which it says shows that the bulk of growth in compensation costs in the decade 1996–2006 went to employer health premiums; in other words, spending on health insurance crowded out growth in wages. The CEA projected that more than 100 percent of the growth in future compensation could go to higher premiums. In other words, wages could actually *decline* over time to compensate for higher employer health costs.

reduction in our company's profitability. But no one really dodged this bullet. Our less profitable company is now less able to afford wage increases over time. And the increase in premium costs had a direct impact on our employees' standard of living this year, as it will continue to in the future.

So what does it mean for Becky? She's certainly aware of the $2,112 she's paying for her share of our insurance premiums; let's also assume she has about $350 in out-of-pocket costs for her deductible. Whether she knows it or not, her compensation is bearing the burden of our $5,679 contribution to her insurance premiums.* But the cost of her own insurance is just the beginning of what Becky is paying into our health care system. Look at her pay stub:

Salary		$35,000
Taxes		−$7,781
State	−$1,276	
Federal	−$3,827	
Social Security	−$2,170	
Medicare	−$ 508	
Other deductions		−$2,112
Medical	−$1,932	
Dental	−$ 114	
Vision	−$ 66	
Net pay		$25,107

* In reality, Becky herself is bearing more; since we hire employees without knowledge of their insurance or family status, we, like most companies, assign an average insurance cost when figuring out the cost of an employee's job. This means that our assumption as to the insurance cost of single employees is higher than what they actually cost us (and conversely, it is slightly lower than the actual cost of an employee who needs a family policy).

If you look closely, there's another $1,909 in health spending in there.

Let's start with Medicare Part A taxes. Becky's share is $508, but our company is also paying an equal $508 that doesn't show up on her pay stub. That makes for a total of $1,016 a year.

Now look at income taxes. Becky will pay $3,827 in federal income tax this year. Approximately 20 percent of the federal budget is spent on health care (that's excluding the amounts funded by Part A taxes or Medicare premiums). Take 20 percent of Becky's yearly federal income tax payments and you have $765. That's another $765 being diverted from Becky's pocket to fund health care.

Becky also pays $1,276 in state income tax; say 10 percent of the average state's budget goes to health care (on average it's a bit higher, even excluding amounts received from the federal government). That's $128 more into the mouth of the Beast.

What is the end result of all these disguised costs? Becky, whose salary is $35,000 a year (and whose real compensation, from my company's perspective, is just over $43,000, including all of her benefits and employer taxes), effectively poured $10,050 into our health care system this year— $10,050! This sum represents more than 23 percent of her true gross income—her entry level, just-starting-out contribution to our economy—going to support our current system of health care. If Becky works for thirty years without a raise, never marries or has kids, and never gets really sick, and if health care prices don't increase at all, she's going to contribute $300,000 into our health care system during her working career. And then she'll pay Medicare premiums.

But of course, all those things will change. If Becky gets married, her premiums will increase by $9,225 a year; if she has kids, that's another $7,231 a year. As her income grows, she'll pay more into Medicare's trust fund (which is now just another income tax) and to the federal and state governments to support Medicare and Medicaid. And when she becomes a senior citizen, she'll pay Medicare premiums plus other expenses. My mother this year will pay $1,572 in premiums for Parts B and D, in addition to the $2,800 she pays for supplemental Medigap insurance and the $1,200 in out-of-pocket expenditures (and she's in very good health).

Let's make a few assumptions about Becky's life. We'll say she gets married at thirty and has two children. She works until she's sixty-five and dies at eighty. We'll also assume her income grows every year by 4 percent, so that at retirement she's earning $180,000 a year. To simplify the analysis, we'll have Becky's husband leave her to join an ashram when he turns sixty-five, so she's responsible only for her own Medicare premiums. Let's also give Becky a stroke of good fortune and say that she and her dependents stay healthy, with no major health crisis requiring large out-of-pocket expenditures.

Now allow me to make a truly crazy assumption just for the sake of argument. Let's assume that health care costs grow at only 2 percent a year—half of Becky's income growth. This hasn't been true for forty-five years, but we can always hope. Given all those factors, how much do you think Becky will contribute into the health care system for herself and her dependents over her lifetime? I'll give you a hint: Becky will earn $3.85 million over her career.

The answer is $1.9 million!*

---

* I suspect that's somewhat more than you guessed. Let me break it down:

Health care payments visible to Becky

Her share of insurance premiums $353,174

Deductibles/out-of-pocket expenses $97,465

Now also remember that $1.9 million was based on an assumption that health costs were somehow tamed below Becky's income growth. In recent years, per capita health costs have actually increased 2 to 3 percent faster than income. If health costs grow merely equal to Becky's income, Becky is looking at an additional $1.3 million in expenses over her lifetime—almost $3.2 million in total. In that scenario, Becky will contribute one out of every two cents she earns to our health care system. Does that possibility sound crazy? The growth rate is less than new government projections for the upcoming decade; the Centers for Medicare and Medicaid Services (CMS) estimates health costs growing at 2 percent more than our gross domestic product, which means 5 percent.*

Becky has no idea she's spending anywhere near this amount on health care. But the math is simple: if our society is going to spend 18 percent of our income on health care—and assume some of the burden for the lowest-income people—then almost all working people must bear a burden greater than 18 percent of their income. How else could an

Medicare taxes	$ 55,831
Medicare premiums	$ 63,690
	$ 570,160

Health care payments hidden from Becky

Employer premiums	$ 957,446
Employer Medicare taxes	$ 55,831
Federal taxes	$ 300,588
State taxes	$ 40,478
	$1,354,586

Though the full cost is $1.9 million, Becky is probably only aware that $570,000 was for health care—her share of insurance and Medicare and her out-of-pocket expenses.

* In the absurd possibility that the 5 percent growth rate continued, Becky would be spending roughly two-thirds of her true lifetime income (including all benefits) on health care.

expense that large be paid for? Of course, most of us think of our health care benefits, not our health care costs. And that is the key to why Becky and the rest of us pay so much.

The great diversion

We may be individually unaware of what we're each contributing for health care, but the growth in cost is clear on a societal level. The share of our GDP devoted to health care has risen from 5.8 percent in 1965 to 17.6 percent today. We now spend $8,166.40 per American on health care a year. Medicare spending has grown to $525 billion and Medicaid to $400 billion in their forty-five-year existence.*

---

* Before Medicare and Medicaid were enacted, government spending on health care was minuscule. The U.S. government spent only 1 percent of its (much smaller) budget on it, and states and localities spent less than 6 percent of theirs. Initial projections suggested that the new Medicare and Medicaid programs would have only minor impacts on government spending.

Shortly after the passage of Medicare, the House Ways and Means Committee estimated that the program's yearly costs would grow to $12 billion by 1990. It hit that estimate sixteen years early; in 1990, Medicare already cost $110 billion—*nine times original estimates* (Sen. Sam Brownback, "Are Health Care Reform Cost Estimates Reliable?" Joint Economic Committee, July 31, 2009).

Only five years after the enactment of Medicare and Medicaid, the dollars spent on them were about the same as those spent by the federal government on education; today, the two health programs together eat up seven times the education budget. Back then, they were roughly two-thirds the size of the welfare program; today, they're double its size. Medicare alone used to cost less than transportation programs; today, it accounts for five times the government spending on transportation. Current projections suggest we still have another seventy years before Medicare and Medicaid account for 100 percent of government spending, but all previous projections of their costs have proved way too low.

These two health care giants make up 21 percent of federal spending: they are bigger than Social Security and our defense budget and dwarf every other domestic program. But just as we saw with Becky's pay stub, the federal government spends money on health care all over its budget. Veterans Affairs itself runs the largest hospital system in the United States, with billings equal to the next two largest chains combined. The Department of Defense's spending on health care alone is now roughly 10 percent of its budget—more than the total military budget of all but four nations. Subtract out Medicare and Medicaid, and federal spending on health care is still almost $175 billion!

Yet for most of us, these huge numbers are mere abstractions. They sound big, but they're difficult to relate to. We get a much better sense of the situation when we see how these costs add up over a single person's lifetime. And we can even more fully comprehend how the cost of health care affects us when we calculate what we are giving up in exchange for this "benefit."

Say, for example, that health care costs had only grown at the rate of the general economy over the past forty-five years—a modest rate compared with health care's actual growth. If such savings were spread equally over the population, the average American would have an extra $4,000 to spend on other things this year. That's $16,000 for a family of four. Per year. One way to understand the burden of health care spending is to think about what you could have done with that money—what else would you have bought or invested in?

When we shift our focus from individual households to our entire society, the cost of the Beast's growth becomes even more shocking. If health care expenses had grown only at the general rate of inflation since the inception of Medicare, America could afford to double our spending on education, buy five times as many new clothes and cars, triple our spending on entertainment and recreation, or wage another war or two. Every single year.

One of the premises of this book is that this diversion of so much of our wealth to health care is done on autopilot. We're not making conscious decisions as individuals or as a society to do so, any more than Becky is. Look at what happened during the recent recession and you'll see how this autopilot works. Almost every sector of our economy shed jobs. From December 2007 to March 2010, almost two mil-

lion construction workers were laid off; 2.1 million manufacturing workers lost their jobs, as did nearly half a million
in the leisure industries and 628,000 in finance; 519,000
temporary employees also found themselves out of work.
Even the federal and state and local governments reduced
employment, despite all their emergency spending. Only
one sector added significant jobs in the Great Recession:
health care, which took on 732,000 new employees while
everyone else was handing out pink slips.

If you're a politician, you may think this is great news:
"Our dynamic health care sector continued to create good
jobs for Americans even during tough times." But step back
and think about what really happened and what it says
about the structure of our economy. Even during a crisis,
when all of us are focused on tightening our belts, health
care demands a greater share of our money. Did we make
a conscious decision to expand health care while reducing
everything else? Or did it just happen automatically?

Automatic growth of this magnitude is inconceivable on
the Mainland. To health experts, it's inevitable: health care
spending grows automatically because our needs are growing with an aging population, the explosion in chronic illness, and the use of innovative technology. But of course,
expanding needs and wants are common to almost all goods
and services. What makes health care truly unique—what
really makes it an island—is the separation of the real consumers from the most important decisions about how much
health care we want relative to anything else. Let's turn to
the massive and varied cost of this fundamental disconnect.

CHAPTER 3

The Disconnect

The absence of consumers in health care

One recent summer, my sister-in-law, Anna, tore her meniscus while visiting us from Russia. Our physician recommended an MRI on Anna's knee to determine what, if any, treatment was appropriate. He referred us to his usual provider of MRI services. As a foreigner, Anna lacked insurance, which meant she would have to pay all her own medical expenses. So it really mattered to us that our physician's usual provider wanted $1,500 to perform the MRI. Fortunately, we'd learned our lesson from the MRI my wife had several years ago: it just wasn't possible that an MRI still needed to be so expensive. My wife called around to other MRI providers for quotes, sharing the previous best price with each new clinic and asking if they could beat it. Several providers gave prices around $1,200, but we were also quoted $800 and $650. Finally, one specialist said he would take $300, but only if payment was by check (not credit card) and only if we could show up at four o'clock the next day.

When I tell friends the story of our MRI price shopping, I get an almost identical reaction: "You can do that? Doctors will negotiate price with you?"

Anna's MRI experience—where she was the true customer—is rare. Almost all our interactions with the health care system occur through insurers, Medicare, government agencies—the intermediaries I call the Surrogates. On our behalf, they negotiate prices, agree on appropriate procedures and treatments, and oversee results. In theory, there seems to be good reason for the Surrogates to serve this role: being large and powerful, they have the leverage to negotiate the best deals with doctors and hospitals. And since they pay for the cost of care over our lifetimes, the Surrogates seem to have a strong incentive to ensure treatments are performed effectively.

This theory—that the Surrogates are more effective health consumers than we as individuals are—is the most important structural foundation of our health care system. It's what justifies having all health care expenses—no matter how routine or trivial—"covered" by insurance or Medicare. It's also the reason that every government solution to the problems plaguing our system involves relying even more on these intermediaries.

After forty-five years of relentless expansion of the role of the Surrogates, we should now admit that this theory is wrong.

Why have the Surrogates failed? First, as I'll discuss in this chapter, intermediaries may have some incentive to push for lower costs, less waste, and higher quality, but these incentives are actually quite minor and are often in direct conflict with the Surrogates' broader goals. More important, the Surrogates have failed because their very existence—

and their relentless expansion—has created the Disconnect. The Disconnect is the gap between health care providers and the one force that is powerful and unconflicted enough to control cost, quality, and waste in a way that can make a real difference.

That power is us. On the Mainland, we consumers—operating as a disorganized and often unthinking mass—exercise highly effective discipline over the industries that produce the goods and services we consume. We're the ones who punish the expensive, the careless, the low quality, and the wasteful. By disconnecting us consumers from the Island economy of health care, the Surrogates' very existence has removed the greatest incentives for good behavior.

Unfortunately, the argument that consumers should play a greater role in health care—that health care should operate more normally—always runs into the same tired counterpoint: consumers lack the knowledge to make good health care decisions. We can't be expected to shop around when we're ill and need care. We'll be taken advantage of by unscrupulous doctors and hospitals. Sure, my wife may have been able to negotiate a 75 percent discount by calling around and paying cash, but doesn't all that work seem like a lot to ask of patients? What if Anna had an advanced stage of cancer or was hit by a bus; would it then be sensible to ask us to comparison-shop?

That argument may sound sensible, but it simply ignores how consumer-driven industries (i.e., every other industry) actually work. On the Mainland, Anna's story is also remarkable, but for the opposite reason: it's amazing that we needed to call so many people to get a 75 percent discount. Isn't it odd that a doctor who could make a profit from a discount MRI didn't seek us out? In what other business does a discounter not advertise loudly to potential consumers that he has lower prices? Where was the ad for the Dr. Crazy Eddie of MRIs, whose prices are so low he's practically giving MRIs away?

In every other business, companies seeking our dollars decide how they want to be positioned—as the cheapest, the highest quality, the most reliable, the most friendly, the most convenient, whatever. They spend fortunes communicating those promises to us and commit their whole resources to living up to them. In every other business, companies chase us.

Not in health care. The Disconnect means we are not the health care industry's customers; the Surrogates are. What benefit does a health care provider receive from being the low-price leader, the quality leader, the safety leader, the comfort leader, and so on? None. And more than any other reason, this is why our health care industry does not bother to meet our demands for lower prices, higher quality, less waste, or greater safety. They are too busy serving the quite different interests of their real customers: the Surrogates.

The rise of the Surrogates

All over the developed world, insurance-based systems dominate the financing of health care, which suggests that there is something fundamentally necessary about using insurance to fund care and intermediaries to negotiate prices. On the Island, every expert agrees that the unique nature of health care requires insurance funding. In the words of the great historian Paul Starr: "In any given year, the most costly 5 percent of people account for more than 50 percent of health-care costs, and the top 10 percent of people account for 70 percent of costs." Insurance is therefore the best mechanism for moving funds from the many well to the few ill. At a conference of Island experts, no other statement is more certain to get you universal nods of agreement.

Hold on. It's true that "in any given year" health care costs are very concentrated. But the sad reality is that we are all virtually certain to be in that 10 percent high-use bracket for one or more years over the course of our lives. Returning to the Mainland allows us to put this in perspective. Health care is a very expensive service that all of us will need. At certain times in our lives, we'll need it often. At other times, we'll require it only rarely. Well, guess what? That's true of all expensive goods and services that are universally used. Think health care is special? Only 11 percent of American households buy a car in any given year, even though almost all of us will purchase at least one over the course of a lifetime. Less than 10 percent buy a refrigerator in any given year. Half of marriages end in divorce, but only half a percent of Americans use a divorce lawyer in any given year. Houses, college education, weddings, you name it: a small percentage of people do all the buying in any given year. In many of these Mainland industries—where annual utilization is far more concentrated than in health care—we use a variety of techniques to spread expenses over many years, but needless to say, in none of them do we rely on insurance to fund purchases.

What makes health care unusual among expensive goods and services is the *opposite* of what the Island believes: it's that we all use health care even when we're not very sick, even when we're not in the top 10 percent of users.*

Now, in fairness—and unlike those who buy cars and have weddings—the top 10 percent of health care users include some people who are very ill for very long periods of time. And for people suffering from these types of long-term illnesses, it may well be that an insurance system is the best approach. But an insurance system that funds every type of expense is not necessary to support the truly catastrophic cases, any more than we need homeowners' insurance to compensate for the times your kids deface the furniture or break windows.

The triumph of the insurance model in health care has moved in lockstep with the rise of the Surrogates as the primary customers for health care. Not only do these Surrogates negotiate prices and preapprove procedures, they increasingly determine your choice of doctors. In the United States, as in most developed countries, governments have also assumed this intermediary-as-customer function in our public health programs. Medicare intentionally resembles an insurer and, like its private counterparts, negotiates price and approves services directly with providers. Medic-

---

* Also, the conventional understanding of the high concentration of annual spending on health care generates a second incorrect argument about the impossibility of transforming health care into a normal industry. Since 90 percent of the population—the overwhelming majority that is not very sick in any given year—accounts for only 30 percent of care, how could a consumer economy possibly be built on such a small share? But do the math: this "only" 30 percent of total spending alone is now $700 billion a year. If $700 billion is not enough consumer dollars to drive transformation, how does any consumer-based industry exist?

In a February 2012 *Health Affairs* interview, the CEO of CareFirst BlueCross BlueShield said that the roughly 50 percent of the insurer's customers it considered "healthy" used 7.2 percent of the total cost of care in the most recent year. Applying just this amount to all of health care spending suggests that even those who are essentially healthy spend almost $200 billion a year—a large industry in itself.

aid is also a direct buyer of health services, contracting with providers on behalf of its clients.

We are so used to the insurance and intermediary functions being combined that it rarely occurs to us that they could even be separated. Although insurers act partially as customers after automobile accidents by approving the specific costs for fixing your wreck, in most forms of insurance—from life to property—the insurer just estimates damages and cuts the insured party a check; the beneficiary figures out how to spend it. And there are plenty of government aid programs—food stamps, welfare, Social Security—in which the government doesn't determine how we will spend its money, much less the prices of goods and services and from whom we can buy them. Why is health care special? Why have we decided to turn our health insurers into Surrogates, rendering ourselves passive as consumers of our own care?

On the Island, the answer is information asymmetry, a fancy term for a situation where the seller has access to greater knowledge about a service or good than the buyer. This difference in knowledge makes it difficult for the buyer to determine the true value of a service and, therefore, a reasonable price. In other words, the ability of consumers to discipline providers in a free market is limited by their ignorance and the providers' superior knowledge.

Of course, information asymmetry exists in almost all markets for goods and services, from used cars to restaurants to watch repair. But a highly influential article written in 1963 by Kenneth Arrow (a Nobel laureate) contended that it was especially severe in health care. Here the "seller" is often a doctor with years of specialized training and experience. By contrast, the customer usually has little information other than the seller's (i.e., doctor's) recommendation. The subject matter—health—is often arcane and highly technical. Further, for many health services, a consumer must make his purchase decision in an emotionally charged state; he may even believe he needs the "purchase" to stay alive.

This is the underpinning of government policies encouraging the rise of the Surrogates. Insurers and government agencies are assumed to be better customers for health care than consumers because it's assumed we're so bad at it. Not only are health insurers and government agencies unemotional, they have the benefit of knowledge that comes from overseeing the treatment of millions. When a provider suggests a course of treatment, the Surrogates can judge reasonableness and cost by comparing it with thousands of other cases. An insurer buying thousands of cardiac bypasses may know more than a cardiologist who has merely performed hundreds.

This is nonsense. The growing dysfunction of our health care system over the past forty-five years did not occur despite the rise of the Surrogates, but rather because of it. Health care has always been expensive, has always been driven by new technologies and products, has always been sold to desperate people. The only truly new thing of the past forty-five years is the now complete domination of the marketplace by intermediaries.

It's like the old joke about the two guys being chased by a bear. One guy stops to change into sneakers. "You idiot," yells his companion, "you can't outrun a bear!" "I don't need to outrun the bear," says the guy in the sneakers. "I only need to outrun you." We as individuals may be terrible consumers of health care—scared, uninformed, and emotional. But so what? The history of the past forty-five years makes clear that the Surrogates are even worse consumers—although for different reasons.

The tragedy of the Surrogates

Anna's MRI experience may be rare, but it's far from unique. In May 2012, the *Los Angeles Times* wrote about a woman who discovered that her co-pay for a CT scan covered by her insurance ($2,336) was greater than the total price she would have paid if she had registered with the facility as an uninsured cash patient (only $1,054). The hospital's finance chief explained: "We end up being forced to charge a premium to health plans to make the books balance." But wasn't the whole point of relying on insurers as purchasers of health care that they could drive better deals than helpless consumers? How can it be that the Surrogates are so ineffective? Or to rephrase the famous comment by a French politician, although it hasn't worked in practice, why hasn't it worked in theory?

The answer is quite simple: the three types of giant intermediaries—private insurers, Medicare, and Medicaid—have minimal incentives to control the size of the health care economy and fundamental incentives to see it expand.

Let's start with private insurers. True, an insurer's profitability in any given year depends on its ability to keep reimbursements for care below the amount charged in premiums. But over time, its incentive is the exact opposite: to see spending on health care increase as much as possible. Why? Like with any private business, insurers require consistent and profitable growth to satisfy their shareholders. And you can't really achieve profit growth by reducing payouts for care—any cost improvements will almost certainly translate to lower premiums. So the only way for the health insurance industry to increase profits is to increase premiums. And there's only three ways to increase this rate base—customers must get sicker, policies must expand to cover new types of care, or prices for care must rise (i.e., the cost of claims must rise).

This point is so obvious, but so poorly understood by Island experts, that it must be repeated: health insurers can achieve long-term profit growth only if the amount of money spent on health care increases. Forty-five years of health care inflation has not hurt health insurers' profits; rather, it has fueled profit growth. Private insurers' profit margins are at the lower range of American corporations (ranging between only 3 and 6 percent of revenues in recent years), so providing returns to shareholders has depended on the massive growth of total revenues—now $850 billion a year.

Of course, we as individuals don't experience insurers as cheerleaders for the growth of health care expenses. They're the ones who refuse to approve reimbursement for treatments recommended by our physicians, who find new and creative ways to reduce the share of approved procedures that they'll pay for. If you are a physician or run a hospital, private insurers regularly demand lower contract rates for your services.

So how can insurers simultaneously be Dr. No and Dr. More?

Three years ago, a pipe burst in my home, causing extensive damage to my kitchen. Less a $2,500 deductible, my homeowners' policy covered the entire cost of the repair—almost $25,000. My insurer had to approve the repair budget and the selection of vendors and materials. In a couple of cases, the insurer required an alternative bid. In short, having accepted that I had a reimbursable claim, the insurer used an adjustment process to keep the size of that claim down. That's what public policy expects insurers to do in health care.

But roughly once a year, I also get a call or letter from my insurer inquiring whether my insurance is adequate. Did I acquire any jewelry, art, or other valuables that should be separately insured? Do I know about new limits or deductibles on my existing policies, and might I want expanded coverage? In the good old days of the real estate boom, they would suggest I raise my coverage amount to compensate for the rising costs of replacement construction. In other words, my insurer wants me to insure as much risk as conceivable—so premiums can be as high as possible— even though that means future claims will inevitably rise as well. Insurers need claims to rise over time; otherwise, premiums and profits can't grow.

As a result, health insurers have, at best, a complex relationship with cost control and, at worst, a fundamental disincentive. Whatever success they may have in negotiating discount prices has been overwhelmed by the expanding definitions of care under their forty-five-year reign. When traditional health reformers talk about insurers' incentives to see customers take better care of themselves, I shake my head in disbelief. It sounds good, but the healthier we are, the less we'll spend on health care. And the less we spend on health care, the less we'll spend on health insurance. That may be a good thing for the country, but why would it be good for insurers? (As I'll show in the next chapter, insurers' interest in our taking better care of ourselves does make business sense if it means expanding the health care pie by selling pervasive "preventive care" testing to healthy people.)*

Even when we look at the major government programs of Medicare and Medicaid, we see how mixed incentives have prevented a meaningful brake on spending. Let's start with the most basic fact about Medicare: it's an entitlement. That means that the program's spending is not limited by a budget approved annually by Congress, the way other spending is. Rather, Medicare has license to spend as much as it must to meet all "needs."

Certainly, the CMS is under some political pressure to cut costs. But it is also facing pressure to make sure that all the health care needs of our seniors are paid for. Imagine you were running CMS and faced both pressures. Which do you think is the more powerful incentive? Now add an addi-

---

* As usual, the language of health care masks the reality of insurer motivation. In July 2012, the Institute of Medicine recommended that contraception be considered preventive medicine and thus included it in the list of services insurers must cover without a co-pay. A typical reaction came from Maryland senator Barbara Mikulski: "We are saying hello to an era where decisions about preventive care . . . are made by a woman and her doctor, not by an insurance company." But this decision is not a triumph over insurers' interests. The more preventive care they are required to cover, the more premiums will have to rise. Profits will, too.

On the morning of June 11, 2012, UnitedHealthcare announced that it would retain three major provisions of the ACA even if the law was struck down: allowing young adults to stay on their parents' policies up to age twenty-six, no lifetime limits on coverage, and preventive testing without co-payments. Within hours, Aetna and Humana said they would also stick to the new rules. A typical reaction came from Chas Roades, chief research officer at the Advisory Board Company: "They're trying to hedge against the possibility that some or all of the law will be overturned and they want to be viewed as doing the right thing."

Well, no. Though Island experts don't seem to understand this, insurers love mandates, as long as they apply to all insurers. Forcing insurers to cover more care merely allows the cost base—and therefore the premium base—to rise. Tellingly, none of these insurers said they would retain the ban on limits for preexisting conditions, as this provision complicates their ability to price policies at a profit rather than merely increasing revenues (Kaiser Health News, "3 Large Insurers Promise to Keep Many Popular Features of Health Law If High Court Strikes It Down," June 11, 2012).

tional fact: you can't possibly run out of money. How good do you think you would be at cutting costs when powerful seniors' organizations could complain to your boss that you were skimping on their care?

Medicaid is also an entitlement at the federal level, although not at the state level, where it is subject to budget pressures. However, as states expand their programs, they are guaranteed access to federal money to pay for at least half. So historically, Medicaid has been afflicted by mission creep, an expansion of its original mandate. For example, in 1984, Medicaid began paying for delivery of children for low-income women. Twenty-seven years later, Medicaid pays for more than 40 percent of all deliveries in the United States. Similarly, at its inception, Medicaid began helping low-income seniors on Medicare pay for nursing homes; today, more than 64 percent of all seniors in nursing homes have their way paid by Medicaid.

The question here is not whether the expansion of Medicaid's services is good or bad but whether it is realistic to look to Medicaid for cost control. I doubt anyone has gone to work for a Medicaid agency because they were motivated to cut services; I doubt we even want people with such motivations going to work for our state aid agencies.

So here's the problem: our reliance on the Surrogates as the customers in health care is based on our faith in their superior judgment in controlling health care spending. But none of them have any real institutional incentive to control spending over the long term. Indeed, continued expansion of the health care economy produces far more benefit for them as institutions, as well as for many of the truly caring people who work for them. Forty-five years into the rise of the Surrogates, we should no longer be shocked that health care prices and health care excess reign unchecked.

Moral hazard

If you've ever had a minor car accident, you've probably experienced how the existence of insurance changes the relationship between a service provider and the customer. Chances are the first question your mechanic asked you was "Is this an insurance job?" If his bill will be paid by an insurer, you are not a price-sensitive customer.

Over my thirty-plus years of driving, I've had a handful of such accidents. The first time, my mechanic suggested we add some small touch-ups here and there that he could convince the insurer were related to the original accident. Other than my fixed $500 deductible, I paid nothing more for these additional services—or so I thought. But then my car insurance premiums immediately rose, and I imagine it was only a year or two before my insurer fully recaptured the extra costs.

I've learned my lesson and have never filed an insurance claim for a fender bender since. Sure enough, my subsequent mechanics have never suggested extra fixes. The prices I have paid have declined as I got wiser as a consumer and learned what to negotiate.

My history with fender benders is an illustration of what is called moral hazard—the tendency of a person to make claims, inflate claims, or tolerate higher costs because he has insurance. Moral hazard is a problem with any insurance product. At its most perverse, it's grist for TV movies, as when people kill their spouses for the life insurance. It can lead a crooked building owner to torch his own property when its market value declines below the insured amount. And of course, moral hazard can also have minor, less dramatic implications for society, as when a body shop repaints a whole car rather than merely the dented area.

In the case of health care, moral hazard can completely dominate an industry's economics and pricing. For every hundred dollars spent on health care in the United States, the patient acting as consumer pays only eleven dollars; an intermediary pays the rest. In fact, when you adjust for those few without any insurance or government assistance, the typical insured American pays much less than 10 percent of the price of most health care services he uses. Because health insurance covers all procedures, not just rare events, the opportunity for moral hazard is uniquely pervasive in health care.

Talking about moral hazard in health care is controversial; a fellow panelist once scolded me for doing so, saying that no one chooses to get cancer or get hit by a bus. That's true, of course, but we don't choose to have auto accidents, either.

Moral hazard in health care is both so universal and so subtle that most of us are unaware of its effect. One morning last summer, I woke up with complete hearing loss in my left ear. It had happened to me a few times in the past, so I knew what it was: a waxy buildup I get after swimming regularly. I also knew what would fix the problem: an ear cleaning by a doctor. My physician referred me to an ear, nose, and throat specialist, who gave me an immediate appointment for this fifteen-minute procedure.

When I showed up for my appointment, I asked the office manager the price of the procedure. She responded that the cleaning was normally covered by most insurance. She also told me that since I was a new patient, the doctor would insist on performing a full ear exam before the cleaning and that insurance would likely cover the exam as well. I explained that since I had a high-deductible insurance policy, I would be paying the entire cost out of my own pocket, so I did need to know the price beforehand. Also, since I had experienced the condition before, I knew what needed to be done and wanted to pay only for the cleaning.

After talking to the doctor, the office manager came back and said that he would perform the cleaning alone and for a reduced fee of a hundred dollars. He mentioned that if the cleaning didn't restore my hearing, he would then recommend a subsequent full exam. The cleaning was successful, the doctor was excellent, and I'd happily use him again.

My ear-cleaning experience was also moral hazard in action. The doctor was not a crook. In fact, one could argue that he was being ethically sound in suggesting a full ear exam before treating a new patient. But his office was willing to quote a price only after I insisted that my insurance wouldn't be paying, and they dropped the required exam only after it was clear I wasn't willing to pay for it personally. The ear exam wouldn't have hurt me—and may well have been beneficial—but it wasn't essential. Although outright fraud is not uncommon in health care (especially in Medicare and Medicaid), most moral hazard is of this more prosaic—and even seemingly justifiable—kind.

We have extensive evidence that the very availability of insurance pushes up the amount of treatment, as well as its price. For example, Medicare spends almost twice as much per patient in Miami, where there is a surplus of doctors and care facilities, as it does in San Francisco, where supply is tighter. Why? Because to make use of spare capacity, doctors in surplus areas order far more procedures than do those in shortage areas. Note that this is the exact opposite of what we experience in any other industry, where excess capacity drives prices down. Here's another example: when Medicare cut reimbursements in 2005 on chemotherapy drugs, it saved almost 20 percent of the previously billed costs. But Medicare's cancer treatment costs actually rose in this period, as the total number of treatments ordered by doctors rose to compensate for lost income from the lower reimbursement rates.

Even if you have trouble accepting that anyone seeks or receives more care than necessary because of insurance, it's hard to argue that moral hazard does not increase the prices paid for medical services. Most of my friends don't even know what they are charged for medical procedures. They may ask what their share of the payment is, but not the total price billed their insurer. It seems that the average insured American and the average uninsured American spend very similar amounts of their own money on health care annually: $654 and $583, respectively. But they spend wildly different amounts of other people's money: $3,809 and $1,103, respectively. If it's true that the insurance system leads us to focus on only our direct share of costs—rather than on the overall cost to society—it's not surprising that insured families and uninsured ones make similar decisions as to how much of their own money to spend on care but very different decisions on the total amount to consume.

Not only is moral hazard especially prevalent in health care, it is also uniquely dangerous. Because we are not cost-sensitive consumers, we are less likely to resist provider suggestions for extra treatment. We are less likely to be skeptical of benefits when we are paying little or nothing for them. So the plague of unnecessary cesarean deliveries, spinal fusion surgeries, and cardiac bypasses can also be viewed as moral hazard in action. But unlike in the case of my fender bender, these "extra fixes" paid for by your Surrogate can actually do you harm.

Yet moral hazard is completely absent from policy debates. No one believes that he gets any health care that isn't absolutely needed. And few doctors believe they are billing for unnecessary treatments. So what politician is ever going to discuss moral hazard, no matter how central it is to exploding health care costs?

What real consumers do

My second child was delivered in the same hospital in which my father was to die only six months later. The difference between the maternity ward and the ICU—in decor, cleanliness, organization, and even the attentiveness of the nursing staff—was astonishing. It was hard to believe they were in the same building.*

Premium hospital service isn't limited to the miracle of childbirth. Current reimbursement policies make certain types of procedures very profitable for hospitals that can achieve high volumes. So it's now common to see hospitals refurbish wings and advertise the quality of the experience and care for treatments such as hip replacement, cardiac bypass and angioplasty, and even chemotherapy. Our

---

* Five years earlier, for the delivery of my first child, we went to a West Coast hospital with a maternity wing that resembled a luxury hotel. For an extra fee comparable to a night at such a hotel, mother, spouse, and child could sleep in a suite and order off a menu that included lobster tail and filet mignon. This may sound expensive but was actually a relatively small charge compared with the high delivery costs covered by insurance.

maternity hospital gave tours of its facilities to prospective mothers.

But almost all of these "green shoots" of competition center on the quality of patient experience, not price. Why? Because you as the patient can decide where to have your baby or your bypass—you have enough advance notice to make an informed decision. But price isn't a factor you need to consider in making that decision: that's an issue between the real customer—your insurer or Medicare—and the hospital.

It reminds me of how airlines acted before deregulation. Prohibited from competing on price, they competed on everything else: the quality of their food, the decor of their jets, their in-flight entertainment, the length of their stewardesses' skirts. Once they were allowed to compete on price, airlines quickly discovered that price was the only thing that really mattered to their customers. Twenty-five years after deregulation, the average price of an airline ticket had declined by almost 40 percent in real terms, while the number of trips taken had grown by 68 percent. However, these statistics don't apply to the one area of the airline business where the person choosing the airline usually isn't the same as the one paying for the ticket: international first class. For this crowd, overwhelmingly made up of travelers whose employers are footing the bill, airlines compete for executives' business by emphasizing—you guessed it—the quality of the seats and food, the entertainment options, and, in our less sexist age, the attentiveness of the cabin crew.

Our policyholders and regulators are aware of all the major problems in health care. Unfortunately, they look for single solutions to these problems—one-size-fits-all, top-down answers that can be imposed by the Surrogates. But getting health care right is rarely a matter of finding the correct answer. It requires putting dynamic processes in place that counteract bad behavior. And the process at the center of most enterprise on the Mainland—the drive to attract customers—is the most powerful and dynamic force we have available. Yet we rarely use it on the Island.

In most industries, the actions of sellers, not the efforts of buyers, are what push down prices and drive quality. Producers of goods and services promote their advantages in price, quality, convenience, sex appeal—you name it—to attract us, the consumers. Take a look at big retailers. Building huge stores featuring a broad category of goods at the lowest possible prices is Wal-Mart's strategy. The company spends hundreds of millions on supply chain management and inventory control to shave pennies off its costs and uses its massive scale to force better terms from manufacturers. It spends billions on advertising to make sure consumers know Wal-Mart has the lowest prices. Wal-Mart's positioning as the low-price leader is not designed to attract consumers who shop around, but rather to assure consumers that if they shop at Wal-Mart, they won't need to shop around.

But Neiman Marcus thrives, too, not despite but because it charges high prices. Neiman's positioning is the antithesis of Wal-Mart's: "We carry only the finest merchandise, much of which you won't find anywhere else." A Neiman Marcus customer receives unhurried service from an elegantly dressed "sales associate" in an uncluttered, uncrowded store.

If Neiman Marcus and Wal-Mart are the extremes, the seemingly infinite options in between are even more instructive. If your prices are slightly higher than Wal-Mart's, then your store needs to offer consumers something else. Perhaps it's bulk purchasing at Costco or a greater emphasis on style at Target or a focus on a single product at Beverage Warehouse or just the convenience of the corner store.

Now, even Wal-Mart doesn't want to compete solely on price. But just as there are few stores that truly compete only on price, almost none of us are pure price shoppers, regardless of income. Some of us will buy only a certain brand of shampoo but happily buy generic toothpaste. Or we complement a diet of cheap pizza with five-dollar lattes. Some people never go out to dinner to save money for a summer vacation; others never go on vacation so they can fund an active nightlife.

No matter where you shop, the mere existence of competing stores benefits you. For example, if you live in a big city, chances are your neighborhood has a convenience store with a limited range of products and relatively high prices. If it's late at night and you urgently need a breath mint or milk for the baby, you may well pay any price. But for most items, you'll have a limit as to how much more you'll pay for the convenience of not having to wait for the supermarket to open in the morning. And the convenience store makes money by selling you more than just what you came in to buy. So the Twinkies have to be somewhat reasonably priced to become tonight's impulse purchase.

What consumer-driven industries do is give us a massive range of choices to match the complexity of our individual preferences and resources. And all of those choices are influenced—at least indirectly—by competition on price, quality, and service. All a consumer has to do is choose, because in a consumer-driven economy the producers and sellers chase consumers, not the other way around.

Perhaps it seems improper to compare competition among retail stores to the industry structure of health care. But let me ask you: Who's the low-price doctor in your neighborhood? Which hospital has the most attentive nurses? The nicest waiting rooms? The smoothest check-in and checkout procedures? Do these questions seem trivial in the life-and-death context of health care? Okay, try this one: Which hospital in your neighborhood has the lowest rate of error-related deaths? That's a piece of information that could well make a difference between a loved one's life and death someday. But the reason you don't know the answer to this fundamental safety question is the same reason you don't know who has the nicest waiting rooms. Health providers, not needing to compete for your business, don't push this information on you.

Our ignorance—our irrelevance—as consumers is the answer to many of the questions regarding dysfunction in health care. The only real reason doctors haven't invested in information technology while dry cleaners have is that doctors can use ridiculous paper files without losing patients. The only real reason the wait is so long at the doctor's office but not at the dentist's is because doctors can get away with it but dentists—most of whose patients pay for their own treatments—can't. The only real reason hospital food is so bad, the decor is so ugly, and the entertainment options are so limited is because they can be—hospitals don't lose patients on this basis. And yes, the reason hospitals kill so many patients is that they can—killing patients doesn't mean they have less loyal customers or that profits decline.

Hospitals don't want to kill patients or even to serve bad food. They just don't face the same discipline that consumer-driven businesses do. Relying on the Surrogates to provide the necessary feedback on quality and service is as useless as relying on them for price discipline; it's the angry, even irrational, consumer that forces a business to be great at service. As absurd as it may seem, the same poor incentives—the same lack of ultimate accountability—that allow hospitals to underinvest in patient comfort also allow them to underinvest in patient safety.

The need for more "waste"

In the mentality that governs much health care thinking, any effort health care providers make to attract patients is simply an expensive distraction from the real mission of providing care. Hospitals and doctors needing to engage in marketing? Wouldn't that just add yet more cost to the system? And wouldn't the pursuit of sexy catchphrases undermine the industry's commitment to medical ethics?

When I was in college, Marxist economists often cited toilet paper as an example of just this type of waste in capitalist economies: all those excessive brands competing on absurd qualities like thickness, softness, roll size, packaging, and jingles. All that pointless marketing, packaging, and distribution expense for a product that everyone needs to buy anyway. Wouldn't it be more sensible to have just toilet paper and use the marketing savings to keep prices down?

My wife grew up in the former Soviet Union, where there was no pointless multiplicity of brands of toilet paper, no class differentiation of thickness of tissue, no wasteful spending on attractive packaging and useless marketing. There was just toilet paper. Sadly, it was expensive, often in short supply, and uniformly rough. The United States has more than fifteen brands of toilet paper. In the grand scheme of things, it truly doesn't matter whose paper is the thickest, the softest, the most absorbent, or even the cheapest. But providing those choices—allowing toilet paper manufacturers to chase consumers on whatever basis they choose—has resulted in all toilet paper (even the unbranded generic product) being thicker, softer, more absorbent, and cheaper than the Soviet one-size-fits-all solution.

Island residents misunderstand marketing because they view it as a wasteful expense. But on the Mainland, marketing revolves around two questions essential for a business to serve customers well: Why should a consumer use my service? And how do I convince him to? Answering those questions means making a promise to consumers and then living up to it; that's what creates real discipline in any business, even one with a product as seemingly generic as toilet paper.

There's already a lot of marketing in health care, but because of moral hazard, it doesn't drive the constant improvement it would in a truly competitive consumer business. Drug companies advertise to get you to ask your doctor for their latest pill, but since you don't bear much of the cost, the burden of their marketing is limited. Hospitals have begun building extra-comfortable emergency rooms for seniors, but their specific goal is to score higher on Medicare's new patient satisfaction surveys—which results in revenue bonuses. A recent *Health Affairs* study even described efforts by hospitals to lure patients with private insurance by offering amenities to the Emergency Medical Service workers who serve better-off neighborhoods.

If health care were a consumer-oriented business, marketing would be the channel of constant improvement.

Some hospital chain would decide to become the Wal-Mart of health care, aggressively driving down costs and passing on the savings to customers. Another chain would decide its best business opportunity lay in becoming the safety leader, capturing patients by bragging far and wide about its record. In this landscape, a third chain would see service and comfort as its best opportunity to create a brand in the eyes of patients. As in every other industry, all three marketing approaches would raise the bar on each of these qualities for all providers. Even if you were hit by a bus and brought unconscious into the nearest hospital, you would benefit from the competition among these chains to capture customers.

A recent survey in Nashville found prices for common preventive services varying by as much as 755 percent across providers. Studies of hospital mortality have found that the surgical death rate for certain procedures when performed at low-volume institutions can be several times the rate for the same procedures when performed at high-volume institutions. Seventy percent of hospitals didn't use electronic records to control the ordering of procedures or drugs as of 2009. And when I recently brought my mother to the emergency room, I was shocked to see that the receiving area was actually marked TRIAGE on a large sign seen by all patients. Can we imagine any of these realities surviving in a competitive, consumer-facing industry that relied on marketing to attract customers?

We all need to change our mentality. A friend of mine recently told me he would be less likely to use a hospital that advertised its services: it made him nervous that its focus wouldn't be on care. I asked him if he was uncomfortable buying his iPad when he realized Apple spent millions advertising its qualities. When your city's safest hospital advertises its success on highway billboards, all hospitals in your city will kill fewer patients.

Our health care policymakers have experimented with countless approaches to improving the quality of health care, reducing the price, and disciplining errors. Why not ask them to try something new? Want providers to offer safer care, lower prices, and better service? Make them chase us.

The passivity disease

The five weeks my father spent in the hospital was a time of great anxiety for my family, as our emotions swung violently with each change in his condition. Indeed, few situations are more stressful than facing for the first time the potential mortality of a loved one. And we were fortunate that—with Dad being a Medicare beneficiary—we didn't have the additional burden of making financial decisions during this extraordinarily difficult time.

But like with so much in health care, our faith in the benefit of not having to worry about money is rooted in a nonsensical fantasy. We all want to believe that there is a single correct course of action for any medical problem and that being assured it will be covered relieves us of stress. But what I found out while attending to my ill father—what I suspect all of us find out in these situations—is that serious illness accentuates our medical individuality, both in how an individual patient reacts to specific treatments and in the patient's individual priorities. So no matter who pays, serious illness requires active decision making by the patient and his family.

When breathing became difficult for my father, an overnight resident suggested we consider a tracheotomy—a surgical incision in his neck that would have opened a direct airway. We didn't do it; of course, with the benefit of hindsight, we've come to see that trying anything would have been better than the ultimate result. But there would have been many factors to consider: at his age, a tracheotomy would have required a long recovery period and might have prevented resumption of his usual activities, including his work.

What still troubles me about the resident's suggestion isn't whether it was the best course for my father's condition at that moment but how quick and casual the conversation was. When I think about the many ways in which my father's hospital service would have been different had he been the true customer, this conversation is front and center. I suspect that my family would actually have had a more complete and structured discussion with the hospital staff on this surgical option if—to put it crudely—the institution had to sell us on a tracheotomy.

I have no way of knowing if a tracheotomy would have saved Dad's life. But I do know that when money is no object, there is less incentive to have the difficult conversations we expect in other expensive services. How much does the course of treatment cost? Are there alternatives? When these conversations don't occur, both patients and providers do whatever is paid for, without really questioning whether what is paid for is really best in a specific situation.

Though Medicare served as the real customer for my father's care—and later paid thousands of dollars for it—Medicare didn't know my father from the forty million other seniors it covers. It had no conversation with the hospital about my father's treatment; it didn't ask for treatment alternatives. Medicare's role was a passive one; in fact, it paid my dad's bill only well after he died (and sent him a follow-up notice informing him of "possible" additional charges three years after he died). In an alarming sense, the hospital's role was a passive one, too; it didn't need to consult with its real customer about my father's specific course of treatment because it already knew what Medicare would and would not reimburse.

Imagine an alternative: instead of paying the hospital, Medicare or your insurer pays you, and you pay the hospital. Don't you suspect that the hospital would be far more active in keeping you informed on what was happening with your loved one and explaining his treatment options? How much personalization of treatment do we give up to avoid personalization of payment?

I think of this as the passivity disease: the false sense of comfort we take from the mistaken idea that the Surrogate who's paying our bills is also assuring the quality of our care and the appropriateness of medical decisions. This false comfort quickly disappears when you first experience a serious illness. Have you ever had a loved one stay in a hospital for an extended period? If so, were you shocked at how much time your family needed to be physically present to prevent mistakes—both big and little ones? My father was taken twice for medical procedures meant for other patients, suffered the same tests multiple times, missed doctor and nurse visits, received incorrectly filled prescriptions, and so on. I now know our experience was typical, not unusual. Even more shocking is how many physicians confirm the need for family members to be present as much as possible to prevent such errors.

Paul Starr has written that "the theory of consumer-driven care rests on a concept of the patient as economic man that does not fit the realities of illness, especially the conditions under which the greatest health-care costs are generated." Indeed, almost all opponents of a greater consumer role in health care cite our alleged incompetence in handling issues of our health. Yet none of them ever address the obvious question: We're incompetent compared with whom? An insurer, perhaps? Does your insurer call you up and say, "Hey, we're concerned about the spot on your forehead. Please have it checked out"? Medicare? Medicaid? None of our Surrogates are—or can be—proactive on our behalf when it comes to our health. Fundamentally, our Surrogates are passive bill payers.

The passivity disease rests on more than a touch of nostalgia. We all remember the days of the general practitioner who did in fact tell us to have that spot checked out, who was invested in our overall health, who helped us navigate the system when specialists were necessary. The reality of our current medical system is that it requires more attention from patients than ever before. With the decline of general medicine and the rise of specialists, we must take on more responsibility for navigating the complexity of the system, coordinating the approaches of specialists who don't communicate with one another, and overseeing hospital care for ourselves and for our families.

And we must be increasingly vigilant when facing a system more likely to sell us unnecessary procedures. Just because a Surrogate will pay for a procedure doesn't mean it's the appropriate course for a patient. This is the ultimate irony: we built the Surrogate system to counteract Arrow's famous information asymmetry problem—that doctors would take advantage of our ignorance to sell us treatment we didn't need—and wound up with ever more waste, ever more excess.*

In an age of heroic physicians, miracle treatments, and breathtaking technology, our health still requires our active participation, from our style of life through our decisions about treatment. We may not like this reality, but hiding from it will not make us healthier. Overall, the Surrogates have done a miserable job of regulating the system's quality, safety, and price. But on an individual level, their performance is even worse. My father in the hospital is not analogous to a car in the shop; his condition, his reactions to drugs and treatments, his tolerance for pain, his emotional state, and his preferences were all unique to him.

Yes, Arrow is right that consumers don't have enough information to be good consumers. But the agents we've designated to act on our behalf have proved to be worse. When it comes to regulating the health care system—providing real discipline on quality, excess, price, and safety—there is no real surrogate. It's a job that only we can do.

---

* Here's just one example: a recent Florida study found that 30 percent of breast biopsies performed over a five-year period were surgical biopsies rather than needle biopsies. This is three times the recommended rate. If that rate held nationally, it would mean that three hundred thousand women a year would be having unnecessary surgery. This, of course, occurs with insurers and Medicare supposedly looking over the shoulder of physicians who order the excessive surgery (Denise Grady, "Study of Breast Biopsy Finds Surgery Used Too Extensively," *New York Times*, February 18, 2011).

CHAPTER 4

The Fallacy

Why we always think we need more health care

> So every night on TV, you see a weird-ass drug com-
> mercial trying to get you hooked on some legal shit, and
> they just keep naming symptoms until they get one that
> you fucking got. Okay? It's like: "Are you sad? Are you
> lonely? You got athlete's foot? Are you hot? Are you cold?
> What you got?" . . . They don't even tell you what the pill
> does. You see a lady on a horse, or a man in the tub, and
> they just keep naming symptoms. . . . I saw a commercial
> the other day that said, "Do you go to bed at night and
> wake up in the morning?" Oh shit, they got one, I got
> that! I'm sick! I need that pill!
>
> —CHRIS ROCK

Imagine a group of investment analysts in the mid-1960s
discussing the future of health care. Incredibly smart and
prescient, they have a unique ability to anticipate almost
perfectly the major developments that will transform the

system. At the time of this imaginary discussion, health care revenue was derived mostly from two sources: highly skilled professionals' (i.e., doctors') time and hospital stays with attendant services. But our analysts foresee that both of these sources of revenue are about to come under tremendous pressure. Doctor productivity will skyrocket as family physicians move from time-consuming house calls to five-minute appointments. Doctors' paternalistic relationship with patients will be eroded as nurse-practitioners, pharmacists, and something called the Internet will take over some of physicians' traditional functions. Information technology will reshape industry, including medicine, allowing patients to own their digital health and treatment records. Perhaps worst of all, giant third-party payers will have enormous market power, forcing physicians and other providers to cut prices.

The business future for hospitals looks even worse. Surgical procedures will become far more effective and efficient, shortening recovery times for even major procedures from weeks to hours.* Even the cost of diagnosis will collapse as extraordinary new machines allow detailed, noninvasive looks into every crevice of the body at low marginal cost. For many conditions, lengthy hands-on treatments will be replaced by pharmaceuticals. At this point, the analysts grouse: everyone knows the economic problem with pharmaceuticals. Like seats on an airplane, they cost a fortune to the airline but have almost no marginal cost to prop up competitive prices.

From the demographic perspective, prospects are even

---

* Almost two-thirds of surgeries no longer require an overnight hospital stay, up from 16 percent as recently as 1980 (*Wall Street Journal,* October 26, 2010).

worse. Americans will be getting richer and healthier. They'll have greater access to better nutrition and enjoy cleaner water and air. They'll have fewer accidents at work and on the roads, and starting in twenty years, there'll be significant declines in violence. They'll be better educated. They'll smoke less—a lot less.

So what do our analysts see? A declining per capita demand for health care as our health and safety improvements are combined with rapid growth in medical productivity. As a result, prices will decline. Health care, our analysts conclude, is a dog—an industry that will be unable to maintain its prices and therefore its profit margins.

Of course, our mythical analysts are truly brilliant in their foresight. Yet somehow they miss one of the greatest industrial growth stories in history—and the chance to invest in an industry in which revenues would grow by sixty times over the next forty-five years. How? These imaginary analysts make only one mistake: they assume there is some set amount of health care that people need.

Our health care policy is built on the same mistake. Every element of our health care system—insurance, Medicare, Medicaid, and regulation—assumes that there is a fixed amount of care that Americans need in a given year and that all we need to do is figure out how to pay for it. But that's a fundamental fallacy.

On the Island, the explanations for the growth of health care all have to do either with health or with care: we're getting older or we have more chronic diseases; effective new treatments cost more than less effective previous ones. But the real explanation is industrial: the health care industry has responded to our willingness to pay for anything labeled "health care" by continuously expanding the definition of health care. As discussed in the previous chapter, we built the Surrogates with the mandate to fund all the health care we need. The ensuing forty-five years have taught us that need isn't independent of payment. That is, as we've shifted more of the direct cost away from patients, providers have less of a hurdle to clear in convincing us that we need more care.

The need fallacy survives because the Beast has expanded subtly: all the new tests, procedures, and pills sure seem medically necessary to patients. And most of this stuff is probably doing people some good. But "doing some good" and "need" are not the same thing. Food and clothing are needs, but that doesn't mean that restaurants and designer jeans are. Yet we could all be easily convinced of their necessity if someone else were paying the bill. That's why no matter how much we keep spending on health care, we never seem to catch up to "need."*

Which came first?

In the movie *Mission: Impossible 2,* the Biocyte Corporation creates both the lethal virus Chimera and its anti-

* Unlike that of our imaginary analysts, most investment research on the health care industry today focuses on the likely increases in insurance, Medicare, and Medicaid payments in determining how much the demand for health care will grow. The real analysts are not subject to the fallacy; they know that if we pay for them, procedures will be performed and billed for.

Business analysts can be far more illuminating on health care than policy experts. For example, a January 2012 research report from Citigroup's health care facilities analysts suggested the following technique for estimating future hospital business: "We specifically focus on 'new' prescriptions, because in the U.S. a new prescription actually requires an actual physician office visit (prescription renewals do not). And we know that the more patients that actually go to a physician's office, the more disease gets diagnosed, the more specialist referrals are made and ultimate(ly) the more hospital visits are generated."

dote, Bellerophon. Tom Cruise's character spends the entire movie preventing a variety of evildoers from capitalizing on this extraordinary profit opportunity. What better business model than the release of a plague for which only your company has the cure? The film, of course, is absurd.

In 1996, Pfizer, one of the world's leading pharmaceutical companies, patented Sildenafil. The drug had not shown much promise in treating angina, its intended target, but it did demonstrate a remarkable ability to induce erections. So in 1998, Pfizer introduced Viagra—its new brand name for Sildenafil—as a treatment for something the company called erectile dysfunction. To date, Viagra and its competitors, Cialis and Levitra, have accounted for an estimated $35 billion in sales.

Pfizer may have coined the term "erectile dysfunction," but it didn't actually cause impotence, which had apparently existed for thousands of years before Pfizer's formation. But the fantasy *M:I-2* and the real Viagra both illustrate something important about contemporary health care.

The traditional understanding of health care is that people get sick and medicine provides a cure. Today, that order is often reversed. With society's willingness to pay for ever more care—a willingness demonstrated by the forty-five-year increase of our spending from $42 billion to $2.5 trillion—much of the innovation in health care is now about the simultaneous search for new treatments and new conditions that require these treatments. It's not that these new conditions are somehow fake illnesses. Rather, illness is increasingly recognized and often only named when a treatment becomes available.

If Pfizer had chosen to market Viagra through sex shops, it's unlikely it would have been able to consistently raise prices even after it lost market share to competitors. The key to its success—and that of its competitors—is that Viagra is marketed as a medicine. The ED drugs have all the trappings of health care. They require prescriptions written by licensed physicians. They look like any other type of medicine, packaged in the iconic plastic prescription bottles. Medicare (and sometimes Medicaid) and many private insurers will cover ED drugs; Viagra and its competitors can legitimately be expensed against tax-advantaged flexible spending and health savings accounts.

Viagra is a classic example of why we seem to need more health care even as we get healthier. Before the treatment was available, most male impotence was seen as a consequence of age. Don't get me wrong: improving the sex lives of older males is a clear social good. But when we first decided to subsidize all health care expenses, would we have considered this problem a health issue?

As we've expanded our willingness to pay for care— through private actions and government support—health care as an industry has met the challenge. It's proved able to absorb our trillions in additional dollars by charging higher prices, convincing us that more expensive options provide better results, and expanding our definitions of "need." In other words, health care has done what any industry does to increase its market and revenue base in the face of rising consumer demand.

But health care as an industry isn't quite like consumer products or automobiles or food. Sure, Procter & Gamble, Ford, and General Mills try to grow by raising prices, introducing new and improved versions of existing products, and extending their product lines. But they must do so in a constant give-and-take with the consumer, overcoming natural consumer resistance to spending more money. As I argued in chapter 3, what makes health care unique is the absence of this consumer in the equation. So health care companies can raise prices, introduce "better" products, and expand the definition of what your health requires without the typical consumer resistance—without needing to prove that a new product is worth a high price.

The most important strategy of the health care industry has been to endlessly increase our demand for health care. To maintain its continued access to the most generous of customers—private insurers, Medicare, and Medicaid—the health care industry must convince us that its services fulfill genuine needs, not merely wants, as all other goods and services do. And once a treatment is considered a need, how can a Surrogate possibly argue it isn't worth paying for?

Chronic conditions

The precise definition of a chronic disease varies, but these ailments are usually identified as long lasting, noncontagious, and resistant to cure. Chronic diseases can range from the primarily annoying (hay fever) to the frequently debilitating (arthritis, diabetes, schizophrenia) to the potentially fatal (heart disease, cancer).

Increasingly, experts on the Island refer to chronic "conditions" instead of "diseases," especially when describing their growth. Roughly half of American adults have been diagnosed with at least one chronic condition; a 2007 report suggests that the number of diagnoses will increase by 42 percent in the next fifteen years. Some of this rapid growth of diagnosed chronic conditions relates to the aging of our population: the average American over sixty-five has at least two identified conditions. But even among younger people—in fact, in every measured age group—chronic conditions are flourishing.

Not only do we all have more chronic conditions, the rate of almost all conditions is on the rise. In the past twenty years, the percentage of Americans suffering from type 2 diabetes and from hypertension has grown from 2 to 10 percent and from 24 to 32 percent, respectively. One out of every eleven children is now considered to have attention deficit hyperactivity disorder.

On the surface, this epidemic of chronic conditions makes little sense. We smoke less, drink less, and work in less physically stressful jobs. Seniors are retiring healthier than they have in any previous generation. How is it possible that we're so much healthier yet have so many more chronic conditions?

I suspect one hint is in the greater use of the word "condition." Increasingly, we've come to describe a broad range of symptomless abnormalities and markers of potential disease as chronic conditions, especially if there is a treatment to manage them. As in the invention of erectile dysfunction, a growing ability to treat—specifically, to manage health issues without curing them—drives an expanding definition of illness.

For example, hypertension is widely recognized as one of the most serious chronic conditions, often leading to heart disease and strokes. It was first recognized in the nineteenth century, but effective treatment is more recent. The spread of blood pressure testing and the introduction of new drugs have allowed hypertension to be managed medically, undoubtedly contributing to the sizable declines in heart attacks and strokes over the past fifty years. But our ability to treat high blood pressure medically has led to an expansion of its diagnosis: nearly a third of American adults today have diagnosable hypertension.

According to a recent article in *The Wall Street Journal*, doctors have now identified a separate issue from hypertension that they call prehypertension—a combination of elevated blood pressure and lifestyle risk factors that may lead directly to heart disease and strokes. Prehypertension doesn't feature all of the usual symptoms of hypertension, so it is regarded as a separate condition. Doctors are still debating the optimal treatment for prehypertension: traditional recommended lifestyle changes (dieting, exercise, alcohol moderation, reduced salt intake) or drugs usually prescribed for high blood pressure. The article notes that while many doctors prefer lifestyle alterations because they have longer-term health benefits for patients, a 2006 study showed clear benefits of medication for prehypertension.

What does this mean for health care policy? Before the identification of prehypertension, people with this syndrome would have been categorized as healthy. But now that doctors have shown that certain blood pressure medications can reduce the chances that some of these previously healthy people will later suffer from hypertension, all of them now have a chronic condition: prehypertension. In short, the growth of chronic conditions is really the march of reclassification: many chronic conditions are simply medicalized terms for the various types of discomfort and risk that people have been dealing with forever. So we now think of these issues as medical ones—as health care problems—even though, in the CDC's words, "four modifiable health risk behaviors—lack of physical activity, poor nutrition, tobacco use, and excessive alcohol consumption—are responsible for much of the illness, suffering, and early death related to chronic diseases."

I myself am a typical example of this. Like an estimated one in four Americans over forty-five, I take a statin daily to control my cholesterol; an elevated level of LDL (or "bad") cholesterol is often classified as a chronic condition. My cardiologist told me that changes in my diet—more fish, fruits, and vegetables; less ice cream, burgers, and doughnuts— might alone be sufficient to lower the LDL level, but he felt that the drug was a safe alternative. So I take the statin, and it works (at least in the sense of lowering my cholesterol; whether it will do anything for my risk of heart disease remains an open question).

Before the invention of statins, someone in my position would have needed to change his diet to reduce the risk of heart disease. The invention of statins provided not only a medical alternative but an alternative that others—through insurance—will help me pay for. My fellow insured Americans would not have been willing to subsidize more fish and vegetables in my grocery cart, but insurance requires them to share the cost of my pharmaceutical alternative.

It's worth thinking about my personal decision for a moment. When I chose a statin, society subsidized that choice at the point of purchase through the tax advantages afforded insurance and my health saving account. If I were a Medicare or Medicaid beneficiary, society's subsidy would have been more direct. Since we all ultimately pay for these subsidies, we should all care about the choices our policies encourage—in this case, more drugs, fewer vegetables.

What does all this mean for our approach to health care?

The issue isn't whether health insurance should or shouldn't cover chronic conditions. The issue is that chronic conditions illustrate why so much medical care cannot be sensibly covered by insurance. Once prehypertension treatment is covered, pre-prehypertension will be discovered. Then pre-pre-prehypertension. Our current level of medical spending means that Becky will have to put at least $1.2 million into the system over her lifetime; how much more will she need to contribute when pre-prehypertension treatment and its like are state of the medical art?

If we step out of the insurance mind-set, the reality of our society's choices is clear. If Becky had $1.2 million to spend on her own health care, she might make different choices with her money. She may decide to pay for treatment of her heart disease but that pre-hypertension treatment isn't as important as eating better, working out more, going to graduate school, or taking more vacations. Any of these decisions may well mean a much better life for Becky. With her money, she can make the individualized trade-offs that society—with our one-size-fits-all approach to care—can't.

Certainly, many of us suffering with chronic conditions have very serious medical issues for which treatment has been essential to survival. And most of us may benefit from treatment: chronic-condition care isn't a fraud, and for some, treatment now could save larger costs down the road. But the very explosion of these diagnoses during a time of vastly improving health should challenge our concept of health care "need."

I don't believe in conspiracies, but it's necessary to point out that chronic conditions may provide the perfect business model for the health care industry. Health care providers now have the equivalent of cheap razors with expensive blades: you'll need to buy refills for these forever. Like a game of health care Whac-A-Mole, the better we get at care, the more conditions we will identify. The more illnesses we can cure, the more in need of treatment we will be. Chronic conditions will continue to replace curable ones until we all require medical management of some form or another.

The rise of pharmaceuticals

Pharmaceuticals are the primary treatment for almost 90 percent of all chronic conditions, and at any given moment, roughly 50 percent of American adults—including nine of ten adults older than sixty—are taking at least one prescription drug. Almost a third of all adults take two or more drugs. About 30 percent of all teens are now on a prescription, as are 20 percent of younger children. America will spend just under $300 billion on pharmaceuticals this year.

To many people, the big drug companies are the chief villains of our health care mess. They convince consumers and doctors to overuse their products. They invest research funds into me-too drugs rather than breakthrough treatments. They maintain absurdly high prices—as is evident when their patent protections expire and generics sell at an average discount of 67 percent.

All of these accusations ring true, but pharmaceutical companies are merely behaving rationally in response to the incentives our system provides. They may be the easiest target for criticism in the system, but that's because, unlike most other health care businesses, they sell an actual identifiable product at an actual price (i.e., not bundled with other services like devices or hospital rooms). The drug business may be the most straightforward example of how our refusal to use price to regulate supply and demand creates excesses in both and discourages innovation.

Let's start with the marketing challenge in the pharmaceutical business. In 2010, drug companies spent over $4 billion on advertising to sell consumers on the virtues of prescription drugs—medicines with easy-to-remember yet medical-sounding names like Lipitor, Flomax, and Lexapro. As much as $272 million has been spent on consumer advertising for a single drug brand in a single year. A 2004 estimate suggested that drug companies spend up to an additional $50 billion a year on their other marketing activities, such as maintaining armies of sales reps who try to convince doctors to prescribe their products (and provide those free samples your physician hands you to reduce the cost of a new prescription).

As discussed in the preceding chapter, I believe there's too little marketing in health care. But pharmaceutical advertising illustrates one of the problems of marketing within our current system. When other businesses try to sell you a product, their implicit message is that the benefits are worth the price to you. But in so much of health care, the price is mostly borne by a third party.* So a health marketer's challenge is simpler: just to prove that the customer will benefit from the product. Drugs are a much easier sell

---

* As drug co-pays have gone up, pharmaceutical companies have looked for ways to help consumers avoid cost sharing. In many drug advertisements, you'll hear an offer to find out if you are eligible for the manufacturer's assistance in handling your out-of-pocket burden. These discounts could in theory be offered to insurers or Medicare, but it's far more effective as a business matter to eliminate consumers' cost concerns and far less likely to be described as a kickback. If it's couched as aid to the needy.

than surgery, as the cost in time, potential pain, and complications appears so much smaller. So drug advertising has a lower consumer hurdle for success, although it's perhaps not quite as easy as Chris Rock suggests at the beginning of this chapter.*

Drug companies spend money on advertising not only to create awareness of these conditions (that is, to stimulate demand for their treatments) but also to brand their products. Though branding is common in consumer products, isn't it a bit bizarre with drugs? After all, drug companies enjoy patent protection on their products; in return for spending an enormous sum of money on research and development, a manufacturer is awarded a monopoly on selling a particular drug for twenty years.† Why would you possibly need to spend all that money branding Lipitor if you have a monopoly on selling the underlying chemical compound?

In drugs, a chemical monopoly is often not really a business monopoly. Because although Pfizer may have had complete control over atorvastatin calcium (aka Lipitor), there were other statin monopolies competing to treat your high cholesterol (most statins have recently become available as generics). In fact, of the top seventy-five prescription drugs sold in the United States, seven treat diabetes, six hypertension, six cholesterol, five asthma, four depression, three heartburn, and three schizophrenia. By definition, these drugs are not chemically identical to one another, yet for

---

* A statistic from the House Energy and Commerce Committee suggests that every $1,000 spent on drug advertising translates into twenty-four new prescriptions (Jerome Groopman and Pamela Hartzband, "Designing a Smarter Patient," *Wall Street Journal,* September 24, 2011).

† In practice, the sales monopoly period is much shorter, often less than ten years, as companies file for protection before entering the lengthy regulatory process.

many patients, they achieve similar results. And all still must compete for patient and doctor attention and awareness.

Pharmaceutical companies spend more than $60 billion a year on research and development of new drugs. The industry estimates that the total cost of developing a single new drug, including research, testing, and the approval process, exceeds $1.3 billion—almost ten times what it was thirty years ago. The industry's trade association notes that the share of sales spent on research and development— 17.4 percent—is the highest among major manufacturing industries.

Why would companies with such high research and development costs chase the same customers with me-too products? Keep in mind that most industries with business models similar to drug companies'—high initial costs, very low production costs, competitive products—have a difficult time maintaining prices (for example, software companies, airlines, and telecoms). A new product creates the risk of a price war. Yet drug companies are able to maintain high prices on their products despite the competition. In 2009, the revenue from each of the fifty top-selling pharmaceuticals increased by more than the drug's total number of prescriptions. That means all of them were able to achieve effective price increases, even in the depth of the recession. Such increases were also the rule for drugs that suffered massive declines in volume (as much as 60 percent!) and for those with clear substitutes.

In theory, providing patent protection for drug companies encourages them to make the risky research investments needed to find the next breakthrough medicine. But the incentives are muddled; the lack of true price competition reduces the risk of introducing a me-too product.

Since a drug company doesn't face the risk of a price war, it overinvests in safer products with established markets and underinvests in riskier ones that may provide greater health benefit.

Pharmaceutical companies do take massive risks in looking for new treatments, and it's not unusual to hear of $1 billion or more in write-offs for an unsuccessful research effort. But they also get excellent returns from large investments in drugs with little marginal benefit over existing options. Without a functioning price system, all they have to do is convince some people to tell their doctors that, say, Crestor is better than Lipitor (which intimidates insurers from denying either in the name of cost control) and to suggest that our ever lower blood pressure or cholesterol levels—or even that rare night of romantic failure—could benefit from medical management.

Preventive care

Hand in hand with the explosion of chronic conditions has been the expansion of what is called preventive care. This term used to refer to specific lifestyle and treatment options for those at elevated risk of certain diseases; the idea was to do everything possible to avoid developing the disease or, in the case of certain cancers, to find it early enough to improve survival odds.

But like so much in health care, the parameters of preventive care have spread well beyond their original definition. Preventive care now seems to include any screening or exam for any potential illness, even if the patient is symptom-free and lacks any meaningful risk factors. When I entered my age and gender on UnitedHealthcare's website, it recommended regular "screening and counseling" for seventeen different issues (height/weight, obesity, vision, dental, blood pressure, cardiovascular disease, cholesterol, diabetes, prostate, colorectal, tobacco/nicotine, alcohol/illicit drug, nutrition, physical activity, sun exposure, depression, and injury prevention) and added one (sexually transmitted disease) if I was sexually active.

Preventive care has become the flavor of the day among health care experts. In fact, the ACA mandates that anything considered preventive be covered 100 percent by insurers. Needless to say, this policy has already set off a scramble in the industry to ensure that all variety of tests and procedures will qualify under this provision.

So what's the problem with some extra screening? Can't hurt, can it?

The ACA policy is based on a fantasy that preventive care somehow saves the health care system money. For people with symptoms or clear risk factors, this may even be true; it usually is cheaper—and definitely safer—to head off heart disease than to treat the victim of a heart attack. But even for at-risk people, studies suggest that much of the benefit has been derived from doctors scaring patients into losing weight, exercising, quitting smoking or drug use, and cutting back on drinking. Society would save a lot of money by paying best friends to perform the same service. And as preventive care has expanded—in Beast-style—to include testing everyone for everything, it can only add massive costs to the system.

Another problem with preventive care is that few of our tests and screenings are truly free in terms of our health. Last year, a study in *The New England Journal of Medicine* reported that imaging tests annually expose four million

Americans under sixty-five to high doses of radiation. About four hundred thousand of them get very high doses, well above exposure limits even for those who work with radioactive materials. The study pointed out that many, perhaps most, of the scans are routine and probably not necessary for diagnosis. But of course, many of these scans will now be eligible for 100 percent reimbursement as preventive care.

A recent study of full-body CT scans illustrates the often misunderstood risk-reward ratios in much preventive medicine. Of twelve hundred scans studied, a full 87 percent showed some abnormality! Yet on further examination, less than 1 percent of these proved to be a tumor of any kind. As Shannon Brownlee points out in her book *Overtreated,* recent studies suggest that having a full-body CT scan every year for fifteen years itself creates a 0.4 percent risk of dying from radiation-related cancer—roughly the same risk of dying in an auto accident.

A third problem with extensive preventive care is that we become "overdiagnosed," to use Dr. H. Gilbert Welch's term. Each healthy person has abnormal levels of something—blood pressure, heart rate, cholesterol, bone density, blood sugar, body mass, hair growth. Remember what normality is: the most typically measured results in a population. But atypical doesn't necessarily mean unhealthy. What is normal—and healthy—is to vary from the mean in at least one thing. Mild variations, without any symptoms of illness, probably require no medical intervention. And the more we test, the more we'll find: Welch notes that test scans on perfectly healthy people without any symptoms have found gallstones in 10 percent, knee meniscus damage in 40 percent, and bulging lumbar disks in 50 percent.

Unfortunately, from prostate growths to polyps to

uterine fibroids, our ability to find abnormalities has significantly outpaced our ability to differentiate between dangerous ones and safe ones. It's a short hop from testing the healthy to magnifying the implications of minor variations ("lowering the threshold of diagnosis," as Welch calls it) to excess treatment.

In addition, treating the healthy ("those who will not benefit") magnifies the apparent success of treatment. Because we now catch and treat so many potential problems before they develop into actual illnesses, it seems as if we're getting better at treating people. Instead, much of our "success" is in treating people who would never have gotten sick anyway. We're so used to the language of preventive care that we sometimes forget that high cholesterol isn't actually heart disease, that above-average blood sugar isn't actually diabetes, and that a diagnosis of low bone density—even if it's now called osteoporosis—is not the same as actually having the symptoms of osteoporosis.

Welch points out that for many conditions (including prostate cancer, melanoma, and kidney cancer), the death rate of those treated has often significantly declined while the death rate across the population as a whole has barely budged. What this means is that even for many serious illnesses, our growing "success" in treatment is illusory; we're merely "successfully" treating those who wouldn't have died. But the excess treatment in itself is dangerous for these success stories. As a recent *BMJ* article put it, "Medicine's much hailed ability to help the sick is fast being challenged by its propensity to harm the healthy."

Finally, just because a test is sensible for some people doesn't mean it should be performed on everyone. We may all know of a friend with no symptoms and no risk factors

who through a test found out about a potentially fatal disease early enough for successful treatment. But the numbers
suggest this is very rare.

Simply put, all preventive care is not equally valuable. We
see this play out in other walks of life every day. It may
make sense to bear the high cost of air bags (including the
chance of injury in deployment) to reduce the significant
risk of dying in an auto accident. And for small risks, such as
carbon monoxide poisoning, it may make sense to bear the
minimal cost of maintaining an inexpensive monitor. But
our approach to preventive care doesn't acknowledge that
the size of the risk is relevant in determining the appropriate
cost in side effects or dollars.

The problems with preventive care are well illustrated in
the recent controversy over a 2009 recommendation by the
U.S. Preventive Services Task Force to reduce the frequency
of mammography screenings. Reversing its earlier recommendation, the task force suggested that asymptomatic
women did not need to begin annual mammograms at forty
(unless they had higher risk of breast cancer) and that a
screening every two years was adequate for women between
fifty and seventy-five. They recommended that women over
seventy-five no longer have mammograms at all.

This proposal to reduce preventive care met with a fire-
storm of criticism. Many accused the nonpolitical panel of
experts of playing politics with health or of trying to save
money, even though the group is prohibited from considering cost in its evaluations. Karen Young-Levi of Breast
Cancer.org had a typical reaction. "If someone ran a computer analysis that determined that wearing a seat belt is

not going to protect you from being killed during a crash, would you stop using a seat belt?" she asked. "My big fear is that coverage will be diminished and that a very valuable tool to detect something at an early stage could be taken away from me."

My mother is a breast cancer survivor, so I'm especially sympathetic to concerns such as those expressed by Ms. Young-Levi. But she and so many other critics didn't seem to be hearing what the Task Force was actually saying: not that mammograms couldn't save some lives through early detection but rather that—when you exclude high-risk women—the benefits were quite small compared with the harm caused by excessive mammograms. Specifically, the Task Force found that the low rate of detection was not worth the regular exposure to radiation, the discomfort of the exam, and, most important, the excess testing, patient anxiety, surgery, and other often toxic treatment generated by mammography's high rate of false positives.

Are they right? If my wife is one of the very few who die from breast cancer because they didn't have a regular mammogram in their forties, I will curse the Task Force. By contrast, if she's one of the many who benefit from avoiding the months of repeat testing and treatment from a false positive, who benefit from reducing their radiation exposure, or who benefit simply from escaping the inconvenience of the test, then I won't even remember there's a Task Force to thank.

Again, it's the insurance system itself that requires a single answer to the question of what's the right amount of mammography, but there isn't one right answer or an answer that addresses all of our risk preferences. Perhaps it would be best for women who need psychological reassurance to get an annual mammogram at thirty and those who would suffer from the anxiety of a false positive to wait until fifty. But this sensible degree of personalization is not what our insurance-based system requires to fund preventive medicine.

Several years ago, the Federal Aviation Administration was considering a new rule requiring that small children fly in a car seat. Who could object to a rule that provided maximum protection to our little ones? It would be coldhearted to point out that there had never been an airline accident in which a child was more likely to survive because of a car seat, or that this new regulation could be quite expensive for parents who would now have to buy tickets for children they might otherwise have held on their laps. Isn't even the smallest additional protection worth it? Fortunately, two clever economists, Richard McKenzie and Dwight Lee, figured out that the proposed regulation was likely to kill many more children than it saved. They showed that the added cost would persuade many parents to drive rather than fly when possible. Since it is far more dangerous to travel by car than by plane, more car trips would mean more children injured and killed.

Perhaps soon someone will make a definitive case that certain types of preventive care also kill more people than they help—that all that radiation, those false positives, and that unneeded treatment cost us more lives than they save. But until then, preventive care may turn into an even better business model than chronic care for the health care industry. Our new love affair with preventive care is creating even more perverse incentives in the system, shifting resources from care of the ill to reassurance of the healthy. In forty-five years, we've gone from claims for only the direst medical emergencies to claims for tests that prove we're just fine.

In *The Simpsons* episode "The Wizard of Evergreen Terrace," Homer decides to become the next Thomas Edison. Among his inventions is an alarm that lets out a loud noise every few seconds as long as everything's okay. Needless to say, in the market-driven world of Springfield, where people spend their own money to buy stuff, there's no demand for Homer's invention.

What works?

John Wanamaker, the department store king, famously remarked, "Half the money I spend on advertising is wasted; the trouble is I don't know which half." In health care, best estimates of pure waste are somewhere between 20 and 30 percent. But as with advertising (at least in Wanamaker's day), we don't have a way to identify which money is well spent. In the past forty-five years, our country has committed an additional $2.2 trillion a year to health care without any effective mechanism for measuring the benefits of that increased spending. True, we're generally healthier, but as noted earlier, much of this can be attributed to lifestyle and environmental changes. Virtually all high-profile studies cite only the greater availability of treatments, not the results of those treatments, as "evidence" for the benefit of health insurance.

Of course, there are effectiveness studies done for many specific treatments, often in connection with regulatory approvals. What is striking to the outsider is how minor incremental improvements can justify massive investments, and how little follow-up research is done after the approval of a new treatment. For example, approximately thirty million Americans now take antidepressants, at an annual cost of $10 billion. Some recent studies suggest that while these drugs may have clear therapeutic benefits for the clinically depressed, they are no better than placebos for the millions of other patients with mere depression symptoms. Yet this hasn't stopped the growth of these drugs, over 70 percent of which are now apparently prescribed without any formal psychiatric diagnosis.*

It's hard to imagine that we would spend anywhere near what we do on health care on anything else without a better understanding of how much good is accomplished. In most markets, this is easy; we expect that if people are spending ten dollars to see a movie, it's because movies give them some pleasure worth ten dollars. But in health care, because most money spent is third-party money, we have no such assurance. Further, given all the harm health care can cause through medical mistakes and excess treatments, developing accurate assessment tools for patients and doctors should be a priority.

Part of the problem in developing better measures of value may be technological, and part may be a lack of social commitment. But much of it is the lack of incentives normally provided by consumers. As chapter 3 describes, consumer-based industries aren't dependent on active con-

---

* There's also $15 billion worth of antipsychotics prescribed each year. It's hard not to suspect that at least one reason for the growth in psychopharmacology is its superiority as a business model over more time-intensive forms of therapy (see Gardiner Harris, "Talk Doesn't Pay, So Psychiatry Turns Instead to Drug Therapy," *New York Times*, March 6, 2011). And it is certainly fertile ground for diagnoses, with claims that as many as one in five American adults has some form of mental illness (see the 2010 Substance Abuse and Mental Health Services Administration survey).

sumers. We consumers are mostly lazy; proving the worth of a product is usually a marketing tool of businesses to attract customers. Unfortunately, health providers haven't needed to develop better metrics to sell us more treatments.

Just before the vote on the ACA, I asked a prominent supporter of the act for his estimate of current health care spending on excess or unneeded care, waste, and inflated prices. He said 30 percent, equal to $750 billion a year. Rather than spend more money on care, I asked, wouldn't it be better to find ways to reduce that waste, freeing up funds for those with limited access? No, he said, the two issues are unrelated. So while Island residents are unable to reallocate spending using measurements and accountable results, we, like Wanamaker, continue to grope in the dark for what is wasted and what is worthwhile.

Are boob jobs health care?

Lounging on the beach one afternoon, my wife suggested that health insurers be required to reimburse women for breast reshaping after childbirth. After all, we treat delivery as a medical procedure and recommend breast-feeding for the health of infants. Why shouldn't fixing a side effect of this necessary biological activity—sagging breasts—also be deserving of insurance coverage? Reconstructive surgery after other medical procedures is reimbursed, after all.

I've been married long enough to know that the correct response to my wife's suggestion did not involve health care policy. After reassuring her that her body was too beautiful to benefit from—much less need—any work, I thought about how difficult her question is given the mechanisms of our current system.

In my gut, something tells me breast reshaping isn't really health care. But why? We already reimburse for a broad variety of cosmetic procedures, usually to fix a congenital deformity, an injury, or the effects of a disease. And no one disputes that breast reconstruction after a mastectomy is a reimbursable procedure, even though its primary function is cosmetic. In the back of our minds, we have a vague definition of medical necessity: if the mastectomy was necessary, doesn't that mean the reconstruction is, too? Since child delivery is necessary, shouldn't my wife's postpartum lift also be reimbursed? Should we pay for prosthetic limbs only if they are functional, or are cosmetic attributes alone worthy of reimbursement? If cosmetic surgery helps a woman develop greater self-esteem or avoid postpartum blues, wouldn't it serve the same purpose as an antidepressant? And following that logic, shouldn't it be reimbursed just like a prescription?*

And what if insurers were mandated to pay for postpartum breast reconstruction? Wouldn't that be unfair to women who were happy with their postpartum bodies, who didn't regard their changed breasts as appropriate candidates for the surgeon's scalpel? Why should their insurance premiums cover the costs for women with different tastes?

---

* The recent rise in weight loss surgery is another example of issues previously regarded as cosmetic morphing into medical ones. A January 8, 2012, *New York Times* article stated that the procedure is now performed on almost a quarter of a million people each year, at a total cost of roughly $6 billion. Its survey of local hospitals suggested that one in twenty is performed on a patient under the age of twenty-five.

You can laugh, but I'm not sure there are clear, consistent, and principled ways to answer my wife's question in the context of our insurance-based health system.

Increasingly, health experts rely on the political system to answer the difficult questions of what should be reimbursable by insurers, Medicare, and Medicaid, but the results haven't been promising in terms of consistency or principle, not to mention control over the expanding definition of care. The fifty states have imposed on health insurers more than two thousand mandates—requirements to reimburse certain procedures—and the regulations required by the ACA will include additional mandates on a national level. Most Americans seem to like mandates; they are always presented as new benefits for the insured, imposed by legislators on reluctant insurers. But of course, politicians aren't merely adding benefits; they're imposing costs through inevitably higher premiums. I suspect that if legislation required all citizens to buy a new suit, most of us wouldn't be celebrating the "benefit" of our new outfit. We'd be complaining that the government had forced us to pay for the outfit. But with few exceptions, no one seems agitated by the government forcing us to pay for coverage of others' procedures—at least not yet.

Many of these existing mandates cover treatments that used to be thought of as cosmetic, optional, or at the very least not medically necessary. Ten states require coverage for hair prostheses; thirteen for in vitro fertilization. Thirty-one mandate contraceptive reimbursement. Forty-six require reimbursement for the services of chiropractors; fourteen for marriage counselors; and four for massage therapists. Arizona mandates the cost of athletic training. Maine mandates breast reduction surgery. The issue isn't whether any or all of these treatments are good or useful: the question is whether we should all be required to pay for some who want them.

Deepak Chopra has said that insurers should cover meditation classes: "If insurance companies paid for lifestyle-management classes, they would save huge sums of money." Almost every request for a new mandate claims it will save money, yet the amount we spend on care keeps rising. But Chopra's comment illustrates the fundamental principle we now apply to judging whether something should be reimbursed: Is it good for us? Not, Is it worth the money, but Is it good, useful, helpful?

Are we really prepared to pay for anybody else's—indeed, everybody else's—idea of what is good and useful?

The health care industry has branched out, expanding its product line from the urgent treatment of illness to the much broader management of well-being and comfort. It's invested in the identification and treatment of chronic conditions—an almost perfect business model in which the patient needs constant treatment without ever receiving a cure. No one was conspiring to broaden health care's reach; no Biocyte Corporation was maliciously locking away the only cure. Redefining health care was a gradual and dis-aggregated process, the rational response of thousands of actors—from doctors and hospitals to drug companies and device manufacturers—to the unique incentives presented in our system of health care. And for the most part, we still don't see it. We still don't understand that no amount of money will ever fill the belly of the Beast.

CHAPTER 5

The Seduction

Forty-five years of Medicare

> The result is a peculiarly American form of ageism. The elderly are afforded anything "approved" that money can buy, even if it affords them no health benefit and places them in harm's way. But the elderly are less likely to be afforded less-costly and less-profitable interventions. The reimbursement schedules caring about them as people and caring for them as patients pale next to reimbursement schedules for interventions aimed at their diseases.
>
> —NORTIN HADLER, *Rethinking Aging: Growing Old and Living Well in an Overtreated Society*

A couple of years ago, my childhood friend Roy and I went to visit his father, Walter, at his Florida condo. Walter is eighty-eight, lives on his own, and looks great despite having suffered a stroke three years ago. In the course of our visit, Roy noticed a folded wheelchair wedged in the corner.

"Dad, why do you have a wheelchair?"

Walter thought for a moment, then remembered. "The hospital gave it to me when I checked out."

"Do you ever use it?"

"I've actually never used it. Forgot it was here."

"Aren't you billed for it?"

"No."

Roy called the hospital to return the wheelchair. He discovered that it was indeed hospital policy to provide wheelchairs to stroke victims on discharge, just in case they needed them. Patients could return the chairs whenever they were no longer useful, but the hospital never asked for them back. By then there was no point in returning Walter's chair: the hospital had been billing Medicare a monthly rental fee, and enough months had gone by that the chair was considered fully paid for. From the hospital's perspective, the chair was now free.

Walter himself placed no value on the chair. He had not asked for it, had never used it, and had forgotten he had it. Like many people his age, he is living on a fixed income and is prudent about spending. My guess is that if he had been required to bear any amount of the wheelchair's cost—even a few cents a month—he would have immediately returned it to the hospital.

This story is a reminder of why so many Americans support Medicare as a pillar of our society's commitment to our seniors. True, Walter has been walking without a wheelchair since discharge, but certainly some seniors do need a wheelchair when recovering from a stroke. Our generosity allows Walter and his loved ones this additional peace of mind at a vulnerable time. After all, the man did have a stroke, and I'd rather see him get some excess and precautionary care than get too little care. It's not as if the unnecessary wheelchair did him any harm or cost him anything.

To most health care experts, Walter's wheelchair is also a good example of the fundamental challenge of Medicare. Our society wants to provide seniors with peace of mind regarding their health, but with its $550 billion annual price tag—one that's rapidly growing—we also need to control the care. Essentially, the challenge, as seen by policymakers, is how to provide wheelchairs to the stroke victims who need them without buying unneeded chairs for people like Walter. This issue has become a familiar battle between those concerned about our nation's fiscal solvency who are looking for ways to control Medicare costs and those advocates for seniors who are fighting against any controls that might deny some of them needed care.

Unfortunately, this battle—which has been raging almost since the first days of Medicare—masks the more important meaning of Walter's wheelchair. As a businessman, I look at the story of Walter and his wheelchair with envy. After all, some hospital and its vendor managed to sell a wheelchair, at a profitable price, to someone who didn't need it and didn't even have to pay for it himself. If only my business had customers like that! The real problem with Medicare is that the health care industry does have customers like this: our seniors through their Surrogate, Medicare.

In October 2011, *The Lancet*, a British health journal, published an analysis of all Medicare patients who had died in 2008. The study discovered that doctors had performed surgery on fully a third of patients in the last year of their lives. Almost 40 percent of sixty-five-year-old patients underwent final-year operations—a statistic that might make sense to many. But 35 percent of eighty-year-olds were subject to this aggressive treatment, and one in five ninety-year-olds had surgery before dying!

By looking only at the dying, *The Lancet*'s study may paint an incomplete picture: we don't know how many patients in 2008 didn't die because they had surgery. Nor do we know how many of the deaths occurred as a result of surgery itself. But the prevalence of aggressive treatment at such late stages in life is so great that the study suggests an extraordinary bias toward such treatment in Medicare. Even assuming that every procedure offered the potential of health benefit, it is difficult to believe that the *health* cost of surgery—with its especially long recovery periods, discomfort, and complications for the aged—could possibly make sense for so many dying eighty- and ninety-year-olds.

In other words, the same factors that allow Walter a free but unneeded wheelchair also tend to subject people of his age to free but ill-advised prostate surgery, coronary bypass operations, spinal fusion procedures, and countless diagnostic scans. The same incentives that discourage a hospital from checking with Walter to see if he needs his wheelchair also discourage them from evaluating whether the risk-reward balance of major treatment is sensible for a man his age. The same weak Medicare oversight that allows for the full purchase of a never used wheelchair also enables an incalculable amount of excess medicine to be delivered in facilities plagued by serious medical errors. And unlike the unnecessary wheelchair, all these excess procedures can harm Walter—or even kill him.

When you switch perspectives on Medicare—from seniors and the government to health care as a business— you understand that Walter's wheelchair is just the tip of a very large iceberg. While we try to find fiscal solutions that will enable seniors to continue their dependency on Medicare for their health needs, we've ignored another dependency. Much of our health care system now relies on Medicare for its revenues and growth.

A growing body of evidence says that this industry dependency explains what should be one of the central questions in health care policy: How is it possible that the healthiest generation in the history of mankind needs so much more health care upon retirement than any previous generation? The answer is that Medicare itself has created an overwhelming economic incentive for providers to find "need" and to treat it. As I discussed in chapter 4, some of this extra care may well be beneficial. Other treatments may be health-neutral (although still wasteful). But with seniors especially vulnerable to the health risks of aggressive care, much of this excess treatment is outright dangerous.*

---

* We do have a lot of evidence of harmful overtreatment. Practically every month brings a study of another test, drug, or procedure widely overused in Medicare. A few recent torn-from-the-headlines examples: nearly a sixth of nursing home residents are treated with powerful antipsychotic pharmaceuticals in doses exceeding recommended maximums (www.nlm.nih.gov/medlineplus/news/fullstory_125718 .html). A quarter of Medicare beneficiaries get colonoscopies more frequently than recommended, including those over seventy-five, for whom the test is not recommended because of exposure to serious dangers and insignificant diagnostic benefit (http://azstarnet.com/news/science/health-med-fit/article_314b1e59 -a748-5d3c-abbd-95c7f5a005b8.html). Of course, that's just part of the growing evidence that our health care system is ever more diligent in looking for conditions—anything—in our elderly to treat. In the past decade, the amount of imaging per beneficiary has increased by almost 90 percent (MedPAC).

Some of the major operations performed on older patients have questionable benefits when all risks are calculated. Many older Americans complain of lower back pain and are often recommended for spinal fusion, even though the evidence is limited that the surgery benefits more than a small fraction of patients. In *Overtreated*, Shannon Brownlee quotes researchers who estimate that as many as 15 percent of elective cardiac catheterizations are inappropriate by cardiologists' own standards. She also notes that roughly two-thirds of the more than one hundred thousand carotid endarterectomies performed annually are done on seniors lacking any symptoms, despite the high (6 to 7 percent) risk of stroke or death from the procedure itself.

We should keep in mind that our seniors are more vulnerable than younger

Unfortunately, we have plenty of evidence that an industry culture that fails to consider the needs of the whole patient is also careless in other essential respects. Medicare's inability to provide normal disciplinary controls allows the current plague of accidents and mistakes of the kind that killed my father, among so many other seniors.

To make it worse, all of Medicare's services—including Walter's wheelchair—are in fact far from genuinely free for our seniors. In our focus on Medicare's ballooning cost to society, we've ignored its ever growing cost to seniors. Incredibly, the percentage of an average senior's income spent on health care is now higher—almost 50 percent higher—than it was before Medicare! Sure, as in so much of health care, these costs are often hidden from seniors themselves, divided among various charges to conceal the total amount. But the plain numbers are unambiguous: even though seniors pay only a tiny percentage of their own health care costs, the explosion of excess medicine, price inflation, medical accidents, and waste means that even this small percentage is now more costly to seniors themselves than when seniors paid almost all of their own health costs.

The pernicious effects of Medicare on seniors are rarely discussed, even among health experts. Medicare is almost universally viewed simply as an invaluable safety net for seniors, not as an industry stimulus that uses seniors as conduits to direct ever more money into health care. So the debate around Medicare continues on a single track—how much of this wonderful benefit to our seniors can our soci-

---

people to the harm of overtreatment. They recover more slowly from procedures, are more likely to suffer side effects, and unfortunately have less time to enjoy whatever benefit treatment may provide. In other words, their risk-reward calculation should often suggest that they receive less treatment than the younger populations, not more.

ety afford? That's certainly an important question, but the more important question is, How much Medicare can our seniors withstand?

The medicalization of senior citizenship

A friend recently told me that her ninety-year-old grandfather was miserable since his doctor ordered the end of his long tradition of a nightly glass of Scotch. The doctor was concerned that alcohol would react poorly with the pills he was taking in the hope of warding off Alzheimer's. No one—not even Granddad—had questioned whether the benefits of the medication were worth giving up the pleasure of the Scotch. In the age of Medicare, it would be rare indeed to put anything before health care for our seniors, no matter what their age or remaining life expectancy.

I see this even with my extraordinarily energetic mother. At 65-plus, my mother still works full-time (and walks to work), exercises several times a week, maintains an active social life, and is a highly engaged grandmother. My mother is also in terrific shape, having never been an ounce overweight. Other than nagging her adult children, she has no bad habits that I know of.

My mother also sees doctors quite regularly. In the past year, she's had roughly a dozen medical appointments: with an internist, an ophthalmologist, a dermatologist, a podiatrist, a gastroenterologist, and a physical therapist. My mother—usually infectiously optimistic and energetic—is left anxious and worried by this regular medical attention. And I can't help comparing her anxiety following any doctor's appointment these days with the extraordinary calm she displayed in dealing with three cancer diagnoses in middle age—or with the joy with which her own mother lived her senior years in spite of severe cardiac disease. (My grandmother suffered five heart attacks, saw doctors only if delivered to them by ambulance, and lived to ninety-one.)

My mom's sister once told me, "Every year, I go into my GP's office a healthy senior and come out of his office a broken-down woman with every illness known to humans." Among seniors, the medicalization of senior years is the rule, not the exception. From 1995 to 2008, the number of annual visits to a physician, clinic, or hospital per person aged sixty-five to seventy-four increased by 30 percent. This explosion in care cannot be attributed to more regular checkups. As recently as thirty years ago, almost two-thirds of seniors' doctor's visits were to a geriatrician or other general practitioner; now more than half are to a special- ist. Moreover, roughly 80 percent of these appointments involve the prescribing of a medication. The amount of all physician services per Medicare beneficiary has increased by almost 50 percent just for the past ten years. Imaging and other testing per senior has almost doubled in a decade. Unlike general physicians, specialists are in the business of selling tests and treatments. So it's no surprise that what CMS calls "major procedures"—especially knee and hip replacements—have grown by 30 percent per beneficiary in ten years.

The conventional wisdom about Medicare is that much of its spending is dedicated to a small percentage of seniors in very poor health. But that's misleading. Some very ill beneficiaries—including those at the end of life—do use a disproportionate amount of care. But what's remarkable about Medicare is how much health care is used by benefi- ciaries in good health. According to the most recent data

(2007), seniors reporting excellent or very good health used approximately $5,500 of health services each year, while those reporting good or fair health used just over $11,000 a year.

All this adds up to $550 billion spent a year on Medicare—and we've spent almost $6 trillion since the program's inception. Most of us assume that this increase in usage of health services is one of the benefits of Medicare. It has allowed seniors to consult with doctors more, to manage their chronic issues, and to catch potentially serious health problems earlier. It may well be that seniors feel they are better off for all this explosion in treatment, but in fact there is little evidence that the improvements in their quality of life can be attributed to all the health care they're receiving.

Penny-wise

For all its failings, Medicare retains many die-hard supporters. Former House Speaker Nancy Pelosi refers to Medicare as a "flag we've planted that we will protect and defend." Like many Republicans, John McCain argued against the ACA because of its Medicare cuts: "All of these are cuts in the obligations that we have assumed and are the rightful benefits that people have earned." A recent *New York Times*/CBS News poll found that only 29 percent of Americans believe that Medicare isn't worth its cost to taxpayers, and a *Washington Post* poll said that 78 percent of Americans opposed cutting Medicare spending to reduce the national debt. In 2009, the AFL-CIO even endorsed extending Medicare to all Americans as the "most cost-effective and equitable way to provide quality health care" for all.

One of the most powerful arguments for Medicare—

and for extending its single-payer model to more Americans—is the program's low administrative costs. Roughly ninety-seven cents out of every Medicare dollar goes to beneficiaries' medical services, compared with the only eighty cents of every private insurance dollar that funds medical benefits. Some experts object that this simple comparison overstates Medicare's cost advantage over the private sector, but I prefer to concede the point of Medicare's supporters: Medicare is cheaper to run than private insurance.* So what? Cheaper doesn't mean more efficient. It may be cheaper to run banks without security guards, hotels without housekeepers, and manufacturers without accountants, but that wouldn't make those businesses more efficient. Cheaper administration is only more efficient if it's able to accomplish the managerial responsibilities fulfilled in more costly administration. And this is where Medicare fails.

At its core, Medicare's limited administrative capability is based on the fallacy I described in the last chapter—the idea that there is a fixed amount of health care to fund. Medicare is essentially a passive funder of care, resting on the comforting assumption that for each illness there's a right approach to treatment and that paying for that treatment is all that's required.

So the more passive Medicare is—the less it spends on administration—the more efficient it seems. But once you understand that the amount of health care "needed" and its price depend on how we pay for care, then Medicare's

---

* For one thing, there are other government programs that contribute to Medicare's services but are not included in the calculation of its administrative cost. And since Medicare spends so much more money per beneficiary than private insurers do, it would probably make more sense to compare administrative costs on a per-beneficiary basis than on a per-dollar-spent measure.

low spending on administration appears penny-wise and pound-foolish—an underinvestment in the management required to make sure that waste, fraud, high prices, and dangerous medicine don't swamp the system.*

Let's start with fraud. Medicare is rife with good old-fashioned criminal fraud: fake clinics sharing money with healthy patients to bill Medicare for phony services; physicians receiving kickbacks for ordering unneeded tests and equipment. Medicare fraud is no longer small-scale; in 2011, the FBI arrested a fraud ring that raked in over $35 million by using stolen doctor and patient identifications to file false claims. Beneficiaries themselves commit Medicare fraud; a recent study by the Government Accountability Office found that 170,000 Medicare beneficiaries receive multiple prescriptions for frequently abused drugs.

Medicare fraud is really only a part of the broader problem of improper payments, which are defined as money paid out without proper billing, or for uncovered services or patients, or in excess of legal limits. In 2008, CMS estimated Medicare and Medicaid's fee-for-service program alone had $24 billion in improper payments (roughly one in every twelve dollars of services). In 2009, the head of the federal government's Office of Management and Budget said Medicare and Medicaid had $54 billion in improper payments.

* It's almost impossible to exaggerate the impact of Medicare's passivity on how health care is practiced in our country. Medicare allows some urologists to own interests in pathology services they use for patient samples. Not surprisingly, urologists with interests in pathology centers order far more biopsies than those who send the samples to an independent lab. And it's not surprising that these urologists have much lower prostate cancer detection rates, as they convince far more healthy men to have biopsies in the first place. But here's an additional fun fact: urologists who own their own labs analyze 72 percent more specimens per biopsy than urologists who don't. Why? Because Medicare pays per specimen (Jean Mitchell, "Urologists' Self-referral for Pathology of Biopsy Specimens Linked to Increased Use and Lower Prostate Cancer Detection," Health Affairs, April 2012).

Claiming that Medicare is administratively inexpensive while ignoring billions of losses in fraud and other improper payments is absurd.

In fairness, Medicare's administrative failings are by design; politicians haven't wanted the agency to intervene in treatment decisions. So CMS's efforts to control costs are limited to visible, big-picture policies, which—for reasons I'll discuss in the next two chapters—can have no meaningful impact on the cost of care. But the toothlessness of our single payer for seniors is not merely a fiscal problem: it's allowed subtle, but disastrous, deterioration in care itself.

Administering harm

To believe Medicare is working is to believe that it is simply funding the right treatment for each senior's specific illness. But maintaining such wishful thinking should be impossible since *The Dartmouth Atlas of Health Care* began publication in 1996. It analyzes Medicare data to compare the cost of a variety of treatments—such as joint replacements and carotid revascularization—in geographic regions around the country. Though we discuss health care as a national issue, the atlas recognizes a key reality of the industry: most health care markets are local. Almost all of us see doctors, get tests, and use hospitals in our immediate vicinity.

From the beginning, the atlas has shown massive—and mostly consistent—variation from one city to another in the amount spent on a Medicare beneficiary to treat any particular condition. What is spent on a patient in some areas can be up to three times the national average. For example, Medicare spends nearly three times as much in Miami as it does in Honolulu.

Why do some regions spend so much more than others on treatment for a particular diagnosis? A variety of factors are responsible, of course, but there is one characteristic common to high-cost areas: the supply of doctors and hospital beds. If you took introductory economics in high school, you would probably assume this means that areas with excess supply of doctors and beds had lower care costs and that areas with tight supply had higher costs. But you—and the laws of economics—would have been wrong. What the atlas consistently seems to demonstrate is that areas with excess doctors and beds spend more money per Medicare beneficiary.

How is this possible? In an area with too many hospitals, shouldn't we see prices lowered by competitive pressures? Sure—if you and I were the customers. But Medicare is the customer. So what we see instead is regions with excess medical resources compensating by performing more treatments—more tests, more surgeries, more acute care—for each type of diagnosis, all covered by Medicare. The atlas gently refers to this phenomenon as "supply-sensitive care."

This is not a mere technical or cost issue. Because of Medicare, if you live in an area with a high ratio of doctors and hospital beds to people, you run a meaningful risk of excess treatment.* Of course, this data-driven picture of the implications of Medicare's lack of discipline conflicts with how our seniors experience health care. They find it hard to believe that the nice young doctor or the comfortable new

---

* Here's further proof of the importance of regional supply in determining how much treatment a patient gets: the rate of drug use by Medicare enrollees varies barely at all by region. An area with surplus doctors or hospitals gets little economic gain from driving revenues to national drug companies.

hospital could really be making financial calculations when determining how to treat their back pain. Some of this is the result of our blind faith in health care, and the absence of the normal skepticism we all have when we're the ones pay-ing for something. Unfortunately, for many seniors, the fact that Medicare is willing to pay for a treatment implies that the treatment is right for them: a dangerous assumption, as it turns out.*

In addition, Medicare has effectively ignored the recom-mendations of government experts on the value and limits of preventive testing. More than 80 percent of cervical can-cer screenings are for women over sixty-five, despite gov-ernment guidance that these tests should end at that age. Even though prostate cancer screening has long been recog-nized as having almost no benefit for men over seventy-five (because the benefits of treating such slow-growing tumors don't justify the painful side effects of treatments), more than a third of Medicare spending for prostate tests is for men over seventy-five. Similarly, 30 percent of spending for colon cancer screening covers people over seventy-five, although the government recommends against testing these people because of the risk of severe complications. Unbeliev-ably, Medicare even pays for screenings for the terminally ill; 15 percent of terminally ill men were screened for pros-

---

* Doctors and hospitals may well have been corrupted by Medicare's perverse incentives, but that doesn't mean they always know they've been corrupted. Eco-nomic incentives work powerfully but often quietly. As Atul Gawande showed in his brilliant *New Yorker* essay "The Cost Conundrum," the incentive for excess medicine can pervert the very professional culture of medicine in a community. Doctors and institutions respond to competitive pressures and Medicare's incen-tives to practice more aggressive treatment; over time, this begins to feel like nec-essary treatment. If you live in McAllen, Texas, you might not know that your hospital performs more procedures per patient than anywhere else in the country. Until Gawande's article, even your doctor might have been unaware of this, having grown accustomed to the local way of doing things.

tate cancer, while a similar share of terminally ill women received mammograms. I'm not sure what's scarier—that these suffering people were given tests or that they may have been further treated in response to the results.

Even where Medicare has identified a clear and serious problem, it lacks the administrative capacity to fix it. For example, more than 5 percent of Medicare patients receiving CT scans of the chest get scanned twice, even though guidelines state that double scans should rarely be used; the percentage has not declined despite Medicare's identifying the procedure as an example of dangerous medical excess.*

For seniors, CMS's inability to safeguard their health is best illustrated by the continuing plague of serious hospital errors and accidents that harm patients. According to a 2010 study by the inspector general of the Department of Health and Human Services, roughly one in seven Medicare beneficiaries can expect to suffer serious harm to their health from care received ("adverse event") during a hospital visit, with another one in seven suffering an event that resulted

* Medicare's bizarre incentives often hurt the most vulnerable. A recent study found that a fifth of Medicare nursing home patients with dementia were sent by nursing homes to hospitals in their final months, usually returning to the nursing home after a brief stay. Why is this noteworthy? First, dying dementia patients should be made comfortable, not subjected to aggressive hospital procedures. Second, Medicare assumes that hospitalized dementia patients are especially frail, so it pays nursing homes roughly three times the normal reimbursement rate for admitting patients from a hospital. Comparing records from various regions in the country, the study's authors found massive variation in the share of advanced dementia patients sent to hospitals. Apparently, in some parts of the country, it is common for nursing homes to send these patients to hospitals just to get the higher reimbursement rate upon their return (Associated Press, "Dementia Patients Suffer Dubious Hospitalizations," September 28, 2011).

"only" in temporary harm. A Medicare patient admitted to a hospital thus has greater than a one-in-four chance of suffering harm to his health from the care received. This study suggested that almost half of these events were preventable mistakes.*

Of course, not all adverse events are created equal. One out of every 165 Medicare hospital patients suffered from "Serious Reportable Events"—or, as they're better known, "never events." They're called this because they should never happen. These include such errors as operating on the wrong body part or patient, administering the wrong drug, or using a toxically contaminated oxygen line.

The study also showed that 1.5 percent of Medicare hospital patients die as a result of a hospital care event. Let's put that number in perspective. Approximately two million U.S. men and women have served in our conflicts in Iraq and Afghanistan; as of this writing, 6,365 have lost their lives. Our hospitals are so dangerous for Medicare beneficiaries that a senior has a greater chance of losing his life from a health care event at a hospital than a soldier has from serving our country in combat.

That may seem like shocking and inflammatory language, but how can we assert that Medicare is efficient without understanding the effects of its inherent passivity?

Many experts—and CMS itself—would have you believe that overtreatment and accidents are mere details, that clever fixes to reimbursement policy or to regulation will fix these side issues. But Medicare's flaws are fundamental; its core

---

* The inspector general's report on hospital error is particularly important because surveys had found that official statistics on errors and resulting injuries greatly underreported the phenomena (see "Hospital Errors Occur 10 Times More Than Reported," Businessweek.com, September 26, 2011; "Report Finds Most Errors at Hospitals Unreported," *New York Times*, January 6, 2012).

incentives for providers, as well as for patients, maximize diagnoses, procedures, and treatments. It lacks the administrative capacity to enforce its own rules, much less to be a positive force for the health of its beneficiaries. Excess care, unnecessary procedures, and sloppy treatment are not side effects of an otherwise well-functioning program; they are inherent in a system that emphasizes and incentivizes quantity over all else.

End-of-choice care

Ever more Americans die the way my father did—in a hospital and only when loved ones were finally ready to concede that no reasonable hope remained. The fact of death may not be a choice, but the exact timing increasingly is. Although some form of end-of-life care has become a common fate, it's not clear that it accounts for a growing share of Medicare spending; CMS estimates have been consistent at around a quarter of Medicare's budget being devoted to beneficiaries in their last year of life. At today's levels, that would suggest that roughly $60,000 is spent on the average enrollee during her last year. Many experts regard this amount as very high and as a potential source of cost savings. I'm not so sure. At $8,000 per American per year, our total spending on health care works out to around $625,000 per lifetime; does using 10 percent of that to cover a final illness seem excessive?*

I believe the bigger issue about end-of-life care is not the cost but how the money is spent. How many of Medicare's beneficiaries would choose aggressive treatment if given

---

* Of course, not all health spending in the last year of life should be described as end-of-life treatment. Much of it occurs before either patient or doctor is aware that a life is coming to an end. Such was the case—at least initially—with my father.

a choice of how to spend $60,000 in their last year? As I watched my father's hopes for recovery deteriorate, I became increasingly uneasy with his care. The only realistic goal of the hospital, I suppose, was to keep him alive, with the hope that, somehow, his body would regain the strength to function on its own. Perhaps this drawn-out process is even essential in helping loved ones cross the emotional bridge to accepting—and, in our time, actually allowing—death.

Yet I couldn't stave off the nagging feeling that my father's hospital death was not what he would have wanted for his end. Like so many, he would have preferred to have died at home and would have liked to have felt his grandchildren near. He didn't see them during the last five weeks of his life, as they were barred from his room by the hospital's ICU visiting policy. I also had a creeping feeling that my dying father was trapped by the system's predilection to perform as much care as possible. On my father's last night—after we had made the euphemistic decision to "make him as comfortable as possible"—an orderly came to administer a blood test. Why? Why give a man with only hours left any additional discomfort, no matter how incidental? Hospital policy, explained the orderly. No way, I responded, physically blocking the orderly.

The medicalization of our senior years thus persists up to death. Approximately 33 percent of our seniors die in hospitals, and 20 percent die in nursing homes. Like so much in health care policy, our debate over end-of-life care is limited to the financial—how much can we afford? The furor over supposed "death panels" during the ACA debate demonstrated how emotionally charged this issue already is. On the one hand, as health care enables us to keep more—maybe even most—patients alive long beyond when real recovery is possible, doesn't Medicare have to impose some restrictions on end-of-life care? But on the other, do we really want Medicare to determine when to pull the plug? I don't believe we'll find a politically acceptable solution to the end-of-life conundrum when it's expressed this way. None of us want the government deciding when to end the life of a loved one, and none of us want to pay unlimited amounts for some other person's "hopeless" treatment. There is no one right answer, no formula that will tell us how much end-of-life care Medicare should fund for each person.

If we leave the Island of Health Care, the end-of-life conundrum appears less perplexing. The issue isn't really how much end-of-life care an individual needs, it's how much an individual wants. End-of-life care isn't accomplishing any traditional medical goals; it's determining the how of a person's death. And in the matter of death, there is a wide variety of patient preferences as to the amount of medical intervention desired. Talk to people who expect they may not have much time left and you'll notice that the desire for end-of-life treatment varies enormously. Some want no treatment spared, to be kept alive as long as technically possible in the hope of some medical miracle. Others want more than anything to die at home, to avoid spending their final days attached to tubes in a hospital. Others want to depart this world as soon as they are unable to engage in favorite activities. And what about the grandmother who'd like to spend her end-of-life resources to fly all the kids and grandkids in for a visit? Should we as a society view her choice as less worthy than hopeless medical care?

Medicare is incapable of functioning according to patient preference. The idea of health care being a want—even a serious want—rather than a need is completely foreign. But with end-of-life care, there can be no disguise—fundamentally, it's all about wants. Since Medicare structurally can't accept that there is no one correct medical answer to the question of how much end-of-life care any single person gets, it has accidentally committed assault on our seniors by pretending there is one. The result is that our seniors are getting a lot of end-of-life care today, much of which is in excess of their wishes and ignores their best interests or comfort. Several studies have shown that many physicians rarely discuss preferences with their seriously ill patients and that many patients who express a strong desire to die at home wind up dying in a hospital.

Like so much in health care, our current approach to end-of-life care is biased toward treatment. Our health care system takes money from us over our whole lives and pays it back for treatment—and only for treatment. If each of us winds up using $60,000 for end-of-life care, then the system is going to find a way to charge us—through premiums, taxes, and so on—at least that $60,000 over our lifetimes. So we put in our $60,000 but get it all back only if we accept aggressive end-of-life treatment.*

---

* As always, Medicare's generosity allows serious abuses in end-of-life care. Brownlee notes that one medical center in Los Angeles charged Medicare an average of more than $100,000 per beneficiary for end-of-life care, with patients in their last six months spending twenty-three days in the hospital (almost half in the ICU) and seeing a doctor ninety-three times (*Overtreated*, p. 115). The *Dartmouth Atlas* finds end-of-life care particularly susceptible to "supply-sensitive care," noting:

> If more hospital beds are available in an area, local care patterns unconsciously adapt to this higher care capacity, and patients are more likely to be admitted. Similarly, research has shown that when ICU beds are readily available, more patients who are less severely ill will be admitted, and they will stay longer. Yet greater use of the hospital or ICU as a site of care does

What if we stopped thinking of end-of-life care as a necessary medical treatment requiring funding and instead
considered it one of a range of options at life's end? Wouldn't
we be better off if that $60,000 was available to us to use
not only for end-of-life care but for preparing our homes
for our final days or for having the grandkids fly in for a last
reunion?

Sure, it's a simplistic idea, and it will undoubtedly seem
absurd to many. But with ever more people fortunate
enough to live to old age, what's our realistic choice? Do we
really prefer for our government through Medicare to make
these decisions for us? Do we as a society really believe that
a central decision maker can honor the range of individual
beliefs and preferences inherent in how we die?

We often group Medicare and Social Security together
when talking about society's safety net for our seniors, but
end-of-life care is a prime example of how these programs
are different. Social Security provides resources to seniors to
use as they wish; Medicare limits their choices if they want
access to the resources poured into the system.

The death of Medicare

Every now and then, some courageous politician will suggest that Medicare is unfair to young people, that it is highly
unlikely that this program to which they contribute so much
will still be there for them when they retire in forty years.
That's wishful thinking. I'm not sure how any serious analysis of Medicare's current finances, of its current spending

not lead to better outcomes on average (*Trends and Variation in End of Life Care for Medicare Beneficiaries*, April 12, 2011, p. 3).

trends, of its anticipated massive expansion, can conclude that Medicare—in anything like its current form—will be there for *today's* seniors. Indeed, for all the political discussion on saving Medicare, fixing Medicare, "Medicare for all," even a cursory look at the finances makes it clear that Medicare is already doomed, a victim of the perverse incentives inherent in its structure.

Medicare gets its funding from three sources. Part A (the hospitalization program) is funded primarily through a dedicated payroll tax charged to all American workers. Medicare's beneficiaries pay monthly premiums for Part B (physician services) and Part D (the prescription drug program). The third source is general government revenues, which subsidize the programs of Part B and Part D to lower the amount seniors would otherwise need to pay as premiums. For 2010, roughly $182 billion came in from the payroll tax, $70 billion from premiums paid by seniors (plus another $14 billion in taxes on benefits received), and $250 billion from the general government budget.

All three of these sources have had to bear the load of Medicare's exploding spending. When Part A began in 1966, the tax on Americans' earnings was equal to 0.7 percent of the first $6,600 in wages; it is now 2.9 percent of all wages (plus, for high-income earners, an extra 0.9 percent on wages, as well as a full 3.8 percent on previously exempt investment income). The initial Part B monthly premium paid by seniors in 1966 was $3, with a $50 annual deductible; this year it is $99.90 for seniors earning less than $85,000 a year and as much as $319.70 for seniors in the highest earning category. The deductible has tripled—a relatively small rise compared with all other elements of the program. In 1970, the federal government added less than a billion dollars to payroll taxes and premiums to subsidize Medicare; this year it will contribute $250 billion.

It would be hard to exaggerate the speed at which Medicare's spending has metastasized. In 1970, the program spent $7.5 billion on twenty million beneficiaries; this year it will spend $550 billion on forty-eight million people. This means that Medicare's spending per person has grown by more than five times in that period, even after stripping out inflation. In the past decade, our economy grew by only 20 percent after inflation; Medicare's inflation-adjusted total spending more than doubled, and real spending per enrollee increased by 80 percent.

This is only a prologue to what's coming soon. There are forty-five million beneficiaries today, but another seventy million Americans will become eligible for Medicare coverage in the next two decades, roughly doubling enrollment. Even "worse," sixty-five-year-olds have seen their life expectancies climb by almost four years, meaning a new beneficiary today can be expected to spend almost a third more time in Medicare than did his 1966 counterpart. Unfortunately for its future, Medicare is the rare insurance business that cannot afford good news for its beneficiaries.

Meanwhile, Medicare's traditional funding sources are drying up. In 1970, there were almost seven Americans in the labor force for each Medicare beneficiary; today, just three workers must carry that burden. Supporters of Medicare take comfort in Medicare's $244 billion Hospitalization Insurance Trust Fund, but this is a false hope. Aware that Medicare's beneficiary population would grow as the baby boomers retired, the government has set the Part A tax at a rate greater than needed to fund each year's hospitalization costs. This surplus is then put in the trust fund to be called down to fund future deficits in Part A.

Perhaps only politicians take the trust fund seriously, because by any common-sense meaning of the word, there is no trust fund at all. Yes, as recently as 2007, the Part A tax (and other revenues) produced a surplus. Do you want to know what happened to that and other surpluses? They were lent to the federal government to fund that year's budget, including, of course, spending on Medicare. In return, the government gives the trust fund a bond, meaning that the trust fund consists entirely of promises by the federal government to pay it back out of general revenues at a future date. How is that more secure than the funding of any other government program? It isn't.

Let's say you promise to pay for college for your young daughter. Each week, you deposit twenty-five dollars in a special account dedicated to her education, earning some interest on the savings. That's probably what most people think of when they hear about the Hospitalization Insurance Trust Fund. But let's say that instead of leaving each week's deposit in the special account, you "borrowed" the money to spend on rent, food, beer, whatever, and left IOUs committing you to paying back each week's borrowed twenty-five dollars, plus interest. When your daughter turns eighteen and wants to go to college, you turn over to her the college "trust fund"—a box with now thousands of dollars' worth of IOUs. If you suspect that this trust fund will not pay for college, you understand the problem with the Hospitalization Insurance Trust Fund.

Medicare's trustees must issue a report each year on Medicare's projected financial health, and they're required by law to pretend the trust fund is real. The trustees' 2009 report—released prior to the passage of the ACA—said that the present value of Medicare's obligations for people alive today exceeded its payroll tax and premium funding by $36 trillion ($90 trillion in total). The ACA does attempt to address this giant hole in the heart of Medicare. The bill provides that, starting in 2015, if Medicare spending exceeds inflation by a certain amount, an independent commission will be required to impose spending cuts, which must be considered by Congress. No specific cuts are identified in the legislation. This would be a lot more reassuring if this method hadn't been tried before without success. In 1997, Congress decreed that in any year in which Medicare spending exceeded its target, reimbursements to doctors would be cut automatically. Congress has "suspended" this "automatic" cut every single year since. This legislation is never going to be allowed to take effect, and I see no reason for any sensible person to believe that the ACA's "automatic" cuts will, either.

As if $36 trillion isn't a big enough hole, even the trustees admit it's likely they have underestimated future spending. After all, essentially every government projection of health care spending has proved far too low, beginning with the estimate made by the Congress that passed Medicare in 1965 that Medicare spending in 1990 would be $12 billion (it was actually $110 billion). All these estimates have the same problem: they assume that there's a fixed amount of health care that seniors will need, rather than that the definition of "need" will continuously expand.

Medicare's supporters remind us that previous predictions of the program's demise have proved unfounded; policy changes have always saved it from the forecasted doom.

But in the past decade alone, we've significantly increased the payroll tax, beneficiary premiums, and government subsidy going to the program. In the next two decades, Medicare enrollees will increase from forty-eight million to eighty million. If their rate of use of Medicare's services grows at the same rate as in the past decade, the 2030 Medicare budget will be $2.8 trillion—in today's dollars!

This is meaningless; such large numbers should make clear to any sensible person that Medicare as it currently functions is doomed. It's common to talk about the government kicking the can down the road, but with Medicare, our leaders are trying to kick an entire can factory down the road. If we don't act soon to restructure the fundamental incentives that have devastated Medicare, the program will be the cause of extraordinary pain, not just for our nation's finances but for seniors themselves, starting with this current generation of seniors.

We can start the process of reform by being honest with seniors. Many are led to believe that they have somehow paid for their benefits and that they have earned unconstrained Medicare. Yet the average person joining Medicare today has paid roughly $60,000 into the program over their lifetime and will use $170,000 in benefits.

More important, we need to be honest about the double-edged nature of Medicare. Yes, it has provided our poorer and sickest seniors some financial security and greater access to health care. But it has done so at unjustifiable cost. Medicare has encouraged the medicalization of our senior years, subjecting beneficiaries to mountains of unnecessary and often seriously harmful treatments. We really have very little evidence that our $550 billion of Medicare-funded health care does much good in terms of life expectancy and vitality and a lot of evidence that a large amount of it does actual physical harm.

Furthermore, with all of Medicare's generous spending, what should be most alarming to seniors is what Medicare doesn't pay for: long-term care. Today, almost six million Americans are older than eighty-five. Their numbers are expected to more than double over the next thirty years. In addition, the number of Americans suffering from Alzheimer's is expected to grow from five million today to sixteen million at midcentury. Many of these seniors are likely to need long-term care, but this is not part of Medicare's current mandate. Beyond being a financial waste for society, the Medicare-funded excessive tests, procedures, and treatments also threaten to crowd out the health services seniors will actually need.

Paying for the privilege

Whether they know it or not, seniors are paying far more for their health care than the architects of Medicare could have imagined. Medicare premiums have risen so sharply that the amount seniors pay for premiums this year will exceed what the entire Medicare program cost in 1985. In the past decade, beneficiaries' out-of-pocket share of their health costs has grown by "only" 46 percent, but far more enrollees are exposed to meaningful financial liability. In 2010, 2.3 million Medicare beneficiaries incurred charges of more than $5,000 in cost sharing; 300,000 owed more than $15,000.

Health care costs are a greater worry for seniors now

than they were before Medicare. In 1970, Medicare premiums and cost sharing used 6 percent of a beneficiary's Social Security check; now it's 25 percent. Prior to Medicare, the average senior used somewhere between 10 and 15 percent of his income to cover out-of-pocket health care costs; today, the average senior uses almost 20 percent! It's worth thinking about that statistic. Before Medicare, when seniors paid almost all of their own health care costs, they had as much as 90 percent of their income to spend on things other than health care. Today, when the government pays for almost all of their health care spending, that little sliver that seniors pay out of their own pockets leaves them only 80 percent of their income for other things. After forty-five years of Medicare—and more than $6 trillion of spending on the program—how many seniors feel more secure about the affordability of health care than their predecessors did?

Most seniors and advocates of Medicare respond to the growing pressure of health costs on enrollees by calling for even greater resources to be poured into Medicare. Like so much of the analysis of our health care situation, this viewpoint sees Medicare as essentially floating on top of the health care economy, forced to respond to the structural elements pushing up need and prices. But of course, Medicare is driving these developments; it can't catch up to growing financial requirements because its lack of meaningful financial discipline—and its unlimited call on the Treasury—is their very cause.

Many years ago, I read an article comparing Medicare to a fictional car subsidy program. Say the government decided that hardworking Americans should be able to afford better cars than the ones their own resources allowed. Every American would receive a matching subsidy from the government, allowing her to buy, say, a $40,000 Mercedes instead of a $20,000 Buick. What happened next is obvious: the price of Buicks rose to $40,000 and the price of Mercedeses to at least $60,000. The beneficiary of this subsidy was in the same place as she was before—the owner of a Buick. It's a beautiful metaphor for Medicare, but incomplete. We didn't notice that most of the benefit of Medicare has been absorbed by excess treatment and runaway prices because this process occurred so gradually. In fact, it happened so gradually that, to continue the metaphor, we not only pay more for the Buick out of our own pockets than we did before the car subsidy but still actually believe we pay less.

Obviously, Medicare has paid for a lot of valuable and essential health care over its existence; in the absence of any other safety net, it may well have made the difference between life and death for many seniors.* There are many thoughtful analyses that argue that Medicare's benefits justify its costs, but most of these are true Island studies, viewing health care as the only thing of value. None of them look at the opportunity cost of diverting so much of soci-

---

* An influential paper suggests that much of Medicare's cost may be justified by the financial security it provides to the small percentage of seniors with very high out-of-pocket costs—that these people were too exposed to bankrupting expenses prior to Medicare. See Amy Finkelstein and Robin McKnight, *What Did Medicare Do (and Was It Worth It)?* Working paper 11609 (Cambridge, Mass.: National Bureau of Economic Research, 2005). Interestingly, the data studied runs only through 2000, before another decade of Medicare explosiveness pushed the *average* out-of-pocket costs for seniors well above pre-Medicare levels. Certainly, we need a safety net that protects the most vulnerable, but as I argued in chapter 3, we've given up a lot of financial discipline and normal economic functioning in insisting that what is best for those most in need should set the framework for how everyone gets care. I'm skeptical that a program that has pushed up seniors' out-of-pocket burden, increased health prices for the whole population, encouraged harmful medicine, and created a massive fiscal imbalance on the federal and state levels can somehow be defended on the basis of providing financial security.

ety's resources—including seniors' resources—away from all the other things that make us happier, more productive, and even healthier.

A friend recently told me that another argument in favor of Medicare's extraordinary level of spending is that it advances the introduction of lifesaving technologies faster than an unsubsidized market would. Fortuitously, that same day, *The New York Times* ran a story about a more effective blood-clotting treatment widely used on the battlefield but barely at all in U.S. hospitals. The problem? The new treatment was too inexpensive to be of interest. Medicare's incentives don't drive better care; they drive more costly care.

Nobody ever asks if Medicare is a good deal for seniors because each year seniors and their advocates must push to expand Medicare just to cover the problem of runaway costs that Medicare has ignited. But if you step back and look at the whole forty-five years of Medicare, it's highly questionable whether seniors are better off for the program's existence. If you had told the seniors of 1965 that they would be getting far more treatment but that much of it would be excessive and dangerous, and that they would be paying a far smaller share of the cost of that treatment but that their share would still cost them more of their income, would Medicare have been enacted in the first place?

Today's seniors weren't seniors in 1965; at today's prices, ending Medicare would seem to ensure only that they couldn't afford any health care at all. But of course that's not possible: seniors are the major customer group for our health care system, and our health care industry would organize itself to serve them at any level of social subsidy. And of course a radical restructuring of Medicare doesn't mean getting rid of the safety net. Better incentives should do more than just save money for society and beneficiaries; they should drive better care.

It will truly be a dangerous failure of our imagination if we remain stuck with an extravagantly costly program that has failed to meet its original objectives, may do as much health harm as good, and is unsustainable for even one more generation. But could any other type of safety net truly do better? Doesn't Medicare already drive the lowest prices in the industry—by some measures, paying less than cost for care? Let's turn to one of the great confusions in health care policy and explore why our obsession with cost inevitably produces higher prices.

CHAPTER 6

The Mirage of Efficiency

Why the cost curve won't bend

I n 1983, the Reagan administration enacted one of the most significant cost reforms in Medicare's history. The new Prospective Payment System (PPS) switched inpatient hospital reimbursement from traditional open-ended fee-for-service to fixed fees paid per diagnosis (technically called payments for diagnosis related groups, or DRGs). In theory, PPS would shift the incentive for hospitals from keeping patients for as long as possible to treating them as quickly and economically as possible. Also, hospitals would now have a financial incentive to force a long-hoped-for Island goal: integrating the care among the various service providers housed under their roofs. With one fixed payment to be split among them, service providers would now be forced to work together when providing care.

This fundamental change in reimbursement certainly did drive extraordinarily large changes in hospital treatment. From 1983 to today, the total number of days spent by Medicare patients in hospitals has actually declined by 40 percent—despite a 60 percent increase in Medicare enrollees. In that time frame, the average length of an inpatient stay has shortened from roughly ten days to just over five days. So did the PPS reforms work? In the simplest measurement sense—the one preferred by policymakers—the answer is an overwhelming yes. Hospitals seem to treat patients more efficiently and are in fact paid fixed fees based on DRGs for most care. These payments seem to average less than what would have been likely under the previous approach. So, success.

On the Island today, it's trendy to refer to reducing the fundamental cost of care as "bending the curve," a reference to an influential 2009 study by the Brookings Institution. The study described nine major ideas that would make health care more efficient and thereby drive down our nation's health care bills. From bonuses for meaningful use of health information technology to comparative effectiveness research, these sensible reforms address many of the most obvious failings of the system.

Of course, everyone wants to bend the cost curve. And who could argue with the idea that more efficient health care would be better for our health and cheaper, too? Unfortunately, looking at the recent history of health care should make it obvious that greater efficiency not only is no guarantee of lower costs but may well contribute to higher costs. It's hard to imagine anything bending the cost curve more than reducing the average number of days spent in the hospital per patient by a half. Yet even this enormous change—this clear objective improvement in the efficiency of care—failed to slow the cost train. Because starting in 1983, the cost of a day in a hospital skyrocketed. Yes, the number of inpatient days declined from 112 million in 1983 to 66 million in 2010, but the amount Medicare paid per day rose from $300 to $1,800.

The simple fact is that the amount paid to hospitals since DRGs were enacted has grown by 700 percent, consistent with all other health care spending. How did hospitals manage to capture so much revenue despite losing so much business? Within ten years of the switch to PPS, outpatient visits, not covered by the reform, jumped from just over 40 percent of hospital business to over 60 percent. (Medicare finally addressed the outpatient loophole in 2000 by extending DRGs to cover such care; by then, outpatients accounted for three out of every four hospital patients.) Second, as noted above, hospitals raised their prices. But what's most interesting is that they raised their "costs" even more. When the DRGs were enacted, hospitals were billing Medicare $4,700 per discharge and accepting payments from the government of $3,000—roughly 65 percent of the bill. By 2010, hospitals were billing $40,152 per discharge but accepting payments of only $9,500—less than 25 percent of the billed amount. So not only are hospitals earning six times their previous per-day revenues, they've somehow managed to claim that Medicare's getting an even better deal than before.

So the PPS succeeded in its policy tactic of reducing hospital days, while failing in its overall goal of reducing total amounts spent on hospital care. And PPS is only the most obvious example of a long trend. Most of the major developments in health care—from higher doctor productivity to diagnostic scans to new pharmaceuticals to minimally invasive surgery—could be described as increasing health care's productivity. But on the Island, none of these achievements in efficiency had any success in bending the cost curve.

But why? Strange as it seems, cost—and the related concept of efficiency—is only mildly relevant to the price of care. The Island's model of cost control is based on the fallacy discussed in chapter 4—that there's a fixed amount of health care we need, so the more efficiently it's performed, the cheaper it will be. This is naïve; it ignores how providers actually respond to changes in their business. So the fundamental "efficiency" reform of PPS was overwhelmed by providers switching their provision of services to outpatient care (outside the price regulation), raising prices of covered services (under the disguise of higher costs), and selling ever more services per patient day.

On the Mainland, we would never assume that greater efficiency leads automatically to lower prices. Wal-Mart may invest in sophisticated inventory control to keep down prices, but movie studios responded to declining costs of computer imaging by making ever more expensive and spectacular films. Airlines achieve greater operational efficiency by building airport hubs, but this gives them greater market power to push up prices. No Mainland analyst would have been surprised by a recent study showing that doctors with electronic access to the results of patients' prior tests actually ordered more costly tests.

Price isn't a matter of efficiency but rather of how efficiency is translated into price through the dynamics of competition. Since these are broken in health care, efforts to make care more efficient have little impact on our total bill. The Island's obsession with costs is more than misplaced; by focusing relentlessly on the cost of care, we actually drive it up—a sort of health care Heisenberg principle. But to understand why this is inescapable, we need to visit the Mainland.

The elusiveness of "cost"

What would you rather pay for the items you buy: whatever price a retailer charges or a small amount—say 5 percent—above the retailer's cost? Take your time: it's a trick question.

Since we know that merchants charge a markup greater than 5 percent above their cost, it seems obvious that the cost-based pricing is the better deal for us. We imagine going into a store, learning that the merchant paid $10 to a manufacturer for a sweater, and buying that sweater for a terrific price of only $10.50. This is what can be called a static analysis of my question—an analysis that assumes everything stays the same when you opt for cost-based pricing.

Then there is a dynamic analysis, which takes the question to another level. Here we understand that merely changing our pricing system from whatever the merchant wants to charge to the cost plus 5 percent will also change all of the economic incentives faced by the merchant: the next sweater his store buys will "cost" him far more than $10 so he can still earn an adequate profit. Though you may find this counterintuitive, moving to the cost-plus system will ultimately produce a much worse deal.

To understand why cost-plus produces such terrible results for consumers, imagine its impact on perhaps the world's simplest business. Your daughter sets up a lemonade stand outside your house. Some lemons, sugar, water, a pitcher, cups, a table—business doesn't get much simpler than this. She charges a dollar a cup. No fancy analysis went into her pricing—that number just seemed right to her. And she does an okay business, selling fifty cups to people passing by each day.

One day your town's mayor passes by the stand. He's running for reelection and he has a great idea: he wants to buy a cup of lemonade every week for all thousand residents of the town. But he doesn't want to pay a thousand dollars every time, so he makes a suggestion: he'll pay your daughter's cost of lemonade plus a "fair" 50 percent profit. He knows each cup of lemonade contains about ten cents' worth of lemons and sugar, so he figures he'll be paying fifteen cents a serving. He's engaging in static analysis of your daughter's lemonade business.

But the moment she agrees to this deal, your daughter's entire business motivation changes. She's no longer trying to sell as much lemonade as possible—the mayor's order ensures she won't need any other customers. Now she's trying to increase her costs as much as possible, because higher costs mean higher profits. So she's better off with more expensive lemons and more expensive sugar. She's going to use larger cups (and maybe even glasses). She's better off hiring someone else to run the stand since those wages will become reimbursable costs. She needs to try to convince the mayor that rental of her family's kitchen table should be included in the "costs" and that the stand needs to buy the new Lemonada 5000 mixer, an expensive machine that guarantees a perfect mix of sugar and lemon in every glass.

The mayor's no idiot; he sees what's happening to his cost of lemonade and realizes he needs a different incentive payment structure. So he renegotiates his deal with your daughter. From now on, her profit is a fixed amount—five cents a cup, regardless of costs. Unfortunately, this also creates perverse incentives. Your daughter can now make more money by accepting the fixed profit and reducing the size of each cup. Or she can cut back on customer service, hygiene, or speed. Or she can cut side deals with her vendors: the lemon seller can raise his prices—passed on to the mayor—and share the proceeds with your daughter in cash kickbacks or through a weekly gift of other fruit for your family.

Of course, the only thing that ultimately keeps your daughter's prices in check is the existence of other normally operating lemonade stands. But if every mayor in every town buys out the lemonade supply at cost-plus prices and enough time goes by, the price of lemonade everywhere—after the dynamics of cost-plus pricing kick in—will be well more than a dollar a cup.

Bizarrely, moving to a cost-based pricing structure not only creates perverse incentives but actually adds a new type of major cost to the lemonade business. Your daughter now spends a lot of time tracking, manipulating, and justifying costs—that effort is itself an additional cost to the lemonade business. That may not seem like much within the context of a lemonade stand business, but in a $2.5 trillion industry like health care, such activities are a major reason that administrative costs exceed $300 billion a year.

A recent *Economist* article on dialysis perfectly illustrates the inflationary impact of cost-plus pricing. Since U.S. clinics are paid on a cost-plus basis, they prefer to use expensive drugs rather than cheaper ones. In fact, many appear to order drugs in units that exceed what a standard dosage requires because they can charge the government for the wastage. Quoting a stock research firm, the article noted that many clinics preferred an injected drug with a price of $4,100 a year over the identical drug in oral form, priced at only $450 a year. Not surprisingly, the manufacturer of the oral drug responded by increasing its price above that of the injected version to make it more competitive!

The cost illusion

Our entire health care system suffers from what I call the "cost illusion"—the seemingly obvious yet always incorrect view that a concrete long-term fixed cost of a service actually exists. Because of this illusion, insurers and regulators believe they can keep prices as low as possible by discovering the "true" costs of a health service and then paying a small spread above that cost. But as the dialysis example demonstrates, every cost is merely someone else's price—the dialysis clinic's cost is the drug manufacturer's price. On the Mainland, prices are in an endless and circular relationship with costs. Yes, the price must reflect cost, but over time, costs themselves are also determined by prices.

To a resident of the Island—indeed, perhaps to most people—this seems backward. How can prices determine costs? So let's return to our friend from chapter 4, Tom Cruise, and look at an exaggerated form of this seeming contradiction in action. If your studio wants to make a movie with Tom Cruise, you will pay him $20 million for roughly four months of his work: that's the cost of Tom Cruise. But why does Tom Cruise cost so much? On the Island, we'd look for some fundamental underlying cost. But Tom contains the same number of molecules as anyone else; he's had some training as an actor, but not so much as to justify $20 million as his cost.

Of course, we all know the answer to this. Tom Cruise's four months cost a studio $20 million because a movie with Tom Cruise will sell a lot of tickets and DVDs. Tom Cruise's cost is directly related to how much money he's likely to make for the studio. So if Tom Cruise goes to work as a janitor, the cost of his labor declines significantly. Importantly,

if fans stop liking Tom Cruise, studios will insist on paying him much less for a film. In that scenario, the cost of
Tom Cruise will have declined, even though Tom himself
remains the same.

What does any of this have to do with health care? Well,
what's the cost of orthopedic surgery? On the Island, the
answer would be the sum of all the costs of the underlying components—the surgeon, anesthesiologist, nurses,
hospital, device, tests, and drugs. But how are these costs
determined? Let's look at the orthopedic surgeon. What's
the value of her time? We may believe there's some objective way to measure the cost of her time—a fair return on
her years of education or training, say—but in reality this
has no more relationship to her cost than acting lessons do
to Tom Cruise's. The cost of the orthopedic surgeon's time
depends on the value of orthopedic surgery to patients. If
more patients need orthopedic surgery, the time of orthopedic surgeons becomes more valuable—just like having more
fans increases the value of Tom Cruise's time.*

In a free market, there are two ways this cost could
decline: more orthopedic surgeons fighting for business or
patients needing less orthopedic surgery. But, in an administered market, our Surrogates substitute their calculation
of cost for the workings of markets. This has the strange
effect of preventing costs from ever declining. Let's say
Medicare sets the reimbursement rate for a hip replacement
at $15,000; that money is fully divided among the surgeon,

---

* In his blog on health policy, John Goodman notes that the technology and skills
involved in a knee replacement for a dog are essentially the same as for a knee
replacement for a human but the price is only a sixth. This makes sense intuitively
but doesn't really fit into the philosophy of our health care system, where some
concept of cost exists independent of value ("Making Sense of Health Care Prices,"
September 21, 2011).

the anesthesiologist, the hospital, the replacement manufacturer, and a drug company. Now say a new drug is invented
that makes hip replacements less useful. In a free market,
the price of the old-fashioned hip replacement is likely to
decline—at least relative to the new drug. The underlying
costs would also decline as doctors and manufacturers were
forced to accept prices that reflect the lower value. But in an
administered system, these prices are viewed as costs, and
once set, what's the mechanism for their decline? Let's say
orthopedic surgeons are now prescribing more of the new
drug and performing fewer surgeries. How will we discover
that their cost of performing surgery has declined? If you're
stuck in the cost illusion, nothing has changed: the same
amount of time from surgeons of the same degree of expertise is still required for hip replacement. So the cost must be
the same. Medicare not only continues to pay $15,000 for
hip replacement but still believes it's getting a great deal at a
price equal to cost.

On the flip side, every underlying price increase in a
component of hip replacement is immediately absorbed
as an additional cost. So let's say Medicare increases the
reimbursement rate for a hip replacement to $20,000. You
might expect that someone in health care is now pocketing
a $5,000 excess profit per patient. But in fact, that wind-
fall would last only about the length of time it took to treat
the first patient. Why? Well, we would imagine that a hip
replacement specialist would now charge more for her time.
But the manufacturer of the hip would likely also raise its
prices to take advantage of the greater demand for the arti-
ficial joint. The hospital, seeing a profit opportunity, might
refurbish its "hip center" and advertise for these profit-

able patients; it will also need a bigger cut to pay for these investments. The diagnostic clinic would raise prices for hip MRIs. Very shortly, if you looked up and down the supply chain for hip replacements, you would find that the cost of a hip replacement was now $20,000. And this is why costs rise as we pour more money into health care. Now, that's the opposite of what Island experts believe: they think that we need to spend more on health care because costs are going up.

The Surrogates claim to exercise their pricing power by paying as little as possible above cost. This concept may be fundamental to our entire health care system, but it's based on a false assumption. We may all think of cost as something fixed—lemons, sugar, glasses, and the lemonade stand—but that's only correct as a snapshot. Prices change constantly in response to value and to other prices. In the context of health care, with our willingness to pay for any care we need, cost can only go in one direction—up.

A fixed world

Think of that cup of Starbucks coffee you had this morning. In the price of your cup was the following information: the prices of its direct components (beans, water, labor, paper cups) and the prices of its shared components (grinding machine, coffeemaker, counter space, store rent). On the Island, this is what is thought of as cost. But the Starbucks price also contains much more information: the value and availability of substitutes (a larger cup, a smaller cup, the distance of Dunkin' Donuts from your nearest Starbucks, a coffee you make at home, the dregs of the office coffee pot, a tea or hot chocolate), Starbucks' cost of capital (interest rates, shareholders' profit expectations), and even the value of the real estate.

Now, of course, it wouldn't be practical for Starbucks to change its prices every minute to reflect changes in any of the myriad factors that go into pricing a cup of its coffee. But over time, if the price of beans declines, Starbucks is likely to try to attract new people to coffee by lowering prices. If a strong competitor opens, Starbucks may lower prices to retain customers or, alternatively, may raise prices to claim the superiority of the Starbucks brew. A new espresso technology may offer the chain efficiencies that it passes on in lower prices or, alternatively, may offer a better product for which Starbucks can charge more. Or both. A recession may lead Starbucks to cut margins; the onset of summer may lead it to raise prices on iced drinks.

Nothing against Starbucks, but the coffee industry isn't particularly complex; yet even here it's impossible to imagine any central price fixer being able to respond to all the changes that Starbucks, its competition, bean traders, the makers of home coffee machines, and milk suppliers do as their full-time jobs. The very power of prices results from their being flexible, with the decisions to charge and pay them spread over an unimaginably large group of decision makers.

That's good in theory, but in health care don't we all benefit from more stable prices? No. Health care is infinitely more complicated and dynamic than coffee. In what other industry is customer demand so individual, innovation so constant, the requirements of cooperation so complex, and skilled labor so transferrable? All this complexity means that imbalances between supply and demand, between resource allocation and need, between technology and price, between demand and quality, will crop up faster in health care than in other industries. And so the impact of turning away from flexible pricing—this powerful tool of rebalancing—has been devastating to health care access, quality, and cost.

Of course, Island experts understand that administratively fixed prices create imbalances. Writing in *The New York Times*, Ezekiel Emanuel, an oncologist, an Obama administration adviser, and a professor of health policy, noted that the price rules governing cancer drugs had led to shortages of older and, in many cases, more effective drugs. He explained that the rules covering Medicare discounts for generics meant these drugs were no longer profitable enough to guarantee sufficient production. He goes on to propose,

> You don't have to be a cynical capitalist to see that the long-term solution is to make the production of generic cancer drugs more profitable. . . . One solution would be to . . . increase the amount Medicare pays for generic cancer drugs to the average selling price plus, say, 30 percent, after the drugs have been generic for three years.

With all respect to the always thoughtful Dr. Emanuel, I'm not sure how someone can get it so right and so wrong at the same time. Yes, prices that are too low do explain why these drugs are in short supply today. But fixing these prices at Dr. Emanuel's 30 percent increase is no long-term solution; in fact, it's just repeating the problem—fixed prices that don't move with changing conditions. We can't even know if Dr. Emanuel's 30 percent is too little—or too much—to induce manufacturers to solve the problem today.*

A fixed price is like the proverbial broken clock: it may be right at the moment it's set, but after that, it's right for only two minutes each day. There is no single price that will ensure the adequate supply of these cancer drugs over the long term. The price that produces that balance between supply and demand will—must—fluctuate, depending on the availability and prices of alternative treatments, the new production technology, the cost of labor and capital, the incidence of cancer itself, you name it. Dr. Emanuel's 30 percent price change may well lead to an increased or even an adequate supply of cancer drugs today. But over time, the new fixed price will—inevitably—lead to periods in which these drugs are overproduced (with the excess almost certainly finding its way into Medicare's total costs) or underproduced (causing unnecessary deaths).

Too little information

Wouldn't it be great if you didn't have to know the price of anything? On the Island, the answer is yes; our entire health care system is designed to shield patients from the pressure of being consumers. Unfortunately, a world without prices is also one that can't achieve the purpose of prices. As I've explained, prices are the tools by which modern economies allocate resources to match what consumers want, understanding that those wants are constantly changing. And a

* This problem appears to be growing, with 267 drug shortages reported in 2011, almost four times the number only five years ago ("Drug Shortages Hit Record Levels in 2011; 2012 May Not Be Much Better," *Modern Medicine,* January 10, 2012).

health care system without prices can't adjust to changes in our health needs.

Let's go back to Starbucks. Notice that some of the information in the price of a cup is about you, not about Starbucks—such as your preference for its coffee over the competition's and over the coffee you make yourself. Because of the size of the coffee-drinking population, no single cup of coffee can accurately reflect that information for everyone. So Starbucks maintains many different prices simultaneously, disguising them as varied beans, preparations, or sizes (your preferences, not the minimal extra ingredients, are the real reason a large is more expensive than a small). In fact, when you consider everything about the coffee industry—from the pushcart outside your office building to the espresso bar on the corner; from the generic freeze-dried instant sold in a supermarket to the whole beans in the gourmet shop; from the free coffee at work to the complimentary coffee at a bar—you realize the unimaginably wide range of prices for this simple drink, each reflecting a different preference for the how, when, and where of drinking it. Every time you pay one of these prices, you are essentially voting for that specific experience, encouraging our economy to devote more resources to that way of making and serving coffee.

On the Island, everything about heath care—need, treatment, and costs—is assumed to be involuntary and fixed. So individual consumer preferences are irrelevant, even dangerous. Since preferences don't matter, Island thinking goes, what good could possibly come from exposing consumers to prices?

Health care prices have literally no meaning relative to Mainland prices. Five weeks after my father died, my mother received a bill for his "treatment"—$635,695.75! The bill was broken down into seventeen items. Had I booked Dad a room at the most expensive hotel in town for those five weeks, filled the room with a million dollars' worth of hospital equipment leased for $15,000 a month, given him round-the-clock nursing care, and paid a physician to spend one hour a day with him (roughly fifty minutes more than at the hospital), it would total roughly $150,000. That leaves a mere $500,000 left over for, say, drugs (billed at $145,431), oxygen ($41,695), and blood ($30,248).

This comparison of the hospital bill to actual Mainland prices is absurd because it assumes that the prices on my father's bill were real prices. But as we've seen, no one was supposed to pay that bill. Medicare paid the hospital according to its established formula. The hospital billed my mother for her share ($992), which she wisely didn't pay and the hospital wisely didn't try to collect. Not only did the prices on the bill bear no relationship to prices as understood in our economy, they didn't even bear a relationship to the exchange of funds for Dad's treatment. Medicare's reimbursement was based on its concept of the hospital's cost. Of course, on the Mainland, there's no question what the competitive price would be for the service of killing my father—zero.

A stunted price system also distorts investment in new health care treatments. America's pharmaceutical companies spent roughly $67 billion in 2010 on research to develop new drugs. But remarkably, many of these new drugs target conditions for which perfectly good drugs already exist. The drug companies, of course, justify their concentrated spending on a few conditions by citing the need to find better treatments. But in fact, it is the lack of consumer prices that explains their me-too approach to research.

Once a new drug is approved, it enters the marketplace at a high reimbursement rate, compensating the manufacturer for its high cost of research. So what's the punishment for entering a crowded market? Very little. Yes, the manufacturer has to bear the expense of marketing, but its ability to maintain high prices significantly reduces the risk of financial failure. Furthermore, even with a promising new entrant, the prices of the existing drugs don't decline; they've already been set to compensate for their "costs." If a product market was crowded in the Mainland, a new entrant would bear not only the risk of a new product being rejected by the market but also the risk of a price war. Not in health care.*

Similarly, many claim that the drug industry is underinvesting in research for new antibiotics to combat infections resistant to older drugs. Again, drug companies' investment priorities are blamed: finding a pill that can be prescribed for years to treat a chronic condition is more profitable than developing a short-term course. In other words, drugs that work partially are more profitable than drugs that work completely. But isn't this fundamentally a pricing problem? In the same way that our administered pricing prevents me-

---

* The rise of a new type of intermediary—pharmacy benefit managers—may be changing the drug industry model by driving discounts on pharmaceuticals at the manufacturer and pharmacy levels. The drug business model is arguably the naturally weakest in health care: these companies are selling pills that cost almost nothing at the margins to manufacture, have products similar to competitors', and are unable to package their products with the services that allow physicians, hospitals, and device manufacturers to expand demand. But it's far from clear whether the pharmacy benefit managers—whose business is increasingly concentrated among three big companies—will use their growing market power to drive prices down to benefit the employer-insurer customers and, ultimately, us.

too chronic care treatments from declining in price, it prevents effective antibiotics from climbing in price enough to provide a competitive return on capital. We may feel good about low-cost antibiotics, but it's a shortsighted victory if not enough are produced.

Administered pricing also explains why our health care industry has so massively underinvested in information technology. Your dry cleaner computerized his inventory system to reduce the amount of lost clothing. Losing a customer's shirt may mean a loss of that customer; at the very least, it requires a refund. Alternatively, a dry cleaner with efficient service could maintain the highest prices. But a doctor who invests in state-of-the-art patient data management can't charge higher prices; insurers won't pay. Nor is there a market mechanism to force hospitals that use paper records to accept lower prices. Without a flexible price system, those benefits never work their way into providers' calculations. So these invaluable investments are never made.

As consumers, we may experience prices as requirements set by a provider, but over time, they're really the prime channel of communication between customer preferences and a competitive industry's services. If we, the consumers, saw and paid prices—if we had a vote in our health care economy—we'd be looking at a very different industry. My guess is that many of us would have "voted" for doctors who spend more time talking to us, for providers who invest in computerized records, for vaccines that work rather than me-too chronic condition drugs, and for hospitals that kill fewer patients. But on an island without prices, we have no vote.

The danger of pricing power

Proponents of a single-payer health care system (sometimes called "Medicare for all") argue that having a single powerful customer—presumably a government agency—would give us the benefits of maximum competition among suppliers and the massive leverage necessary to drive down prices.

That's simply not realistic, as our current system proves. True, it's not single-payer, but for most health services, ours is already a few-payer system. In many regions, there are only one or two private insurers operating, which means that for most medical services, a hospital, physician, or clinic may have only three or four customers: the insurer(s), Medicare, and the state Medicaid agency. Medicare is already especially powerful; it provides 20 percent of the money spent on patient care, and its system of coding services for billing is now the standard for all other payers. For many hospital services, Medicare's customer share is so large that the other payers essentially set their prices in reference to Medicare's payments.

I'm pretty sure I've never heard a single-payer proponent cite the success of the single-payer model in the defense industry, but I suspect the experience here—where the U.S. government is essentially the only customer for advanced weapons systems—should be sobering. The private defense industry has met the challenge of dealing with one customer through endless consolidation. On most major projects, only two suppliers compete—and they tend to compete on features rather than price. National security considerations may require a nonmarket defense procurement system, but does anyone believe that the United States is getting the best possible prices for military hardware as a result?

All-powerful customers are in many ways weaker—
less free to act—than consumers in normal markets. The
Defense Department can't buy weapons the way you buy
toothpaste—by simply looking for the best price. If you
don't buy your tube at the local store, the store stays in business as long as it provides value to other customers. But if
the government doesn't buy a manufacturer's warplane, that
company may go out of business—which could leave only
one provider for the next plane. So by being the only customer, the government is in effect a partner of its vendors—
their survival is essential.

It's similar in health care; the Surrogates can push their
power only so far. And in health care—unlike defense—
there are many providers, so it's impossible for Medicare or
Medicaid agencies to negotiate with individual suppliers to
establish prices. Most must be fixed centrally, even if efforts
are made to reflect varying local conditions. And although
private insurers do negotiate terms with powerful local hospitals or drug manufacturers, for most small providers—
physicians' groups and clinics—insurers can usually set
reimbursement terms unilaterally.

As a result, even without a single-payer system, almost all
prices in health care are now fixed either directly by the Surrogates or in negotiation with other large institutions, rather
than being established in any kind of competitive marketplace. But as in defense, the Surrogates must consider what
is required to keep these many suppliers in business.* Which
of course means setting prices that reflect their "costs."

So the result of having all-powerful Surrogates setting

---

* The Surrogates have an important political consideration here as well. Private
insurers operate on a state level and are subject to extensive regulation. Driving a
local high-price hospital out of business is rarely a practical option.

health care prices is that health care resembles your daughter's lemonade business after her deal with the mayor. In health care, the negative impact of our few-payer system is subtle but pernicious. Few-payer pricing has directly established many of the perverse incentives that riddle health care—widespread incentives to inflate costs, overtreat patients, cut corners, and use enormous resources just to justify that it's all needed. Moving to cost-based pricing changed more than the economic deal between your daughter and the mayor; it changed the recipe, serving size, and quality of the lemonade itself. As we'll see, in health care, our Surrogates' search for costs on which to base prices has done the same thing—it's changed the nature of care itself.

CHAPTER 7

The Tyranny of Rules

Why everything is so complicated

> A shift last year by the federal government in how it pays for drugs to treat dialysis patients may have had an unintended and potentially dire consequence, according to new research: a significant jump in blood transfusions for patients who now may not be getting enough of the medications. The findings are seen by some experts as a stark illustration of how the government's reimbursement policies can drive the practice of medicine.
>
> —KEVIN SACK, "Unintended Consequence for Dialysis Patients as Drug Rule Changes," *The New York Times*, May 11, 2012

A pediatrician friend recently told me about a young child with cystic fibrosis who was being fed through a surgically implanted gastric tube. The patient, an active child, pulled out the tube. My friend decided to try feeding him orally, but his young patient refused to consume any formula, except for an orange-flavored one that happened not to be on the insurer's list of reimbursable formulas. Insurers have medical officers who are responsible for listening to appeals of reimbursement decisions, so the pediatrician contacted him and argued his case. If the insurer didn't approve the orange formula, the hospital would need to reinsert a tube, at greater discomfort and risk for the patient and at a greater total cost for the insurer. Without giving a reason, this medical officer refused the appeal.

My friend told this story in disbelief; looking for any explanation for this decision, he speculated that because the insurer's medical officer was trained as a geriatrician, he didn't understand the particular challenges of child patients. Who reading this story isn't frustrated by the irrationality of this decision and by its impact on a sick child? But who doesn't also find it easy to believe? Who hasn't experienced the irrationality of our health care system in ways both large and small? Certainly, in this story we have a clear villain: an unfeeling bureaucrat at an impersonal insurance company who was perhaps overtaxed by the burden of balancing medical need with policy. But the fact that we all have similar—if less painful—experiences should tell us that this child's story doesn't dramatize just one bad decision.

The real story here isn't about money: the insurer could have saved money by making an exception. Rather, it illustrates what happens when you try to govern something as complex as health care—and as individual as our 310 million bundles of health care needs and preferences—through centralized management. On the Island, it's obvious that the only way to handle such complexity is through a central authority (and that is the role of the Surrogates). But as health care consumers, we see a different reality. In almost every interaction with the health care system, we see how inflexible rules interact with the always varying real world of human needs to create irrational and self-defeating complexity.

In 2010, President Obama appointed Donald Berwick to head the Centers for Medicare and Medicaid Services, the agency that runs these massive medical programs. A practicing pediatrician, Berwick cofounded and led the highly influential Institute for Healthcare Improvement. He is a clinical professor of pediatrics and health care policy at Harvard Medical School and a professor of health policy at the Harvard School of Public Health. Berwick has published countless articles and several books on issues ranging from heart disease in children to health care regulation. By all accounts, he is an extraordinarily talented, knowledgeable, and ethical man, as was his predecessor under George Bush, Mark McClellan (also a Harvard-educated physician with a doctorate in economics from the Massachusetts Institute of Technology). McClellan had brought to CMS an equally impressive list of medical, academic, and public service accomplishments.

We are fortunate to have extraordinary people in positions of responsibility throughout our health care system. But we're going to have to face an uncomfortable fact: even the most motivated and highly knowledgeable health experts cannot overcome the dysfunction that arises from perverse incentives. Indeed, many of the biggest problems in health care today result from the very efforts of these smart and dedicated people. How can this be? Because their efforts are confined to the impossible task of overcoming the negative effects of bad incentives without changing the fundamentals of the system.

In America, there are approximately one million physicians in forty-one specialties, 5,754 hospitals, 12,751 FDA-approved prescription pharmaceuticals, and several hundred thousand Class III medical devices all treating 14,568 possible diagnoses in 310 million patients. John Goodman* estimates that Medicare sets six billion individual prices. When you appreciate how difficult it has been for the government to effectively regulate the supply and prices in the electric power industry—an industry with few providers and a single product that never changes—doesn't it appear impossible to govern this most complex and innovative of industries through centralized purchasing and regulation?

Modern economies generally handle the extraordinary complexity of balancing the diverse needs and preferences of large populations and massive but varied production resources by relying on the disaggregated decision making that implicitly arises from trillions of individual transactions. This is also known as the free market.

Of course, markets do operate in health care, but they are massively distorted by an extensive array of rules. So they rarely give us accurate information about people's needs and preferences, the relative scarcity or surplus of resources, or the best allocation of capital and labor. Instead, the logical operations of health markets produce results based on the

---

* John Goodman, "Three Simple Ways Medicare Can Save Money," *Wall Street Journal*, August 11, 2011.

system's "instructions" as to needs, resources, and incentives. And not only are these results often terrible—shortage or excess of care, high prices, and poor safety and customer service—they aren't corrected by the feedback loop (aka consumers) that dominates other markets.

So we require our best minds to compensate for the lack of a normal feedback mechanism by writing rules to address the various shortages and excesses, the carelessness, and the limited accountability. Unfortunately, rules—no matter how precisely designed—never function only as intended in a system as complex as health care. Imposing these rules creates a new reality and a new series of incentives, which often lead to even more imbalance, which then must be addressed by yet more rules.

As discussed earlier, the only reason anyone even thinks something as complex as health care can be managed by centralized rule is the fallacy that our population needs a fixed amount of care: the rules then merely determine how that fixed need is addressed. But as we've seen, the structure of our health care system—including its myriad rules— drives both the amount and the type of care needed.

Equally important is what a rules-based system discourages: the diversity of care models that are essential to true innovation and improvement. Rules favor uniformity, not flexibility. And the administrative burdens of a rules-based system favor those with the resources to manage complex reporting requirements, and, in turn, disadvantage doctors, clinics, and innovators. Substituting rules for consumer feedback makes our system less responsive to the needs of patients and providers and less comprehensible to us. And all this seeming addiction to complexity has a high social cost—not just in our difficulty in navigating the system as patients but in our ability as a society to understand and fix what's truly wrong.

Mispricing care

I have argued that our health care system is plagued by excess—excess tests, excess procedures, and excess treatments. Yet some areas of the country also suffer from a severe shortage of primary physicians. In some states, the wait for a new patient to see a primary doctor is as long as ninety-nine days. Roughly sixty-five million Americans—20 percent of our population—live in what has been described as "primary-care health-professional shortage areas," and the share of doctors now practicing general medicine has declined slowly but steadily over forty years. There are only 7,160 geriatricians—one for every 2,620 Americans seventy-five or older. This ratio is expected to worsen over the next two decades, to one for roughly 3,800. The percentage of doctors practicing family medicine has declined. Both of these problems are direct results of mispricing physicians' time—itself a result of using rules rather than markets to determine prices.

A shortage of primary care physicians has a meaningful impact on the way our system delivers care. Health issues best addressed through lifestyle changes (recommended by primary care physicians) are now treated by medical procedures (performed by specialists). No one makes the connections between disparate symptoms, which is of particular concern to our seniors, who often have related symptoms missed by specialists. Your specialist is less likely to tell you that a symptom is better left to work itself out, that surgery is too dangerous, or that a procedure is an unnecessary risk.

How is it possible to have such a shortage in a sea of excess?

Superficially, the answer is obvious. For almost two generations, medical school students have known that most medical specialties will offer them a higher income than primary care. A recent survey showed that, on average, family practitioners annually earned $175,000, pediatricians $209,000, and geriatricians $188,000. By contrast, radiologists, cardiologists, and gastroenterologists, among other specialists, enjoyed incomes more than double those of primary care physicians. Orthopedic surgeons and neurologists made more than three times as much! Not only has this pay gap persisted for many years (at least since 1995, when first measured), it has actually widened.

Now, even if the services provided by specialists are viewed by patients as more valuable than those of primary physicians, the relationship between the incomes of primary and specialist doctors would be dynamically adjusted in a functioning marketplace to prevent long-term shortages. As primary care physicians got busier, they would raise their prices well before such a shortage developed. That may sound bad for you, but the effect would be observed by that year's class of medical students, more of whom would then choose primary care.

But with our powerful Surrogates, the pay gap between primary and specialist physicians has persisted even beyond the point of shortage. Why?

Medicare bases its reimbursement rates for doctors on the "relative value unit," which in theory equalizes payments as a "function of the time it takes a practitioner to perform each service." But in practical terms, not only does this approach fail to balance supply and demand across different services, it doesn't even set coherent rates for the same service. So the reimbursement for a procedure performed in a hospital on an outpatient basis will be almost double that for the exact same service performed in a doctor's office. In our few-payer system, the feedback mechanism of primary doctor shortages leading to higher incomes is impeded; we have to wait for the Surrogates to notice the long waits for appointments before any action is taken.*

And once they notice the shortage, what happens? Well, in the case of Medicare, they rely on experts, including committees of medical professionals. That sounds good; surely experts will know how to restore balance. But in reality, experts have little to go on—after all, the absence of a functioning marketplace means they don't have meaningful price signals on which to base decisions. And because experts are also people, it turns out that many of these experts are themselves specialist physicians who aren't especially enthusiastic about changing the primary-to-specialist reimbursement pay ratio. In the end, Medicare adjusts prices as a result of compromise among its various stakeholders; such compromises are a much less powerful tool than markets in enforcing the price shifts necessary to prevent excesses and shortages.

Finally, economic value doesn't drive prices in an administered system. Leverage does. Yes, our few payers have meaningful pricing power, but that power doesn't work equally. Your family doctor—practicing by herself or with a few partners—is what's known as a price taker; she accepts

* A *Health Affairs* blog post shows this differential in action. Medicare rates are $836 for a routine cataract removal, which takes ten to fifteen minutes, but only $111 for a primary care visit, which can last twenty-five minutes and include a broad variety of diagnostic and treatment complications (John Goodman, "Three Simple Ways Medicare Can Make Money," *Wall Street Journal*, August 11, 2011).

the Medicare or private insurance reimbursement rate or loses you as a patient. A large local hospital has far more power to resist imposed prices—it may even be a monopoly in your community. So does a major pharmaceutical firm, offering branded drugs backed by big advertising budgets. Even a device manufacturer, whose prices are usually bundled in someone else's costs, has more power. And because Medicare is a dominant payer, these players back up the leverage they get from size with large lobbying budgets.

Spending on Medicare and Medicaid has exceeded projections essentially since the first day each program began operations. The rates private insurers charge their corporate customers have for decades risen faster than inflation. So the Surrogates are under some pressure to cut costs—at least visibly. And the easiest way to do this is to cut doctors' reimbursements. This is partly because doctors have less leverage and political power but also because, as discussed above, it's hard to cut back on treatments with seemingly more tangible costs. It's relatively easy to demand cuts in the reimbursement rate for a doctor's time. Unfortunately, time is what primary care physicians sell. A 2006 report estimated that physicians' income declined in inflation-adjusted terms by 7 percent between 1995 and 2003, and while this sharp decline seems to have abated, hospitals, pharmaceutical companies, and device manufacturers still capture more of our health care dollars than doctors do. It's a major reason that doctors have been selling their practices to the institutions implicitly favored by the Surrogates. As recently as 2005, half of physicians owned their own practices; estimates are that by next year, only a third will.

Primary care physicians have been hurt most. They have only sixty minutes to spend each hour, and their work requires time spent with the patient. They can reduce and have already reduced the minutes they spend with each patient, but many say they are already bumping up against the minimum required by professional responsibility. They can also invest in costly diagnostic equipment to capture more of the revenue they would typically refer to clinics— an option that exacerbates our Surrogates' preference for procedures over care.

Meanwhile, specialists have a broader range of options for reacting to price pressures. They can recommend (i.e., sell) more—and more extensive—treatments. They can demand better terms from hospitals for bringing in more patients. They can enjoy volume discounts (aka kickbacks) from device manufacturers by using more of their implants or equipment.

Many experts consider the imperfections of the Surrogate-based administrated price system to be a matter of money, a tawdry issue of who gets what in our health care industry. But unfortunately, as the above demonstrates, the real problem with an inflexible administered price system is its effect on care itself. Because our Surrogates have so much pricing power, we have fewer primary care physicians, who, in turn, have less time to spend with their patients. We have more physicians incented to order too many tests and too many procedures. And more of our care is delivered by large institutions, with their associated problems of safety and service. That's the health impact of getting just one administered price wrong. Make just one mistake and it will set off a chain reaction and be compounded by the lack of the natural feedback loop that on the Mainland we call the market.

The unintended consequences of discounts

As if maintaining a single administered pricing system isn't impossible enough, our health policy effectively creates three different administered price regimens. Medicare demands a discount below what private insurers pay for all procedures; only Medicaid agencies can be charged less than the price Medicare pays. Medicare and Medicaid are the biggest customers of the health care system, so there's certainly an argument to be made that they deserve a volume discount on services. And they certainly seem to get these discounts.* But the cost is high: three different levels of pricing may not deliver true discounts on care but rather unintentionally produce three different levels of care.

On the Island, the issue of the three prices is thought to have a direct and straightforward impact on financing care. Many hospitals now contend that they lose money on the low reimbursement rates paid on Medicare patients. Two years ago, CMS reported that the average hospital's margin (Medicare's payments less a hospital's costs) was as low as −7 percent. A growing number of providers are refusing Medicaid patients because they say reimbursement rates are too low. And health care experts attribute some of the rise in private insurance premiums to cost shifting, by which hospitals require private insurers to bear some of the costs

---

* Precise numbers are hard to obtain, but MedPAC data suggest that on average Medicare pays 88 percent of what commercial insurers pay, with Medicaid paying between 66 and 72 percent of Medicare rates (www.statehealthfacts.org /comparetable.jsp?ind=196&cat=4). A 2005 Michigan State Medical Society survey reported that for a diagnostic colonoscopy, Blue Cross reimbursed $209, Medicare $175, and Medicaid $91. For an appendectomy, the numbers were $784, $676, and $336 (Vanessa Fuhrmans, "Note to Medicaid Patients: The Doctor Won't See You," *Wall Street Journal*, July 19, 2007).

of public patients not fully reimbursed by Medicare and Medicaid.*

It's an interesting (and endless) discussion, but there's only one problem: none of this makes any sense. Hospitals lose money on their huge number of Medicare patients? Then why is it that more hospitals have opened than have closed each year for the past decade? Medicaid beneficiaries are unable to find providers? Then how has the number of Medicaid treatments skyrocketed? Private insurance rates have to bear the cost shifting from Medicare and Medicaid patients? Why would private insurers agree to pay for someone else's patients?

It may be true that many health care insiders obsess over these phenomena, but that doesn't mean they really exist across the board. Island experts assume that the health care industry has responded to the three-price system by merely accepting its objectives, by simply pricing the same service at three different levels. But here's a more plausible view: the industry has responded to the three prices by offering three different tiers of service, with each one structured to be profitable to the industry. Let's see how this would work.

Patients with private insurance tend to get relatively good treatment and service from their doctors and hospitals; they are regarded as the full-price-paying customer but also the one most likely to question appropriateness of extra procedures. Medicare patients can also produce an attractive profit margin even at lower prices if these patients can be sold enough additional tests and procedures. In other words, by paying a lower price for Medicare services, the

---

* Some experts believe this is a social good—that those fortunate enough to have private insurance should subsidize those on Medicare and Medicaid by paying more through cost shifting.

government is providing an accidental incentive for providers to perform more services on Medicare patients. Which is probably why hospitals continue to serve these patients—and build new beds for them—despite Medicare's belief that they are doing so at a loss.

Medicaid patients present a different customer profile to the health care industry. Because their reimbursement rates are so much lower, it only makes sense—makes a profit—to accept a Medicaid patient under certain circumstances. Medicaid patients are profitable for providers in specialties that allow for high-volume medicine, for those willing to cut corners, and for those whose reputations or geography prevent them from attracting higher paying private and Medicare customers. Medicaid beneficiaries have a hard time finding providers in primary care and certain time-intensive specialties, since these providers are unable to make up low rates with higher volumes. Since Medicaid patients have less choice in all forms of care (as other patients offer a greater profit opportunity), it is unsurprising that the quality of care, the attentiveness of physicians, and the state of the facilities serving large numbers of Medicaid patients often do appear to be of lower quality. And this explains the simultaneous existence of physician shortage and exploding procedures; Medicaid's across-the-board discount ensures that its beneficiaries receive lots of treatments, but little care.

Nobody wanted to create three different levels of quality and service in our health care system. Of course, variation of quality, service, and price can be found in many industries on the Mainland. But the insistence on across-the-board discounts for Medicare and Medicaid without the disaggregated disciplinary force of consumers produces perverse results, including the broad incentive for excess care in Medicare and the shortages of primary providers in Medicaid. As in any other business, health care providers respond to rules that seem to reduce their prices by finding ways to restore profitability. And because those responses can be so powerful, the perverse incentives can overwhelm even good intentions.

A final irony: the government's insistence that providers give Medicaid the lowest prices has the accidental effect of discouraging any discounting at all to anyone else. In Clayton Christensen's words:

> Most Medicaid programs stipulate that, at the end of each quarter, the prices they pay to suppliers must be written down to the lowest prices charged to any other customer. While this ostensibly ensures that Medicaid automatically pays the lowest price for everything it buys, its inadvertent effect is to make discounting extremely expensive for providers of health-care products and services. It instills extraordinary pricing "discipline" among competitors in the hospital, pharmaceutical, and medical device industries that executives in other industries . . . can only dream about.

The impossibility of simplicity

My single favorite provision in the ACA—because it so perfectly illustrates our policymakers' refusal to consider the dynamic effect of rules on incentives—is a requirement that insurers pay out a certain percentage of their premiums on health care claims. This medical loss ratio (MLR) rule requires that insurers pay out at least 85 percent of their premium income from larger employers and 80 percent from smaller employers and individuals. In other words, no more than 15 or 20 percent of premiums can be used for marketing, administration, and profits; the rest must go to care. The penalty is straightforward: insurers who fail to meet these minimums must refund the difference. The MLR rule caps the profits of the insurance industry, at least as a share of premiums, forcing it to control its administrative and marketing expenses and leaving more resources for health care. The rule returns "excess" health care premiums to those who deserve them: policyholders. And better yet, the new rule is simple and straightforward.

That's the argument, at least. But I don't understand how the MLR provision can accomplish any of these goals, even in theory. Even more, when you think through the likely responses to it, you can appreciate how even a simple rule must have complex results; indeed, this rule adds levels of cost and complexity that are likely to overwhelm its purported benefits.

Consider the hypothetical El Diablo Health Insurance Company, which serves the small-business market. Today, El Diablo has $1 million in premiums, pays out $750,000 in claims (a 75 percent MLR), spends $150,000 in expenses, and has $100,000 in profits. The MLR rule makes a typically static analysis of the situation: El Diablo seemingly needs to shift $50,000 from expenses and profits to benefits for policyholders to achieve the 80 percent ratio. But of course, El Diablo has another alternative: it can raise premiums by $250,000 and pay out the difference in additional benefits. In this circumstance, El Diablo has $1.25 million in premiums, $1 million in paid claims, and the same $150,000 in expenses and $100,000 in profits. It might be hard to accomplish that full increase in claims paid in the first year (and in fact some insurers are likely to pay out some rebates in the initial implementation of the ACA). But if you ran El Diablo, what do you think you'd do?*

It's unclear exactly what problem the MLR rule is intended to fix. Did Congress believe that insurance companies were wasteful in their back-office operations and marketing? Insurers already get to take 100 percent of any savings they achieve as profit; how can a payout rule fix a supposed inefficiency when the profit motive didn't? Or are we concerned that health insurers are inadequately motivated by profit?†

An ACA supporter might counter that if an insurer winds up raising premiums and payouts to meet the requirements of the new MLR rule, that's not so bad, is it? At least more health care is paid for. But if we've learned anything from health care's history, it's that undermining an incentive to be disciplined leads to inflation in the price of care. And— paradoxically—the MLR rule lessens every insurer's incentive to be disciplined about the cost of care.

The MLR rule does create a powerful new incentive for

---

* A recent Kaiser study suggests that insurers will have to pay almost \$1.3 billion in rebates on individual policies in the first year of the ACA. "This alone is not going to make health insurance affordable for large numbers of people, but it is getting excess administrative cost out of the system," the study claimed (Julie Appleby, "Checks in the Mail," Kaiser Health News, April 26, 2012). I doubt it. More likely is that the rebate possibility will offer insurers future cover for higher premiums (something like: "If these premiums turn out to be too high, don't worry: you'll get a year-end rebate in that case").

† Some advocates of the MLR rules contend that insurance profits are too high, and that the rule will discipline excess profits. But this is typical static analysis. Over time insurers measure profits as return on equity, like all other big companies. So if margin declines are not associated with premiums increases (as in the hypothetical El Diablo example above), we would expect capital to exit the health insurance business. This would make the business even less competitive, and in a dynamic world, such a development is rarely associated with profit declines.

insurers: to lobby endlessly for favorable interpretations of the rule. Within days of the ACA's passage, the major insurers were besieging regulators to ensure definitions of each part of the ratio that best suited their particular interests. Should all of an insurer's plans and markets be pooled in calculating MLR? Are health quality initiatives part of medical claims? Can unusually large claims be carried over from year to year?

These definitions are not merely a matter of enforcement. Each regulatory decision will create a new set of incentives, which will shape what kind of care is funded. For example, many insurers are experimenting with wellness programs that give discounts to beneficiaries who don't smoke, who maintain healthy weights, or who commit to an exercise program. Should the money spent to fund these programs be included in the definition of benefits, even though that would reduce the amount actually spent on care? If regulators rule against inclusion of wellness programs, insurers will likely drop them and society will lose the beneficial effects of these initiatives. If regulators decide to allow inclusion, insurers may well overinvest in wellness programs beyond their beneficial effects. Of course, without an MLR rule, insurers would have been free to experiment with wellness programs until they found an efficient balance. In other words, not only is the MLR rule unlikely to reduce costs, it is certain to add one major new cost to health care—the cost of managing claims to comply with the MLR rule.*

---

* One ironic consequence of the MLR rule is that it implicitly acknowledges that health insurers aren't really in the insurance business. All types of insurance are subject to strict regulations that cap the *maximum* amount an insurer can pay in claims, not that specify a *minimum* amount, as the MLR rule does. Why? In real insurance, the regulator is concerned that an insurance company is paying out too

The MLR rule will also provide a clear illustration of how even a single detail contains the seeds of perverse results. Congress did recognize that insurers serving small businesses and individuals have higher costs than those serving large employers. So it quite sensibly allowed companies serving these customers a lower MLR of 80 percent. But even if that seems like the right thing to do today, this legislation will be the rule of law for years. So that ratio of 80 percent to 85 percent is now frozen. How will it affect insurers' willingness to offer insurance in these respective markets over time? To invest in efficiency in each of these markets? To offer new products? We have no idea. All we know is that the relationship between these ratios is fixed by law, although all of the underlying factors—the cost of health care, technology, wage levels, the cost of capital, and so on—will continue to fluctuate. It's an extraordinary amount of potential mischief from just one simple rule.*

---

much in claims to attract business and that too high a payout leaves too little in reserves and profits to ensure its ability to meet future claims. Insurance regulation has always been primarily concerned with the safety and financial soundness of insurers. The MLR rule forces insurers to pay out more than they otherwise would, without concern for whether insurers can meet their future obligations. It's an accidental reminder that health insurance operates primarily as a payment management system, taking money from us each year and paying it out each year for expected services.

* Another small rule with the potential for unanticipated mischief is that companies that are self-insured are exempt from some of ACA's more important insurance regulations, including the MLR, minimum benefits, and annual fees. While previously only the largest companies were self-insured, it seems as if many companies are now examining this option. Some of ACA's advocates have already called for this "loophole" to be closed, but its original inclusion reflects its sponsors' fundamental misunderstanding of employer insurance. Any company with more than a handful of employees was already effectively if not technically self-insured, in that any unusual increase in its costs in one year would be added to their premiums in

Rule of rules

Now, all institutions need rules, of course, and all rules have the potential for abuse or misapplication. We can shake our heads at kindergartners suspended for "sexually harassing" a classmate with a kiss, at an NBA player drawing an offensive foul with an obvious flop, or at the divorce proceeding that lasts longer than the marriage. But in health care, excessive rules can cost lives.

The story about dialysis at the beginning of this chapter is instructive. The federal government pays all of the dialysis costs for most kidney-failure patients, but it has had trouble getting the economic incentives for providers to match patient interest. It had paid for antianemia drugs separate from treatment but found this was causing dangerously excessive prescribing of the drugs. So it changed the reimbursement formula, packaging the price of the drugs with the treatment. This, of course, produced the exact opposite problem: a dangerous underprescribing of the drugs.

One could write a separate book just on such stories of dysfunctional health care rules. But what's the alternative to a rules-based system? Flexibility. The average supermarket stocks 48,750 items and gives its employees rules as to how to order these items and where to place them on the shelves. But what's most important is the possibility of change: that faster-moving items will get more shelf space in more prominent locations. That prices will change. And that new items

---

the next. So it's usually a small financial step to move from effective self-insurance to actual self-insurance, with the insurer taking on the technical role of payments manager (some employers may buy "stop-loss" insurance to protect them against true health catastrophe). In other words, ACA's exclusion provides the little incentive needed to drop the fiction that companies are truly passing on financial risk to their insurer when they buy health insurance for employees.

will be added and old ones dropped. Supermarkets—like all businesses on the Mainland—are in the one-size-fits-only-some business.

Essentially, everything we've done in health care points in the other direction—toward more uniformity. It's an inevitable consequence of our greater reliance on the Surrogates to serve our role; they can't deal with us—or represent our needs—as individuals. They need rules. The only way around this is to get rid of the Surrogates and embrace the flexibility, dynamism, and accountability provided by real customers.

CHAPTER 8

Last Gasp

The ACA and the insurance fixation

> Two New Russian businessmen encounter each other at the airport in Zurich. The first says, "That's a nice tie."
>
> "Thank you," responds the second man. "It's an Hermès."
>
> "May I ask," says the first, "how much did you pay for that tie?"
>
> "A hundred and fifty dollars!" answers the second man proudly.
>
> "You idiot!" says the first man. "I bought the exact same tie, but for two hundred and fifty dollars!"
>
> —Russian joke from the mid-1990s

If you like your health plan, you can keep it," President Obama famously promised when kicking off his drive for new health legislation. The president's words signaled that he had learned an invaluable political lesson from Bill Clinton's 1993 health reform failure: most Americans have health insurance, and they are afraid of losing their benefits through reform. There was another difference from the Clinton approach: the Obama administration locked up early support from the health care industry—most prominently the hospitals and pharmaceutical companies—with the promise of an expanded market. And so this time, although by the narrowest of legislative margins, a Democratic administration was finally able to pass what it regarded as comprehensive health reform: the Patient Protection and Affordable Care Act of 2010 (the ACA). Many on the Island saw the ACA as a major victory because it seemingly expands access to affordable care for the poor and uninsured; in practice, however, by retaining all the perverse incentives of our current system, the ACA may well have the opposite effect.

History weighed heavily on ACA supporters. From Congress's first serious consideration of national health insurance in 1935, through Truman's 1945 proposal for national insurance and the 1965 passage of Medicare and Medicaid, up to the failure of Clinton's plan, the battle for universal health insurance has been portrayed as a kind of unfinished civil rights struggle.* Senator Tom Harkin expressed a common feeling of simple justice in claiming that the ACA "get[s] rid of that shameful divide within our American family. With this bill, we say that for every member of our family, access to quality, affordable health care should be a right, not a privilege." America, with its partial and reluctant commitment to health coverage, has compared poorly

---

* This from *The New Republic:* "For generations, health care reform has been a signature cause of liberalism—a campaign to redress a great moral failing of our democratic capitalist order, and a unique failing of our system when judged next to its peers in the industrialized world" ("Obama in the Balance," January 27, 2010).

with other developed nations. Germany enacted national health insurance in 1888. Most European nations adopted universal, publicly funded systems starting in the 1950s. Our neighbor Canada had national coverage by 1961. In signing the bill, the president remarked that "after almost a century of trying . . . health insurance reform becomes law in the United States of America."

Narratives matter in politics, and for supporters, the ACA narrative was straightforward. Though true universal coverage is not quite achieved, the bill's proponents estimate that an additional thirty-two million Americans not currently insured will ultimately be covered by private insurance and Medicaid. Just as important, in principle, the goal of universal access—even if achieved through our current hodgepodge of private insurance, Medicare, and Medicaid—is now law.*

The political fight over the ACA was unusually bitter and partisan, although the opposition's narrative was often incoherent.† Yet for all the heated rhetoric on both sides, the ACA as legislation—not as symbol—has remarkably limited objectives. What proponents call "reform" is essentially a synonym for the single goal of insurance expansion. The ACA is also designed to be "revenue-neutral," meaning the explicit cost to the federal government (but not to

* The thirty-two million estimate was calculated before the Supreme Court's decision allowing states to opt-out of ACA's Medicaid expansion. At this writing, it is unclear whether any states will ultimately opt out and what effect that would have on the numbers of uninsured.

† Some Republicans decried a government takeover of the health care system, even though our government already funds a majority of care. Others claimed the new coverage was budget busting, even while criticizing the bill's potential curbs on Medicare spending. Some weirdly read horrific "death panels" into the legislation, even while criticizing the bill's lack of effective cost controls. Conservative scholars questioned the constitutionality of the ACA insurance mandate, ignoring the idea's roots in conservative think tanks.

state governments) is matched by explicit revenue increases or anticipated budget savings. The only taxes raised are on medical device manufacturers, certain insurance plans, the investment income of high earners, and—weirdly— tanning salons, which means few Americans will experience direct tax increases as a result of the bill. Much of the ACA's true financial burden is—in the grand tradition of health care financing—hidden from those who will ultimately pay. With its new insurance mandates and regulation, ACA's greatest cost impact will likely be on insurance premiums, which can be blamed on insurance companies rather than policymakers.

And for all the rhetoric about reshaping how health care itself is practiced, the major initiatives of the ACA are best described as baby steps. Integrated medicine, best prac- tices, promotion of primary care—all the conventional care improvement ideas from the Island—get only "pilot pro- gram" treatment from the bill, not enough to genuinely transform anything. The ACA may suggest a different future of medicine, but it doesn't mandate enough change to have risked the political opposition of industry interests. (I'll dis- cuss a few of the higher-profile initiatives in appendix 2.)

Indeed, the ACA's most obvious characteristic is its continuity with our existing system: a continued reliance on insurance as the funding mechanism for all care. On employers as the source of this insurance for most Ameri- cans. On unreconstructed Medicare for seniors and on Medicaid for the needy. On premium subsidies, tax breaks, and cost-sharing limits to maintain the illusion of afford- able care. On the Surrogates to discipline the cost of care (even while reducing their ability to say no to anything). On a raft of rules to overcome the inevitable imbalances, distortions, and waste. Step away from the sound and fury of politics, and the ACA is laid bare as a technocrats' approach to saving our current system while expanding it somewhat to cover more people.

Which is why the ACA, at the end of the day, is unlikely to matter much at all.

Narratives may be important in politics, but reality matters in policy. The triumphalist narrative of the ACA's sponsors ("We finally achieved health reform") ignored how much the health care landscape had shifted beneath their feet—not just since FDR's administration first proposed national insurance but even in the short time since Bill Clinton's failure. In 1993, Americans spent $3,500 per capita on health care; we spend two and a half times that today. Back then, Medicare and Medicaid represented 15 percent of federal spending; today, it's 23 percent. In 1993, employers paid an average of $4,404 as an insurance premium for an employee with a family; today, that premium is $15,073. In the intervening years, we've come to recognize that the cost of health benefits has significant impacts on employment, wages, and U.S. industrial competitiveness.

We've also become aware of the physical toll of our health care system's carelessness. In 1999, the Institute of Medicine published *To Err Is Human,* which first documented that up to ninety-eight thousand people were killed each year by medical errors. The intervening years of higher estimates and failed regulatory solutions means that medical errors alone have killed between one million and three million people since Bill Clinton proposed health reform—more than have died in all of America's wars combined.

Looking outside our borders at recent trends should also have modified conventional wisdom. Yes, the national health systems of other countries continue to achieve broader guaranteed access and health results (to the very limited extent that these are measured) similar to those in the United States at much less cost.* But the past decade has also seen rapid increases in health costs, regardless of the system model.† Health spending in other advanced countries appears under control only in contrast to the United States. Looking forward, which nation can be described as confident of its ability to manage health care costs?

Further, another piece of conventional wisdom has been turned on its head since the Clinton years; in 1990, Americans funded 20 percent of their own health care costs, one of the highest out-of-pocket percentages in the developed world. Today, our health care system is so expensive that the massive amount we fund out of pocket is only 11 percent of total spending—among the lowest in the developed world!‡

* One of the constant questions in health care policy is how other nations are able to achieve similar or better results in national health data yet spend so much less on care. An implicit assumption is that these two sets of data are related: that health care drives health results and therefore health data. But for much of what we measure—life span, infant mortality, contraceptive use, infectious diseases—health care is far less a driver than are the measures of wealth, lifestyle, and public health (such as vaccination). The ones most related to health care are specifically about health care, not health: doctors and dentists per population, government spending on health care, and so on (World Health Organization statistics).

† In a decade, the United Kingdom, with its government-run health system, has seen health care rise as a share of GDP by 36 percent; Canada, with its national health budget, by 30 percent; France, with its national insurance system, by 17 percent; and Germany, with its price-controlled private insurance system, by 13 percent. Canadian health spending now accounts for 46 percent of provincial governments' budgets, up more than 10 percent in a decade. In the United Kingdom, 11 percent of patients now wait more than four months for treatment; almost 4 percent wait more than six months.

‡ It should be noted that measuring national out-of-pocket data is difficult, but the trends are consistent: the share of out-of-pocket spending has been declining in the United States as it stays constant or even rises in nations with national health systems. The most recent data available from the Organization for Economic Cooperation and Development (from 2009) shows that only France (7.3 percent) and the United Kingdom (10.5 percent) have out-of-pocket shares less than

In the years since the defeat of the Clinton health plan, the real fundamental problems of our health system should have come into full relief: perverse incentives that encourage excess treatment, high prices, poor service, and dangerous sloppiness; disincentives to control costs and increase efficiency; the lack of a trade-off mechanism between health care and society's other goals; incomprehensible complexity; and a flawed safety net. But to all problems and issues, the ACA has the same two answers that would have made complete sense to any of the reformers in 1994: more insurance and Medicaid and more top-down cost control.

So despite all the noise, all the drama, all the promises of paradise and the warnings of apocalypse, I suspect the most accurate description of the ACA is that it is profoundly old-fashioned. And no part of it is as tragically old-fashioned as its equating insurance with access. The explosion in the cost of care over the past four decades now means that having insurance is no guarantee of either access or affordability. Insurers are an easy political target, but it's absurd to believe that health insurance can somehow be made affordable when health care isn't. So to achieve its twin goals of affordable insurance for all without anyone seeming to pay more for care, the ACA is fundamentally an exercise in Rube Goldberg–like financial engineering. As with so many of these schemes in our history of health care policy, the very complexity and attendant unanticipated consequences are likely to undermine achievement of the fundamental goal of expanding access. (In appendix 1, I'll discuss how the sum

ours (12.3 percent). Figures from 2008 show that national insurance systems with greater out-of-pocket expenditures than ours include Canada (14.6 percent), Germany (13.1 percent), and Japan (15.8 percent). The out-of-pocket share in the United States is much less than it is in Switzerland (30.5 percent), Italy (19.7 percent), Belgium (20 percent), and Finland (19 percent).

effect of the ACA's mechanics might even have the unintended consequence of reducing the share of the population with health insurance.)

Supporters may believe that all the costs, complications, and mistakes of the ACA are worth it if the bill merely expands our insurance system to cover many of those not covered. But the bottom line should be health and health care, not the quantity of insurance. If the ACA places more of the burden of health care on the poor and the middle class, diverts resources into waste and unnecessary treatments, coddles an industry culture of dangerous sloppiness, and crowds out all other social priorities, then it will have actively hurt the very people it was intended to help.

Monomania

Nothing better illustrates the flaw at the heart of the ACA than its treatment of Medicaid. There may be no element of our current system more dysfunctional or plagued by runaway costs, quality issues, unimaginable complexity, and outright corruption. But the ACA ignores these fundamental issues and instead mandates a massive expansion of the program. Indeed, Medicaid's growth is expected to account for roughly half of the thirty-two million newly covered under the ACA.

Enacted along with Medicare in 1965, Medicaid may be the most complicated program ever designed by the federal government; it's run by the individual states, with each state having its own eligibility requirements, coverage definitions, and payment policies. Less than 10 percent of the population is eligible for Medicaid in Nevada; in neighboring California, it's just about 30 percent. The average annual outlay per beneficiary is less than $3,000 in Wisconsin but more than $10,000 in Washington, D.C. The federal government sets broad guidelines and pays for between 50 and 74 percent of a state's total costs, depending on—you guessed it—a complicated formula.

As a result, what we call Medicaid has, to date, really been fifty-six separate health care aid programs. Only low-income adults with certain conditions—such as pregnant women and the disabled—have been automatically eligible, although states are allowed to adopt more generous eligibility standards. Children can be eligible for Medicaid even when their parents are not. Certain Medicare beneficiaries, known as dual eligibles, also qualify for Medicaid.

Since its inception, Medicaid has funded treatments connected to certain specified diseases or conditions; it has paid for much of AIDS treatment (now shifted to Medicare) and funds 40 percent of U.S. births. Medicaid also supports almost two-thirds of nursing home residents, although only those dual eligibles who can prove they have spent all their available assets (generating a good business for financial advisers expert in secretly transferring assets to family members). As recently as 2009, roughly two-thirds of Medicaid spending was for the blind and disabled, seniors eligible for Medicare, and foster children, leaving only a third for what most Americans think Medicaid is for: support for the general health issues of America's neediest.

To those needy Americans who would benefit most from a straightforward and predictable assistance program, Medicaid has instead offered an almost incomprehensible patchwork of eligibility rules, coverage guidelines, and service providers. One of the main goals of the ACA was to expand Medicaid's coverage and establish it as a more reliable and straightforward safety net for people of lower income.* Under the ACA, any citizen with income less than 133 percent of the federal poverty level (which would equal just under $15,000 for an individual or $31,000 for a family of four today) will qualify for his state's Medicaid program. This simplification of eligibility is good news and should improve the operation of the program.

Unfortunately, for all its restrictions and exclusions, Medicaid was already very expensive; in 2010, the states and the federal government spent a combined $405 billion on their Medicaid programs, up from $206 billion only a decade before.† Though the federal government will initially pick up all the additional bills for expansion, some states are already resisting this mandated expansion (and the recent Supreme Court decision will allow them to opt out of the expansion). Most states were already struggling with their existing Medicaid costs—and many have been reducing their reimbursements. Arizona froze enrollment and stopped reimbursing for many organ transplants, even when death is imminent. Florida cut the number of hospital days it will cover by half. California's governor proposed limiting doctor's visits.

For our purposes, though, the key question is this: Why has Medicaid's cost grown so rapidly? As with Medicare, it

---

* Studies have suggested that 15 to 45 percent of adults eligible for Medicaid haven't applied for coverage (summarized in Sommers, Kronick, et al., "Understanding Participation Rates in Medicaid: Implications for the Affordable Care Act," ASPE Issue Brief, Department of Health and Human Services, March 2012), and the Department of Health and Human Services has estimated that five million eligible children are unenrolled (quoted in "Enrolling More Kids in Medicaid and CHIP," Health Policy Brief, *Health Affairs,* January 2011).

† During the past ten years, the growth of spending on Medicaid has outpaced all other categories in state budgets, according to *The Fiscal Survey of States* prepared by the National Governors Association.

doesn't seem to make sense that a population that is getting richer, that has greater access to better food and cleaner water, that works in less physically dangerous occupations, that doesn't smoke or drink as much, and that has longer life spans should need so much more health care. With the economic downturn that began in 2008 the number of Americans turning to Medicaid has grown, but the program's increase in costs—and the growth of beneficiaries—was outsize even during the boom years.

On the Island, one speculation is that poor Americans receive little primary care, meaning that health problems are addressed only after they become severe (and more costly to treat). Another is that the disproportionate incidence of obesity among low-income people suggests that their lifestyles have become less healthy, even as income levels rise. In other words, maybe people are less healthy.

But like Medicare, Medicaid is an entitlement at the federal level, so it's fertile ground for state governments looking for funds for a variety of programs. Incredibly, my household is a Medicaid beneficiary despite my CEO-level income; the tutoring provided by our local public school to our son is partially reimbursed under our state's Medicaid program.

More important, Medicaid's growth is an inevitable consequence of the undisciplined demand for care that pushes up prices in the Medicare and private insurance markets. In providing health assistance to the neediest, governments face a health care industry that enjoys the ability to sell excess care at high prices to other customers.

With Medicaid now consuming more than a fifth of most of their budgets (or 14 percent, excluding federal contributions), state governments have been desperate for ideas to reduce its cost. Many are simply continually reducing the amounts they reimburse for specific procedures. In the previous chapter, I discussed how low Medicaid reimbursement rates, combined with the limited accountability inherent in a large government program, create an opening for low-quality providers to dominate Medicaid services. Only physicians and other providers able or willing to engage in extremely high-volume medicine—or that have difficulty competing for higher-paying private patients—do well in Medicaid. Further, as I'll discuss below, Medicaid coverage is no guarantee of care; many physicians now refuse to treat Medicaid patients, and this problem was getting worse even before Medicaid expansion.

Several analysts have argued that the wait lists for Medicaid patients and the often low-quality care they receive suggest that being on Medicaid may be worse for most people than being uninsured. Essentially, their view is that because Medicaid is usually a direct purchaser of care, the distortive effects of its cost-savings measures and the inflexibility of its rules can have such a deleterious effect on care that a patient would be better off negotiating directly with providers. This, they argue, explains why so many who are eligible for Medicaid have not actually enrolled in the program. Interestingly, much of the response to this argument has focused on Medicaid beneficiaries' greater access to preventive care—most of which, by definition, goes to the healthy.

As long as waste, excess, and price inflation dominate health care, ever more Americans will need to rely on some form of public safety net to obtain care. And those same factors will change the nature of care available through Medicaid relative to that available to the rest of the population. Expanding Medicaid may allow us to claim that more people are covered, but the real issue—the quality of care actually available to our neediest—can be addressed only by fundamental reform of the whole system.

The problem of the uninsured

For the proponents of the ACA, the problem of the uninsured is straightforward: when they get sick, they have no access to health care, with potentially fatal consequences. Thus expanding our insurance system is as simple a moral issue as there could be. As one journalist wrote in *The New York Times*, "Thanks to the Affordable Care Act, some unquantifiable number of people will live who would otherwise die." That's a very morally compelling argument. But there's a good reason the writer refers to the number of lives saved as "unquantifiable." Even after forty-five years of an insurance-dominated health system, we don't actually know if having insurance saves any lives.

How can that be? First, the uninsured encompass a broad range of people, which makes a simple comparison impossible (more on that below). Second, lacking insurance truly isn't the same thing as lacking health care, no matter what the politicians say; the real issue is to what extent being uninsured means actually receiving insufficient or inadequate care that meaningfully affects health.

In other words, the problem of the uninsured is more complex than the politics of health care reform would suggest. I have argued that excessive insurance is a central cause for our health care dysfunction. Yet, like almost everyone with the choice, I take a comprehensive policy offered by my employer. I don't have a cost-effective alternative to opt out of the system, so as an individual I'm a part of the system even if I believe the societal cost is excessive. However, that doesn't necessarily mean that for those outside this system, merely joining it improves their own situation. Because the uninsured are not a simple monolithic group, both the costs and benefits will land unevenly.

When policymakers talk about the uninsured, they usually are referring to people who lack private insurance—purchased directly or through an employer—and who are not enrolled in Medicare, Medicaid, or another government program. The most recent estimate is that roughly 16 percent of the population can be considered uninsured. That's a lot of people—about fifty million—lacking access to the health safety net at any one time. The ACA's sponsors believe this number will shrink to eighteen million under the new legislation.

But "at any one time" is not the same as permanently; the uninsured are not some type of lifelong disadvantaged minority. Almost 20 percent of our population lacks insurance at some time during a given year, but 40 percent of these people are uninsured for less than one year. This means that many uninsured people are likely to have had similar access to health care as the always insured over most of their lives. (This is a major reason that measuring the health impacts of lacking insurance is so difficult: an uninsured person this year may well have been insured last year and will be again next year.)

In addition, people aged eighteen to thirty make up about a third of the uninsured. They are less likely to have jobs with coverage and more likely to consider insurance an unnecessary expense. Remember also that virtually no seniors are uninsured, because they receive Medicare, while most of the uninsured who suffer disabilities become eligible for Medicaid or Medicare. Strangely, then, as a whole the uninsured may be healthier than the general population: 90 percent of the uninsured describe their health as good to excellent.

Then there are the long-term uninsured; for them, the story is likely to be quite different. Roughly half of the uninsured at any one time—twenty-five million people—are estimated to be without coverage for three years or more. We can assume that lacking insurance for this long an interval would have a significant impact on health care choices and options. The long-term uninsured are disproportionately poor, suffering long periods of unemployment and often working in low-wage jobs without health benefits. While government programs now cover two-thirds of poor children, the remaining uninsured youngsters are very likely to be in poor families with long-term insurance gaps. Furthermore, low-income people—regardless of insurance status—are more likely to suffer from chronic health problems relating to lifestyle issues: hypertension, diabetes, and heart disease (this is another major reason that measuring the health benefit of insurance has been so elusive: it has proven difficult to separate the effects of lifestyle from those of health care).

In short, as the ACA was being written, the uninsured consisted of at least three very different groups: young people with low health risks; people of all ages (except seniors) with average health risks but uninsured for only a short period of time; and low-income people with high health risks and long periods spent outside the insurance system.

If viewing the uninsured as a monolithic high-risk group clouds our understanding of the issue, viewing them as having no access to care is even more deceptive. Because whatever the political rhetoric, lacking health insurance is not the same as lacking health care. A 2008 study (the "2008 study") estimated that those uninsured for a whole year averaged $1,686 in health care spending, a little over 43 percent of what was spent by those privately insured ($3,915).*

At least on average, the uninsured appear to be getting more than only 43 percent of the care of the insured. For example, 48 percent of the insured and 42 percent of the uninsured reported one to three visits to the doctor in the most recently measured year. A recent study of low-income uninsured people found that roughly 70 percent of those with diabetes reported a regular source of care (as opposed to 90 percent of Medicaid beneficiaries with diabetes).

A study now under way in Oregon (the "Oregon study") may answer many of the questions regarding the health cost of lacking insurance. Fortuitously, the state conducted a lottery to pick 10,000 Medicaid beneficiaries out of a pool of 90,000 uninsured eligibles; so researchers can compare the health results of people who differ only by winning or losing the lottery. One year in, the study has shown that the Medicaid beneficiaries were 15 percent more likely to use prescription drugs, 20 percent more likely to get cholesterol monitoring, 30 percent more likely to have been admitted to a hospital, and 35 percent more likely to have visited an outpatient facility.† It's too early in the study to find definitive health results of this higher level of treatment, but the

---

* The study's authors divide the uninsured into full- and part-year uninsured. The part-year uninsured receive levels of care closer to the insured (roughly 31 percent less).

† Medicaid beneficiaries in the study are also 60 percent more likely to obtain mammograms despite the U.S. Preventive Services Task Force recommendation against regular mammograms for women under sixty without specific symptoms.

study's authors note that the covered respondents on average say they feel healthier than do the uncovered.

Overall, the uninsured certainly seem to receive less care than the insured, especially preventive and chronic condition care. But certainly not so much less care as to explain the massive differences in spending by the insured and uninsured. And certainly not enough to explain the cost of the ACA's efforts to expand insurance. The government has estimated that the legislation will provide coverage for thirty-two million at a cost of $200 billion: $100 billion in government funds (assuming the ACA's highly dubious cost control provisions are effective) plus $100 billion in the newly insured's own money. That's $6,250 per person, just a small amount less than the total cost of health care for the insured.* How is it possible that "15 percent more likely to use prescription drugs, 20 percent more likely to get cholesterol monitoring, or even 30 percent more likely to being admitted to a hospital," and so on can translate to an extra $6,250 in cost per person?

As I have suggested several times in this book, let's turn our attention away from the needs and resources of patients and toward the motivations of the health care industry. Look at how the uninsured pay for their care today. Some of their spending is out of pocket, although the 2008 study concluded that the average uninsured person paid less out of pocket than insured people did ($583 a year compared with $681). But this still represents $30 billion of demand in the health care cash economy, where providers cannot rely

---

* Personal health expenditures per capita in the United States are $8,445 in 2012, but if you exclude people 65-plus (almost none of whom are uninsured), the per capita number drops to around $6,850 (to calculate this number, I applied the same age spending ratios as in the 2004 National Health Expenditures published by CMS).

on any source of payment other than their patients' own resources. And while experts on the Island view this $30 billion as blood squeezed from stones, in many communities with large numbers of uninsured, it means a cash health care system exists. For example, driving around a neighborhood with a large number of immigrants in Broward County, Florida, I saw a billboard offering a full maternity package for $4,995 cash, all expenses included.

The 2008 study's authors also estimated that the uninsured received $56 billion in "uncompensated" care a year. What is uncompensated care? Mostly, it is care provided by hospitals for free; existing rules essentially give the uninsured guaranteed access to emergency room and hospital treatment for acute conditions even if they can't pay. There are many distortions in care and pricing resulting from this rule, which exists only as a way to disguise from taxpayers the true cost of caring for the needy.*

* U.S. hospitals (technically only those that treat Medicare patients) are required to treat anyone showing up at their doors with an emergency condition, regardless of ability to pay. An estimated eight million uninsured Americans received such treatment in 2007 (CDC NCHS Data Brief, "Emergency Department Visits and Visitors," which also says that 18.8 percent of uninsured used emergency rooms in 2007).

Though the rule is simple, the hospital service safety net has at least two long-term implications for the delivery of health care. First, it encourages massive overuse of emergency rooms, as the rule makes these the gateway to free care. Second, because the uninsured are not evenly distributed around the country, it appears that the weight of the financial burden of this hospital obligation depends on where a hospital is located. An inner-city hospital is likely to have far more uncompensated emergency room traffic than a suburban institution. In certain cases, it appears that some urban hospitals may have closed because they treated too many patients for free.

Hospitals and many physicians also offer charity care—free or discounted service to low-income individuals for a wide variety of conditions (that is, not only emergency conditions). But hospitals are not required to perform charity care, and low-income patients cannot count on its availability. Some states do insist that nonprofit hospitals provide some amount of charity care to maintain their tax-exempt status, but recent data suggests that nonprofits and for-profits provide similar levels of charity. Considering the lengths to which some hospitals go to col-

But here are a couple of important facts to keep in mind when understanding uncompensated care. First, it *is* compensated—at least partially. Under a variety of state and federal programs (including Medicare and Medicaid), hospitals receive lump payments tied to geography, income of their patient population, and evidence of above-average uncompensated care (which, of course, incents them to exaggerate the cost of such care). A recent estimate is that hospitals provide $34 billion of uncompensated care and receive payments, through a variety of programs, of roughly $25 billion to help them deal with the burden of uncompensated care. Second, uncompensated care generates much of the confusion about the real cost of the emergency room. Island experts insist that emergency care is the most expensive type of care, whereas anyone visiting an actual emergency room—with its fixed-salary employees, train-station-like waiting rooms, interminable delays, shared resources, and minimal amenities—is pretty certain it must be the least costly. Hospitals have every incentive to load costs onto their emergency and uncompensated operations, as their losses provide support for special treatment from legislators and regulators.*

---

lect unpaid balances from even low-income uninsured patients, one could suspect that charity care is a disguised form of price discrimination—keeping facilities full at discounted prices without upsetting the overall price structure.

Wouldn't it be far better to pay directly for the care provided to the needy? Of course. But then we'd have to admit that we're paying for needy people's care—far better to pretend that the hospitals are doing it for free.

* If you look at hospitals' financial statements, you can see why simple claims about the cost of uncompensated care are difficult. For example, HCA, the biggest private hospital chain in the United States, shows uncompensated care in 2011 totaling $11 billion, a full 27 percent of revenues. However, the company estimated the cost of providing this care at only $2 billion when it applied its 18 percent ratio of care costs to patient charges. Also, a full 50 percent of the uncompensated amount relates to discounts provided to uninsured patients "similar to those provided to many local managed care plans." In other words, these patients paid

When you exit the Holland Tunnel in New Jersey, you see a digital clock showing the current ER wait time at Bayonne Medical Center. I highly doubt this clock is for the benefit of those in cardiac arrest; it must be for those who use emergency rooms as primary care, many of whom are uninsured or Medicaid beneficiaries. So if it pays to maintain the clock, at least some of these patients must represent business worth attracting.*

Though some may in fact be profitable, uninsured people are overall the "worst" customers of our health care providers—less likely to sign up for preventive tests and voluntary procedures, more likely to demand price discounts and even free care. Further, providers have little incentive to perform extra care on the uninsured; there is no moral hazard problem without third-party payers. If the commonplace statement that 25 percent of our spending on health care is waste is true, then it's hard to believe the uninsured account for much of it.†

So what does it all mean? When you move away from the misleading idea that having no health insurance is the same as having no health care, the mixed purpose of the ACA is clear. The uninsured do already receive a meaning-

---

for their care, just not at the billed level. Further, a quarter of what HCA lists as uncompensated care is write-offs of receivables from patients; to the extent some of this write-off relates to privately insured, Medicare, or Medicaid patients who didn't pay their cost sharing, the chain itself received compensation for the bulk of these patients' "uncompensated" care (HCA Holdings Inc. 10-K as filed with the SEC February 24, 2012).

* Of course, it probably wouldn't make sense to maintain the clock on the other side of the tunnel—New York City—where too many patients using the emergency room is being blamed for deteriorating hospital economics.
† On leaving office, CMS head Donald Berwick said 20 to 35 percent of health care spending is waste, including inefficiency and bureaucratic cost. "Much is done that does not help patients at all," Dr. Berwick said, "and many physicians know it" (Robert Pear, "Health Official Takes Parting Shot at 'Waste,'" *New York Times*, December 3, 2011).

ful amount of health care, but for certain types of treatment (especially for care poorly served by the hospital safety net—preventive and chronic conditions), it appears that many have real difficulty paying for essential care. So there is a problem for the uninsured, but for industry there is also a problem of the uninsured. For the care that they do get, they are the system's discount customers—far less profitable in terms of price and quantity of services sold than mainstream insured customers. And when you look at the 2008 study and the initial results from the Oregon study, it's hard not to conclude that more of the massive new spending under ACA will go to paying higher prices for these low-price customers than to additional care.

We certainly hope that some of that additional spending will improve health and even save some lives. But what we do know is that now every dollar spent by each previously uninsured person on health care—not just the incremental care he'll receive but all the care he buys—will now occur under the mainstream system, with all its incentives for waste, excess, and price inflation. From the industry's perspective, we've turned bad customers into good ones.

The hospital and pharmaceutical industries were important supporters of the ACA, with the latter providing major financial support for a public advertising campaign. On the Island, this unusual support was explained by these industries' enlightened understanding that reform will bring them new customers.* But a better explanation is that reform will

---

* I have focused here on hospitals' profit benefits from the ACA. The pharmaceutical industry was playing defense in reform, because of the weakness of its business model. As discussed earlier, with the marginal cost of manufacturing pills almost zero, drug companies might have trouble maintaining prices in a competitive market. Since the management of chronic conditions is the most important hole in the hospitals' safety net for the uninsured—and drugs the leading treatment for

turn their discount customers into full-price ones. A recent Citigroup research report explains it best: while hospitals face uncertainty about the implementation of the ACA, if the results of the new health reform follow the projection of the Congressional Budget Office, they will see profits rise by 43 percent.

The Russian joke at the head of this chapter plays off our assumption—a widespread one on the Island—that spending more must mean getting more. Now, I don't want to get carried away with this; there is no question that many uninsured face an impossible burden in managing certain ongoing conditions and that the emergency room safety net is not the most desirable option for many types of treatment. All other things being equal, I—and probably everyone—would rather have health insurance.

But all other things aren't equal. Now we can return to the paradox at the beginning of the section: despite the rhetoric surrounding the issue, no study has ever demonstrated a real link between lack of insurance and poor health results (perhaps the Oregon study will break new ground here). And not for lack of trying.* The biggest problem in find-

---

chronic conditions—a more targeted reform might have enforced deep discounts on pharmaceuticals for uncovered people. Certainly, the companies have shown a willingness to offer discounts when they can be achieved through a back door (i.e., a reduction or elimination of deductibles to needy beneficiaries). But the ACA explicitly walked away from requiring such discounts—or using the pricing power of Medicare and Medicaid to achieve them. Recall that unlike other health providers, drug companies are unable to package their products with expanded services, so they are less able to do what the rest of the industry does: accept discounts on specific goods while expanding the definition of "essential" services.

* A series of studies using data from the 1980s did suggest that lack of insurance contributed to a higher death rate. An Urban Institute report in 2008 updated these studies to produce an estimate of twenty thousand incremental deaths among the uninsured annually—a statistic regularly quoted in the debate over the ACA. But as Megan McArdle argued in *The Atlantic,* the original studies on which all later estimates were based have a fundamental problem: they didn't properly

ing a simple connection is that the most vulnerable uninsured are most vulnerable not just because of health issues
but because of low incomes, financial insecurity, and the
lifestyle choices and stress associated with poverty. To the
extent the uninsured have higher incapacity and even death
rates, it is mostly because they are poor and have unhealthy
lifestyles, not because they lack insurance.

As I'll discuss below, there's no group more hurt by the
Beast's consumption of ever more of society's resources than
our low-income citizens, no matter how these expenses are
shifted around. And of course, the ACA is far from universal: an estimated eighteen million will be left uncovered.
How will their ability to pay for care be affected by turning
another thirty-two million into price-insensitive customers?

Ignore the rhetoric: the ACA is not about the health issues
of the poor, much less the underlying lifestyle issues frequently associated with poor health. The ACA is only about
insurance, as we could expect from an alliance between
experts stuck in the belief that coverage and care are identical and more practical industrial interests looking to protect
their business models. Coverage, not health or even health
care, is the metric by which the ACA's sponsors measured
their success.

---

control for other factors that significantly affect the death rate with or without
insurance ("Myth Diagnosis," March 2010). In other words, the higher death rate
was likely to be attributable to being poor, lifestyle choices, and unemployment.
These high-risk factors are more prevalent among the uninsured but are not a
result of being uninsured. McArdle notes that the one study that controlled for
these factors showed no difference at all in death rate from lack of insurance.

McArdle is not arguing that lack of health insurance makes no difference; her
slightly different point is that we don't actually *know* that extra health care makes a
difference. If the insured indeed spend too much on health care, then the fact that
the uninsured spend less doesn't necessarily tell us that they are worse off for it.

The illusion of access

Perhaps the most significant development ignored by the proponents of the ACA is that insurance itself no longer ensures access. To build support for the bill, the president's website featured dozens of personal stories—many truly tragic—about Americans' problems with the system. Reading through these, one is struck by how many of the respondents had health insurance. Many stories involve people with very high out-of-pocket costs and procedures excluded from reimbursement. The ACA does attempt to address some of these concerns through regulation, requiring, for example, insurers to cap the amount any beneficiary must pay out of pocket. But this will merely drive up premiums for all, with predictable consequences.

A second issue reported by the already insured should have suggested the problem with expanded coverage as the primary goal of the ACA. Many covered people reported trouble finding doctors who would treat them or insurers that would recognize the validity of their needs, while others were put in desperate financial straits despite having insurance, as even their limited share of medical expense was unsupportable. An *Archives of Internal Medicine* study found that only 88 percent of doctors were willing to take patients with private insurance. A 2011 report from the Medicare Payment Advisory Commission (MedPAC) showed a sharp rise in Medicare beneficiaries reporting a big problem finding a primary care physician (traditionally a strength of Medicare). In California, 25 percent of Medi-Cal beneficiaries reported problems finding a primary physician who would see them, and more than a third had difficulty finding a specialist. More than 10 percent of privately insured

Californians had trouble finding a doctor who would take them.

The proponents of the ACA could have gathered this from even the brief example of a similar reform in Massachusetts. Though the state had the lowest rate of uninsured in the country, Massachusetts enacted a law in 2006 that required all residents to have insurance. Its proponents would call the legislation a success: roughly 98 percent of residents are insured now, up from 90 percent. Since residents already had access to care for serious conditions through the hospital safety net, the main benefit of insurance should have been improved access to routine care. But early reports suggest that primary physicians are increasingly unwilling to accept new patients or those covered by the state's Medicaid program.* The Association of American Medical Colleges was projecting doctor shortages would double over the next decade to more than 100,000 even before the passage of ACA; the bill will accelerate and deepen the problem. So which is the better measure of access—provider availability or insurance coverage? The ACA attempts to improve access to primary care by enabling its beneficiaries to afford primary care. But a growing shortage of primary care physicians will defeat that objective. In a normal market, we would be confident that, over time, supply would expand as more consumers had more money to spend. However, in health care, we can have no such confidence. With the ACA anticipating

---

* According to a controversial study by the Massachusetts Medical Society, the share of primary physicians willing to accept new patients has declined from 70 to 47 percent. The average wait time to see a family medicine provider is thirty-six days; for an internal medicine provider, it's forty-eight days. Only 53 percent of family doctors are even willing to accept Mass Health, the state's Medicaid program and a key plank of expanding coverage. Several experts have criticized the study's methodology and findings, even if its overall message about declines in access may be accurate.

a 40 percent increase in Medicaid enrollees, how can this real access problem not worsen? In the words of an Arkansas hospital CEO: "I worry that the Medicaid card will be like Confederate money. You won't have anywhere to use it, and it won't be worth anything." Of course, there are solutions to this problem, but merely expanding our current system exclusively to achieve more coverage isn't one of them.

Even if the ACA may do more for hospitals and drug companies than for the uninsured, and even if insurance may no longer guarantee equal access, doesn't society have a simple fundamental moral responsibility to include everyone in our health care system? Even if we can't prove that the insurance will make a clear difference in health outcomes, isn't it worth the cost just in case? So what that we may spend $200 billion more to get our neediest only $70 billion in additional real care—isn't it worth it?

As a liberal, I would have said yes to any of those questions even a few years ago. Now I suspect these questions are out of date. Our health care system no longer neatly divides between the insured and the uninsured. After all, the financial burden is already crushing—directly or indirectly—for all but the richest Americans. With the system's warped financial incentives, your odds of getting appropriate care— rather than excessive and uncoordinated care—depend more on the professional culture of your providers than on your insurance status. How many more of these best doctors will choose to work outside of the insurance system, especially if the effect of the ACA is to increase the numbers who choose to forgo coverage? And of course, with the sloppiness inherent in the whole system, your chances of avoiding a serious medical error are a matter more of luck than of your insurance status.

The ACA is just the latest in a long line of legislation that drives resources from all other goods into health care. To those who think health care should never be a matter of money, I can only ask: Can you think of any other use of $200 billion a year that would have less of an impact on the lives, not to mention the health, of these mostly low-income Americans? The $100 billion a year in government spending could lift the disposable incomes of ten million American families with children by 20 percent. It could buy a gym membership for forty-two million Americans and pay them ten dollars an hour to exercise three times a week. It could put fresh vegetables on the table daily for every child in America. These figures don't even include the $100 billion now in their pockets that the ACA will make them spend on health insurance!

Like so much of health care policy, the debate over the uninsured is stuck in a time warp. If heath care costs were a reasonable percentage of our economy, then the money-is-no-object-when-it-comes-to-health argument might make more sense. But with these costs 18 percent of our economy, the decision to shovel more money into health care through insurance will have a powerful impact on job creation, wage growth, and disposable income. All of these issues are more important to the well-being of the long-term uninsured—even to their health—than more health care.

In fact, there's a meaningful possibility that many of the uninsured will be worse off because of the ACA—that the cost of the individual mandate, the additional job-creation burden of the new employer mandate (which also acts as a tax on hiring), and the impact on wage growth of higher insurance premiums will overwhelm whatever benefit they get from being able to spend as much on health care as the insured. In other words, the costs these families will bear off the Island of Health Care will be greater than the additional benefit received on the Island. But as with all health care discussions, anything off the Island is irrelevant.

Last stand

Included in the ACA was the Community Living Assistance Services and Supports Act (CLASS), which established a new form of insurance covering long-term care. With the aging of America's population—and especially the growing proportion of people living into what had previously been considered extreme old age—the need for such care is expanding rapidly. These services are only partly medical in nature, often including assistance with daily tasks such as eating and bathing. Yet Medicare provides for only a few of these services, and Medicaid pays for out-of-home assisted living only for those who have already exhausted their assets. Private insurers have begun to drop long-term care coverage, as the growing cost of such care—because of ever extending life spans—makes it unprofitable.

Under CLASS, the government was charged with setting up an insurance pool and designing premiums and benefits. Like any insurance pool, the CLASS pool would have to collect enough premiums from people who do not currently need long-term care to fund the expensive support of those who do. So premiums needed to be low enough to attract fully abled people but high enough to fund current care levels. In October 2011, the Obama administration announced it was giving up on the whole idea: there was no solution to this particular equation.

For some people, the abortive launch of CLASS is merely a failed first effort to address the long-term care issue. But it actually represents something much bigger: the government's first recognition that the problem of our undisciplined health care system cannot be solved through mere financial engineering. Long-term care isn't insurable for the reason that most of health care isn't really insurable: it's more about inevitabilities than about actual risks.

Long-term care is one of the most important health issues that seniors face, just because of their age. It can be the difference between an ever larger share of our population continuing to function in society and their abandonment to incapacity. Our government will spend $620 billion on Medicare this coming year. Medicaid will spend another $88 billion on seniors. Seniors themselves will spend another $183 billion on their care. So we'll spend roughly $900 billion on care for our seniors, with almost nothing available for one of their greatest true health needs.

Before the ACA, our undisciplined health care system was already harming us through its extraordinary expense, depriving all of us of many of the other good things in life. Our undisciplined health care system was also harming us physically through excess treatment and carelessness. The ACA attempts to move thirty-two million Americans from their current status as low-paying uninsured people to much higher-paying insured people. Whether this does anyone other than the health industry much good is debatable. At the same time, the ACA adds additional expense to the system by mandating that more money be spent on favored categories of care, such as preventive services, and greatly ratcheting up the administrative cost through a complex of new regulations. The ACA anticipates that health care's share of GDP will pass 20 percent in the next couple of years, growing to 23 percent in a decade.

Yet at the same time, the Obama administration abandoned CLASS because it understood that the program could not be sustained without an unlimited government subsidy. And the government cannot afford another open-ended commitment.

The conflict between the goals of the ACA—no matter how well motivated—and the reality of our highly flawed Surrogate-based health care system will now be visible in a new type of harm.

As society runs up against its ability to spend on health care, cuts will be made in what insurers and Medicaid can afford to fund. Nothing in the ACA changes the fundamental incentives that have so warped our health care system. So we have no reason to believe that growing cost pressures will lead to cuts in excess medicine, waste, inefficiency, dangerous treatment, and price inflation. The CLASS failure is our first real taste. We're running up against limits. Bad health care is crowding out needed care. The supporters of the ACA should have considered how cost pressures were eating away at the safety net elements of private insurance and Medicaid. They should have seen how Medicare's entitlement mentality was exposing its beneficiaries to rafts of unnecessary and often dangerous treatment. They chose to focus on other issues.

Denial

It's easy to criticize the legislative designers, managers, and regulators of our health care system, up to and including the architects of the ACA. They are obsessed with an insurance model to the exclusion of all other alternatives. They make static rules for a dynamic world. They misunderstand the role of prices and assume an impossible confidence in their ability to set them. They underestimate the power of flexibility, variation, and markets. They revel in complexity. Intellectually, they have isolated themselves on an Island, assuming that health care is so special that there is nothing to be learned from the Mainland.

Each of these criticisms is true but, at the same time, quite unfair.

The dysfunctional, unsustainable, and dangerous health care system America has built is not merely a result of the errors of our leaders; it was designed in service to a wish—our wish. We don't want to know the truth about health care, so we've built a system whose main accomplishment is shielding us from reality.

We want to believe someone else is paying for our care, so we operate an employer-based insurance system, as if those premiums don't reduce our compensation. Or we impose treatment mandates, coverage requirements, and maximum cost sharing, as if the cost of each of these isn't merely added to our premiums. Or we demand tax benefits for health spending—for everyone—as if their effects don't drive up health prices, not to mention other taxes.

We each want to believe we're not paying for someone else's care, so we operate a Medicare program based on the obvious fiction that it's funded by a trust fund endowed by seniors themselves. Or we exclude many of the needy from Medicaid and require hospitals to treat them, as if hospitals don't have to make up the money from other government payments.

We want to believe that someone is watching out for our health, so we let the Surrogates manage our relationships with doctors, hospitals, and the entire health industry, even though they know nothing about us as individuals. We allow the system to overtreat us, as if the very fact that the Surrogates are willing to pay for something means we should undergo it. Despite being surrounded by efficient, service-oriented industries, we accept the sloppiness and even the danger of our health care system as inevitabilities.

Whatever their own mistakes, our experts are required to try to make health care work without shattering our illusions. It is a job that forces them to create an ever more complicated, ever less comprehensible, ever less functioning system. We can blame them for the system's addiction to complexity, but it's the inevitable cost of our own denial.

To fix our health care system, we'll have to start by facing reality. Our society can easily afford a lot of health care for every American, almost certainly enough to meet any objective need. But paradoxically, the only sustainable way we can meet those needs is to wind down health care's special treatment in our society. Since we are unable to repeal the economic laws of gravity in health care, it's time to embrace them, to build a more normal system of financing care—and a more normal system of weighing its value and holding its providers accountable. Only by embracing such normal reality can we develop an alternative to our current system that is financially sustainable, dynamically disciplined, and flexible enough to allow the true innovation that offers so much promise for our future.

CHAPTER 9

In Search of Balance

How should we pay for health care?

My friend Bill is rich. As cofounder of a very success-ful investment firm, he has become accustomed to only the best. As a result, his first major interaction with our health care system was more than a little disorienting.

Bill is obsessed with staying in top physical condition, and so he quickly noticed when elements of his exercise rou-tines left him short of breath and coughing. Bill's primary physician assured him the problem was nothing more than exercise-induced asthma (although Bill had no family his-tory of asthma) and gave him an inhaler to help with the symptoms.

His symptoms grew progressively worse; on a ski trip, he experienced a frightening feeling of asphyxiation. He saw a pulmonologist, who found evidence of major impair-ment in Bill's lung capacity but was unable to make a diag-nosis. Over the course of the next three months, Bill saw three other pulmonologists, a hematologist, and a cardiologist. He received a number of possible diagnoses, including lymphoma, a congenital heart defect, and a variety of lung ailments.

Interestingly, one of the first specialists he saw got the diagnosis correct: a serious, though treatable, form of sarcoidosis, an accumulation of abnormal tissue that impairs lung functioning. But because this particular physician's manner was so imperious—and his interest in treating the problem so limited—Bill felt compelled to seek another opinion. Finally, Bill was able to use his connections to get an appointment with one of the country's leading pulmonologists. Not only was this doctor calm and compassionate, he also confirmed the early sarcoidosis diagnosis and oversaw the steroid treatment that made the problem manageable.

"What surprised me is that there was no quarterback," Bill told me. "Here was a life-threatening situation, and no one was coordinating what the doctors were saying or recommending. They didn't even communicate with each other. They kept me waiting for hours. And the bedside manners left something to be desired. One doctor told me and my wife that I had only a few months to live as if it was no big deal." Bill was surprised how even highly regarded specialists had difficulty thinking about possibilities beyond their areas of expertise: "Everybody is myopic—they can only see five feet around them."

Bill is a realist about his health, so he wasn't expecting to be able to buy better results. But he was surprised that he couldn't pay for more coordinated service. He was already seeing the most expensive doctors, and he didn't need to think about the cost of his co-pays or what amount was covered by insurance. But it was shocking how much work he had to do himself, from hounding doctors for appointments, to making sure their test results were communicated to the other specialists, to wading through mountains of online data to determine the best treatment options.

Fortunately, Bill has been able to manage his condition with medication. So in this critical sense, his care was successful. But as a businessman, he found that his experience with the health care system felt like a visit to a "different planet." For people to whom money is essentially no object, our economy has developed services to find them the best seats to the big game, the best table at the finest restaurants, the most luxurious vacations, the finest tutors for their children, the most tasteful furniture for their homes. How is it possible that no one is willing to take their money to create a seamless, reassuring experience surrounding what may be the most difficult time in their lives?*

If you're an Island resident, you might be rolling your eyes at Bill's complaint. After all, he was correctly diagnosed and got the right treatment, and his condition is under control. Isn't that all that matters? This is health care, not the Four Seasons. But as I've argued, service is not an extraneous detail in health care, or in anything else. It's a key component of provider responsiveness to customer need, an indication of quality of care and accountability. Good service in itself is therapeutic, especially in a difficult time. Bill noted that he was fortunate in having a supportive family, a flexible work situation, ample resources, a network of connections, and a positive attitude. For anyone without these advantages, the chaotic and demoralizing experience may have produced less fortuitous results.

---

* In fact, high-end concierge services, discussed in the next chapter, are now developing to serve this very need.

Now, if you're not a member of the 1 percent, perhaps you have a different reaction to Bill's story. Perhaps you are reassured by the egalitarian element, that a rich guy cannot buy himself out of the miserable service our health care system offers (although it's worth noting that a rich guy's connections did ultimately get him to the right care). But turn the whole issue on its head—do you think any industry is ever going to be good at service for anyone if it's not even good at serving the rich? Is it genuinely reassuring that the Andy Warhols of our world have as good a chance as us of dying of a hospital mistake?*

The irony is that when it comes to health care, we're all rich. We're all Bill. Remember that Becky is going to put at least $1.2 million into our health care system over her lifetime. That's likely to be much more than she'll spend on anything else—and it may be more than she spends on everything else combined. My father spent the final five weeks of his life in a hospital; Medicare paid roughly $60,000 on his behalf. Other than for our home, my father had never before paid $60,000 for anything in his life! Even a healthy person uninsured his whole life until being eligible for Medicare will probably incur a six-figure lifetime health care bill.

In health care, all of us are spending insane amounts of money. Yet the system makes us feel like paupers, as if we should be grateful for whatever we get. And the cost of this attitude isn't merely the superficial realities of indifferent or even rude service. It's the deeper implications of a culture lacking customer accountability: high prices, excess,

---

* Andy Warhol died of heart failure in 1987, three days after entering a hospital for gallbladder surgery. His family's wrongful-death lawsuit against the hospital was settled out of court without a hospital admission of error.

errors, underinvestment in information technology, lack of follow-up.

I've described how we got to this state in health care and how solutions developed on the Island only get us in deeper. But how do we get out? How do we get the benefits we all deserve as rich guys putting big money into the health care system?

We will be treated as good customers only when we are actually writing the checks, rather than having someone else do it for us. Instead of having our insurers, Medicare, and Medicaid take our $2.5 trillion from us, waste a large chunk on administration and excess, and spend the balance on our care, what if we took back the $2.5 trillion and spent it ourselves? Replacing the Surrogates with ourselves as the true customers of health care would set off an accountability revolution among providers. But at what cost?

The exception that disproves the rule

On the Island, it is common to describe the United States as unique among developed nations in providing no guarantee of health care (or coverage, to be precise) to its citizens, in relying on so much private spending, and in exposing its citizens to such high out-of-pocket costs. We all have a sense of how the rest of the developed world works—centrally administered systems with governments either directly providing or financing all care.

So Singapore's statistics suggest health care from another planet: the nation spends under 4 percent of its GDP on health care. The next most efficient rich country spends twice as much; if the United States spent only 4 percent of

GDP on health care, we'd have around $2 trillion a year (just about $6,500 per person) to spend on everything else!

How is it possible for a country to spend so much less on health care? Yes, Singapore is much smaller than the United States, but its population of 5.2 million enjoys an average per capita income of $50,000 and life expectancy of eighty-two years—roughly the same as in the United States. And its health care results are just as good if not better than ours in almost every category (although as discussed earlier very little of the data on health outcomes tells us much about health care anyway). Singapore has slightly fewer doctors than we do: one for every 550 people, as against our one for every 420. But this difference certainly doesn't account for 14 percent of GDP.

Singapore's system of care is unique and doesn't fit into neat ideological categories. There are three characteristics that differentiate its approach. First, for all types of care—regardless of provider or funder—patients make a meaningful financial contribution at the point of purchase. Individuals are the direct purchasers of care even when insurance or state subsidy is involved. In our terms, all patients in Singapore have a lot of skin in the game.

Second, all health care is not treated the same, with a single payment model covering all treatment. As will be discussed below, the type of financing available for care depends on the nature of care. Further, providers of acute care vary charges based on level of service provided to the patient, a policy encouraged even in the structure of the government's subsidy programs.

Third, the government itself directly provides care through its own facilities alongside the private sector. Not only does this have the effect of guaranteeing care for all, but it provides a powerful low-price competitor to the private providers.

Singapore's system has five major elements. All employees are obligated to put between 6.5 and 9 percent of their earnings into health savings accounts (Medisave), which can be used for most medical treatment for their family. Medisave accounts can also be used to fund premiums for the government-sponsored Medishield, a catastrophic insurance plan that provides defined-benefit financial support in the case of major illnesses. The government also maintains an insurance pool covering severe disabilities (ElderShield) and a fund to help those unable to pay their bills (Medifund). An unusual feature of Singapore's program is that even the core health savings and catastrophic insurance carry limits on how much can be withdrawn to pay for care; this ensures that even someone with a fully funded health savings account bears meaningful additional expenses at the point of treatment.

These four programs all feature an extraordinarily high level of personal responsibility but exist within the framework of a heavily subsidized provider sector. These subsidies—the fifth pillar of Singapore's system—vary along with service level. For example, patients opting for private hospital rooms with all the amenities and their choice of doctors will pay their bills with no government subsidy. Those willing to be treated in open wards with few amenities and an assigned staff physician will see most of their bill covered by a government subsidy (with subsidy levels also tied to the patient's income).

A 2003 study shows that, in practice, Singaporeans pay a lot of their health care directly from their current income while enjoying the security of the government-mandated savings systems. At that time, 60 percent of health spending was derived either from out-of-pocket payments or from benefits provided by employers. Only 8 percent came from Medisave accounts, with only 2 percent from Medishield or Medifund. Government subsidies accounted for a full 25 percent of spending, while private insurance provided 5 percent. The study's authors estimated that citizens had accumulated total balances in their Medisave accounts equal to more than six times the total amount spent annually on health care.* Today, Singapore's Ministry of Health claims that the average citizen has enough saved to fund eleven hospitalizations. Further, even though Medisave and Medifund are entirely supported by savings, less than 5 percent of patients need to turn to Medifund for their hospitalization bills.

In short, in Singapore the price of services *always* matters to the patient, even if ultimately the patient is paying little of it. In that sense, it's the opposite of our system, where price is never supposed to matter, even if the patient is ultimately paying for most of the care (as I have shown is in fact the case for most of us). Singapore is certainly seeing the cost of care rise somewhat as its population ages and demands more care. But because it spends so little on health care, Singapore has extraordinary flexibility in addressing challenges. The bottom line is that health care in Singapore is high quality, high-tech, and, by international standards, cheap. Genuinely cheap, not just misleadingly cheap at the point of purchase.

---

* For perspective, translating this ratio to the United States would imply $15 trillion in private health savings.

Singapore is different from the United States and other developed countries in many ways, of course, and it would be facile to suggest that a system that worked so well in a small, rich island state could simply be transported here. But it's worth noting that Singapore didn't start with its system—it was evolved from a more traditional form of government-sponsored care that existed at the nation's founding in 1965—and also that underpinning Singapore's system of care is a realistic philosophy that our system explicitly discourages:

> Singaporeans are a pragmatic lot and understand that trade-offs are an inevitable fact of life. They under-stand that whether the burden falls on Taxes, Medisave, Employer benefits, or Insurance, it is ultimately Sin-gaporeans themselves who must pay—since taxes are paid by taxpayers, insurance premiums are ultimately paid by the people, and employee medical benefits form part of wage costs—and that overburdening the state or employers would affect the competitiveness of Singa-pore's externally-oriented economy and ultimately, their own livelihoods.

Consumer-driven health care reform in the United States

Over the past decade, several innovative health experts (including Regina Herzlinger, John Goodman, Michael Cannon, Michael Tanner, John Cogan, Daniel Kessler, and Glenn Hubbard) have proposed a variety of consumer-driven health reforms to our existing system. They have pioneered the argument that consumers will make better

choices if required to spend their own money and that providers will have to work harder at cost and quality control
to serve them. Their work has led to the establishment of
consumer-driven health plans (CDHPs) as an alternative to
the typical insurance or HMO plans.

For the most part, these CDHPs consist of health insurance with a higher deductible than traditional plans—
usually $2,500 or $5,000 instead of the more typical $500 or
$1,000. Because a high-deductible plan carries much lower
premiums, the beneficiary has savings from lower premiums
available to deposit in a health savings account (HSA). The
HSA covers expenses below the deductible, and HSA funds
can be accumulated tax-free for future use. So unlike with
regular health insurance, someone who uses our health system rarely—or is more vigilant on the prices she pays—can
build a substantial health nest egg. And in theory, society
also benefits because these beneficiaries act as more careful
shoppers for health care (aka consumers).

Political realities have constrained the structuring and
adoption of CDHPs, leaving them tax disadvantaged against
more traditional insurance. For example, our company and
an employee together pay $22,182 a year for an employee's
premiums for traditional family insurance coverage. That
entire amount is tax-free to that employee. If that employee
instead chose a high-deductible plan, her insurance would
save us $7,540 in premiums, but the most we are able to con-
tribute tax-free to her HSA is $6,200. If Congress were will-
ing to give CDHPs a real shot against traditional insurance,
it would equalize the potential tax benefits. This would
allow employers to offer plans with truly high deductibles
(say $10,000 or even $25,000); as terrible as these plans

may sound in today's marketplace, they would carry very low premiums, allowing even entry-level employees such as Becky to accumulate very large amounts in an HSA.

There's a great deal of debate about the benefits of CDHPs. The largest and best-known study, RAND's analysis of more than eight hundred thousand households from 2004 to 2005, confirms the basic conviction of advocates that CDHPs can produce significant cost savings (14 percent in one year for any plan with a deductible over $1,000). But opponents also saw support for their views that requiring people to pay for their lower-level health expenses might cause them to scrimp—although just slightly in RANDs conclusions—on preventive care.*

I see in my own company that CDHPs seem to make our employees more aware of their health expenses and, in that sense, less likely to spend money (full disclosure: I'm enrolled in our CDHP). For some, that may well mean somewhat fewer diagnostic tests a year, but the view that the right amount of preventive care is the greatest amount is Island nonsense.

The real problem with CDHPs is excessive expectations:

* See "Healthcare Spending and Preventive Care in High-Deductible and Consumer-Directed Health Plans." The authors' related article states "that CDHPs reduce spending without unduly restricting access for lower income and chronically ill populations. However, in all groups, there is evidence of a small reduction in receipt of high value preventive procedures" (Amelia M. Haviland et al., "Consumer-Directed Health Plans and Vulnerable Populations," *Forum for Health Economics and Policy* [2011]).

Opponents of CDHPs seem to regard any reduction in preventive care for vulnerable people as a definitive argument against these plans, which I don't understand. There is no health care system that can protect all people against their choices, nor any system that can provide everybody with everything. If CDHPs can bring consumer discipline to our care system, the benefits—even to vulnerable populations that may cut back a little on preventive services—should be far greater than the costs. But as so often in discussions of care, any possible reduction in care for anybody is viewed as a disqualifying consideration.

slightly changing the motivations of a minority of consumers won't transform health care into a consumer-driven industry. We're not yet ready to consider a true shift to a consumer-driven health care world. We still hold conventional views about health care uncorrected by forty-five years of contradictory experience. We see health insurance as essential to secure our health care future. We suspect big insurers and Medicare are better than we are at driving quality. We see our current system as fair, distributing resources from the rich to everyone else (even Becky probably believes this). We're accustomed to someone else seeming to pay for our health care. As a doctor who recently switched to a no-insurance practice told me, "I've lost some patients who wouldn't think twice about dropping three hundred dollars on a hairdresser once a month but couldn't conceive of paying two hundred and fifty out of pocket once a year to see the physician of her choice."

It may take a true disaster to consider a real societal commitment to a consumer-driven health model, but a glance at Medicare's finances or the potential for dysfunction in the ACA's perverse incentives suggests we may get that disaster in the foreseeable future. So what would a true consumer alternative look like?

The sensible approach in proposing an alternative to our current system is to respect what's called path dependence. This is a fancy way of saying that societies don't get a chance to genuinely start anything over again—that reforms must be built on top of existing structures, recognizing their established political support and existing ways of doing business as limitations on any changes. It's what all the smart analysts do, limiting the development of alternatives to those that are considered realistic.

So let's not do the smart thing here. Let's not be path dependent. If we somehow could truly start over, what kind of health care funding system would we create? Then we can ask a more realistic question: Can we get there from here?

Becky's ideal

Americans will spend roughly $8,500 per person on health care this year. Of course, this money will enter the system from a variety of sources: insurance premiums, out-of-pocket payments, taxes, Medicare premiums, even charitable contributions. Let's wish all that away for a moment and say instead we go to Becky and offer to give her newborn daughter $8,500 a year for life to spend on health care. What system would she set up for Becky Jr.?

Obviously, if Becky Jr. is like most of us, she'll need much less than $8,500 in health care in almost all the years of her life. So the first thing Becky wants to confirm is that Junior's annual health grant can carry over, that the amount she doesn't use this year can be used in future years. Some type of Health Account must be a foundation of this system.

With a Health Account, Becky now thinks about health care differently. She no longer thinks of Junior having $8,500 a year but rather $680,000 over her expected eighty-year life. This is crucially important. As discussed in chapter 3, Island experts think insurance is necessary to fund health care because, in any given year, the overwhelming amount of health expenses are concentrated among a small share of the population. That small high-use group would not be able to afford its massive health care expenses during that year. But Island experts confuse the risk of a person suffering a major illness with the risk of suffering a major illness in a given year. Because all of us are likely to have large health needs at some point in our lives, we all will spend a few years in that high-spending group. This isn't a risk at all; unfortunately, it's a certainty. The risk relates to our suffering our inevitable major illness in any given year, but insurance is an incredibly costly, inefficient, and distortive way merely to move funds among years.

Becky can see this immediately. She wants to make sure Junior has access to the $680,000 when she needs it, and she knows she has a guaranteed $8,500 annual health grant. So she knows if Junior's Health Account is ever too small to cover a major medical expense, her best bet is to borrow the money, with the future grant serving as collateral. A Health Loan is a low-cost way to transfer money from a future health grant to the present.

So with the annual grant, the Health Account, and the Health Loan capacity, Becky Jr. now has access to $680,000 in health funds to be used anytime over her life—whenever it's her turn to need major medical care. Remember, this dream proposal is per person. So when Junior gets married and has her two kids, her family has a total of $34,000 a year in health grants. For at least 95 percent of Americans, this simple system would provide for all their conceivable health needs over their lifetimes. Without any insurance. So for almost everyone, just the money we're spending today will create a huge surplus.

Becky hopes her daughter will spend relatively little of her health grant every year. She knows some of this depends on good luck, but she will raise Junior to be careful about her health and a thoughtful consumer of health services. Becky understands that even trusted medical professionals are in the business of selling tests and procedures, so she's naturally skeptical when care is suggested. She has friends who don't take care of themselves, have every test and procedure offered, and are spendthrifts when it comes to health care. She understands that their profligacy explains why the annual grant is so high; as a result, she believes that at some point in Junior's life she should be able to use at least some of the large accumulation of money in her Health Account for other purposes. Or at least be allowed to leave the unused balance to a loved one in her will.

But what if Junior is one of the unlucky ones; what if she develops a health problem, or a series of problems, that will cost more than $680,000 over her lifetime to treat? Becky will want to protect Junior against this risk. So we will need to introduce some kind of health insurance into even this, our dream scenario. Here Becky has two goals. First, she wants to protect Junior against truly catastrophic health circumstances. Second, she wants to spend as little of Junior's money on premiums as possible, preserving as much as she can in her Health Account.

In other words, Becky wants health insurance that covers as little as possible. She understands that health insurance is high cost (even under the new ACA rule, only eighty cents of each premium dollar will be spent on care). Junior gets to spend on care all one hundred cents of every health grant dollar she doesn't spend on premiums. So Becky wants insurance that covers only any care Junior might need that is not covered by her lifetime health grants. As perverse as it seems to our current way of thinking, Becky wants insurance with as high a deductible as possible so that Junior's premiums—and therefore her losses to the costly administration of insurance—are as small as possible.

Now let's design that insurance policy. Say that for 95 percent of the country, the $680,000 lifetime health grant will more than adequately cover their health needs. But for the unfortunate 5 percent, the average need is much higher, requiring, let's say, a total of $2.58 million in lifetime care (in other words, roughly an additional $2 million). Assuming insurance administrative and profit costs are 20 percent, the premium for Junior for protection against being one of the high-cost 5 percent should be about $120,000 over the course of her life—or $1,500 a year. And the lifetime deductible (because in a system where money can be moved through loans from one year to another, lifetime deductible is all that matters) will be $500,000.*

On the Mainland, this type of insurance would be called catastrophic insurance because it insures against a risk that is very remote. On the Island, the term "catastrophic insurance" has been hijacked to mean (slightly) higher-deductible insurance. On the Mainland, no one with real catastrophic insurance expects ever to make a claim against the policy. On the Island, everybody with a catastrophic insurance policy expects to make a claim most years. So let's call this new type of health policy True Catastrophic Insurance (TruCat).

All of the elements of Becky's health care system are effective from cradle to grave. Junior is born with a Health Grant, a Health Account, and a TruCat policy. If she's unfortunate enough to be born with a very serious illness, she can claim against TruCat from her first day. There are no milestones

---

* Obviously, all these numbers are simplified for purposes of illustration. But let's do the math. If 5 percent of the population needs an extra $2 million in lifetime care, then spreading that care over 100 percent of the population will cost $100,000 per person. Adding 20 percent in insurance administrative costs makes the premiums $120,000. So what does Becky have now? She has $680,000 in health grants, of which $120,000 goes to her insurance premium, leaving $560,000 to spend on her own care.

that alter Junior's status in Becky's dream health system; reaching adulthood, switching jobs, or becoming a senior citizen are all irrelevant. Chances are that Junior's first years of life—well into middle age—are likely to involve low health expenses and a growing accumulation of funds in her Health Account. After middle age, her health expenses are likely to increase, gradually diminishing the balance built over the previous years. Junior almost certainly will turn sixty-five with several hundred thousand dollars in her Health Account—far more than is spent on beneficiaries even by today's undisciplined Medicare program.

So what do we have? Becky's daughter enjoys a health system that uses exactly as much money as is used today. It is straightforward, with no variation for age, work status, health status, or anything else. It has cradle-to-grave coverage. And it involves very low administrative costs, as insurance is held to a minimum and simplicity substitutes for the administrative complexity of modern health care finance.

Becky's principles

Becky's dream health system is just that—a dream. But in trying to rebuild our existing system, which of the principles from this ideal should guide us?

One is security against catastrophe. Anyone can be struck down by serious illness or accident, or have a child born with severe health problems. It may not exactly be a lottery—we have some ability to shape our health probabilities through lifestyle choices—but severe illness is a universal risk.

As we have seen in the health care systems of other developed countries, the need for protection against the risk of catastrophe easily morphs into the desire to be protected against all bad events. Island experts would argue that expanding security beyond true catastrophic risks to cover mere certainties is a matter of societal generosity. But the past forty-five years suggests they are wrong: protecting against catastrophic risk and protecting against certainties are trade-offs. As we've seen, the cost inflation, inefficiency, sloppiness, and danger inherent in trying to cover too much in the name of security weaken our ability to compensate for true catastrophe. Most Americans may believe that the problems they face in getting good health care could be solved by more insurance. But the crisis in health care in America—and in all developed countries—has only grown as we have expanded the range of noncatastrophic events covered by health security tools; the ACA further broadens this burden. Becky's system asks insurance to do only what insurance can do (cover true risk) and not what insurance can't do without massive distortion (protect against certainty).

As mentioned, Becky's is a cradle-to-grave health system: all its requirements and guarantees are permanent for the individual. Our existing health system, of course, is not structured this way. Though most Americans would agree on some basic health care for all Americans, the structure of that health safety net could not be more complicated. The type of access you have to our health system depends on your age, your job status, your insurance status (or that of other family members), your income, and your health. Over the course of her lifetime, Becky may be covered by her parents' policy, a school policy, four or more job-based plans, COBRA, individual coverage, a spouse's policy, and then Medicare and Medigap. For good measure, she's also likely to have at least one health savings and one flexible spending account.

How much of the inefficiency, cost, and incomprehensible complexity of our system derive from these needless, pointless transitions? Not to mention the hardship experienced by people who happen to be ill when one of these transitions occurs. And all of this complexity exists only for one reason: to maintain the fiction that someone else is paying for your health care. Becky Jr. has a lot more to spend on health care because her system has dropped the fiction.

Becky's dream system also features breathtaking simplicity. In the past couple of decades, billions of dollars of value have been created by Apple, Amazon, Ikea, FedEx, Southwest Airlines, Google, all the major credit card companies, and countless others simplifying something complicated. In health care, no company in any sector can make this claim—or even seems interested in pursuing the goal. The Island experts revel in our system's complexity like priests of ancient religions, jealously guarding their exclusive relationship with the gods.

Medicine is complicated enough without making the payment system incomprehensible. Whatever your views about the more state-oriented health systems of other developed countries, at least they are easier to understand. The beauty of Becky's dream system is that all of us will be able to understand what we have.

Most Americans probably share the broad goals of Becky's system, even if our current predicament makes them almost unattainable. But what should be most transformative about Becky's system is that it has transformed Junior from a mere patient into a customer. Becky's system gives all health care providers a new boss—and a whole new set of incentives on price, quality, service, and safety.

As a customer—as the new boss—Becky Jr. is likely to insist on several features totally foreign to our current system. One is accessibility. Becky herself is used to information being accessible every second, from her up-to-the-minute credit card balance to the precise location of a gift she's shipping to a friend. She gets and pays her bills online and expects to be able to click through to the underlying explanation of any charge.

Becky is also used to choice among a wide and easily searchable list of alternatives, whether for entertainment, clothing, housing, or potential dates. She customizes her sneakers at Nike's online site and picked her courses in college after reading other students' online reviews. Becky expects Junior will be able to choose her provider from a variety of bundled services and billing plans. After all, it's her money.

This is all good for Junior, but in designing our health system, we as a society would add a couple of other principles. Related to the idea of security is a society's obligation to all citizens. Any acceptable health system should offer to all in society who are ill the resources to cure or at least alleviate their suffering. So it's not enough that Becky's system works for Junior; it has to be applicable and beneficial to everyone.

Of course, society's willingness to provide security for all presents a "free rider" problem. Even people who choose not to help pay for care know that they will have a claim on health resources. This free rider problem can take a variety of forms—from the refusal to pay for insurance or set aside funds for care to an unwillingness to take care of one's health. In our current system, responses to the free rider problem often create more problems, unfairness, or hardship—from the mandate that hospitals provide care for anyone dropping into an emergency room to insurance companies' exclusions on preexisting conditions in new policies. As in Becky's system, any system that accepts a responsibility for all citizens must also require participation by all.*

Becky's system is based on the dream premise that instead of collectively spending $2.5 trillion a year on health care, we could magically distribute that money equally to each individual to spend on his or her own care. While it might be ideal if everybody could each start with the same level of resources in health care, that would have been possible only before the great health care inflation. Today, the key is not that everyone have the same resources but rather that the system work for the person with the least resources. Junior's fictional health grant enabled us to give her insurance with a $500,000 lifetime deductible; in the real world, appropriately designed insurance would need a deductible that served as protection for those less fortunate. I'll turn to that issue in the last chapter, which addresses how to create something approaching Becky's dream system from today's reality.

Becky's system introduces something our current auto-pilot system does not allow: a trade-off between health care and the other good things in life. It accomplishes this in a

* An individual mandate was one of the most contentious elements of the ACA, with some arguing that its imposition was unconstitutional. If that is the case, it just means that a true catastrophic safety net would have to be a public undertaking rather than a private one. There's no argument about the government's right to require citizens to participate in a government insurance scheme.

couple of ways, one obvious and one subtle. The obvious way is that we've allowed Becky Jr. to leave the balance in her health account to her survivors (and perhaps even to access some for other uses once it reaches a certain level of surplus). This money no longer has to be used only for health care. As Becky saves money in her health account, she knows it will at least become part of her estate. Maybe that's not very satisfying—or motivating—to many people. But remember that we made a big assumption: that demand for health care continues at our current level of $8,500 per person per year. What if Becky's system achieves what we've seen in HSA experiments to date: a 10 to 30 percent reduction in health spending? Then we'll need to put aside much less in our Health Accounts, freeing up resources to be used on everything else.

A second element of "withdrawal" of resources from the health care system into our general needs is more subtle. For some of us, health is a matter of luck (or the predetermination of our individual genetic makeups). But much is attributable to how well we care for ourselves—our diet, physical activity, risk-taking, avoidance of excess, ability to eliminate or manage stress. On average, people choosing healthy lifestyles will need less health care and will thus have more of their Health Account money to devote to other things.

One of the unusual elements of Becky's system is that health becomes a financial asset for each of us as individuals in a more explicit way. And like everything else in life, there are individual trade-offs that will affect our individual valuation of our asset. No one regards good health as the only goal in life, any more than anyone values money as the only goal.* Both are sometimes—even often—subordinate to our interests, life goals, affections, and even vices.

My grandmother may have been right that health is wealth, but of course wealth is for spending, not just accumulating. Becky's system allows us to make our own health primarily our own concern. It restores health to its proper place in our lives: an important value, yes. But only one of several.

Financing a lifetime of care

In our current health care system, we rely on only two forms of finance: insurance, which pays for most of our services, and out-of-pocket expenditures (aka income), which pay for the small balance. On the Mainland, consumers use five basic financial tools to pay for goods and services.

Income is the default financing mechanism. For most routine, predictable, small-ticket needs and wants, we just pay out of pocket from our current income.

Savings are used as either a rainy day fund for any unexpected cost (repairing a broken appliance, for example) or to build for a specific goal (such as a vacation or down payment on a house).

Debt also typically has two purposes: as a short-term

---

* Employers have been experimenting with wellness initiatives that reward employees for losing weight or exercising or giving up smoking. Some Island experts dismiss the value of these approaches with the sensible observation that bad health outcomes would seem to be a greater disincentive to bad habits than a small financial reward. But the whole question is stuck on the Island, as if health outcomes are the only thing that do—or should—matter to people.

Everything in life involves a trade-off. No one decides to become a soldier or a police officer or a war-zone aid worker for her health—much less for money. We don't choose to hang glide, party, or even watch TV for our health. And we all have vices—many of which harm, at least a little, our health probabilities. Only on the Island is health seen as of sole importance.

bridge to spread out payments on a higher-ticket item (such as when a credit card is used to buy a dress) or as a long-term arrangement to supplement savings in buying a very expensive item with long-term value (like a car or a house). Debt is used to spread out expenditures over time.

Insurance is used to finance major, unpredictable costs (such as an accident or theft). Unlike other forms of finance, we pay for insurance knowing that we may never receive anything of tangible value for our payment. Insurance is used to spread rare expenditure over populations subject to the risk of those expenditures. Insurance is highly inefficient at financing certainty because it adds so much administrative cost; it can efficiently fund only those costs that are unexpected.

Aid is typically provided to those in need and unable on their own to afford or access some or all of the other financing tools. The various levels of the U.S. government will spend more than $1 trillion on health care this year, almost all of it as a direct purchaser of care. One trillion dollars is a lot of money—so much that it would allow the government alternatively to make an $8,000 annual deposit into the Health Accounts of 125 million people—a full 40 percent of our population.

Because health care consists of so many different types of goods and services used at so many different stages of life, an efficient health care system will employ all of the first four of these tools—matching each to the type of health expenditure it most efficiently finances—with aid to the neediest provided in the same forms that we use to fund our care.

Income: Any routine medical expense should ideally be funded out of pocket from a patient's income. This would include regular checkups and testing, the few likely annual visits to the doctor for the flu or a child's cold, and treatment for a minor accident or two.

Insurance: At the other extreme, all truly major and unpredictable health events—including cancer, massive trauma, and disabling illness—should be covered by insurance.

Savings: Major costs that are predictable are more inexpensively covered by savings. Most of us are now fortunate enough to live long enough to face the question of end-of-life care. As a result of its near universality, end-of-life care cannot be financed efficiently by insurance—too many dollars go into administration. Similarly, all of us are going to die of something, so conditions that may seem appropriately covered by insurance early in life—when they cannot be anticipated—are more efficiently covered by savings later in life. In this sense, health insurance should be more like life insurance: it protects against the possibility not of getting ill but rather of getting ill before we've had the opportunity to set aside enough savings to cover it. A heart attack at forty may be financially devastating and therefore should be heavily protected by insurance; at ninety, however, we would expect that most of its costs would be covered by a lifetime of health savings. As we saw with Becky's system, choosing the most appropriate form of finance for any health expenditure allows society—and us as individuals—to bear less cost.

Debt: Outside of credit cards, we don't have much debt financing available for health care. In part, this is because health services lack an associated tangible long-term asset—such as a car—that can secure a loan. But if possible, using debt for someone with inadequate health savings in health care would be a much cheaper way to finance small but unexpected expenses, such as a broken bone, a child with pneumonia, or even a pregnancy (and in chapter 11, I'll describe how to make this option feasible).

Of course, many health care expenses fit into several of these categories and are best funded by a combination of the four tools. Let's look at the most prevalent: the broad category called chronic conditions. As our definition of chronic conditions continues to expand, it becomes ever more likely that every one of us will be diagnosed with at least one; already almost half of the population has a chronic condition. By definition, this means insurance will be an inefficient way to pay for chronic conditions; they've become certainties, not risks. To build a low-cost system, we each will have to set aside some portion of our income and savings to fund the management of a typical chronic condition, with the more serious conditions covered by insurance.

If you're stuck in our current mind-set, this all sounds nuts. Pay for end-of-life care out of savings? That can cost $100,000—who has that kind of savings? Borrow to finance a pregnancy? Now you have to bear the burden of a new family and pay off a loan? Pay for your statins out of pocket? Where can you find the extra $100 a month? But of course, that ignores the key to Becky's system, which is to take the massive amount of money you're already paying for health care—but don't realize it—and put it in your bank account. And with all of us spending the money directly, what do you think would happen to these absurd prices?

Back to reality?

Unfortunately, we can't implement Becky's health system for Junior from scratch today. After all, only four million of us will be born this year. The rest of us are well on our way through our health journey. Those with congenital conditions already have them and face an insurance system desperate to exclude them from coverage. Our seniors are spending massive amounts on care today. Health care is too expensive to gamble on the hope of consumer-driven savings. And none of us have any health savings, much less enough to accept a truly high deductible catastrophic insurance policy.

But Becky's dream system—and the more concrete example of Singapore—illustrates that it is theoretically possible to fund most of our health expenditures the same way we fund most things on the Mainland and also to protect people against the circumstances that make health care unique. But what do we do now? Is it possible to create the foundation for a new system while still making sure people get the care they need today? The question resembles the problem we have with highway repair—how do we conduct necessary repairs without losing use of the highway?

The first ingredient in rebuilding our health care system is patience. It has taken us forty-five years to build this behemoth; it will take a generation to rebuild it in a sensible way. We will need a long transition period. But unlike with highway repair, even the first steps to a more responsive health care system could produce benefits that exceed the initial inconvenience. America remains an extraordinarily dynamic nation, and amid the rot of our health care system are promising developments that—with the right encouragement—portend a much brighter future. Let's turn to some of these "green shoots."

CHAPTER 10

Green Shoots

Foundations of a better system

My family visited a small beach town in Morocco last year. We stayed at an eight-room family-owned inn, with beautiful views of the water and simple but tastefully furnished rooms. The staff was very attentive to the guests and prepared excellent breakfasts. As I was checking out, I complimented one of the owners on the inn. "Thanks," she replied, "but it would be really great if you would say it on TripAdvisor."

TripAdvisor was founded in 2000 with a simple idea: to let travelers post their reviews of almost every imaginable destination and vacation experience online to be read by others planning their vacations. In just ten years, it has become a major force in the travel industry without owning a single plane, hotel, or attraction.* Roughly fifty mil-

---

* Full disclosure: I sat on the board of TripAdvisor's former parent company, Expedia, from 2005 to 2007.

lion people a month visit the website, which features sixty million reviews and more than six million photos that have been posted about 460,000 hotels, 650,000 restaurants, and 125,000 attractions in more than eighty-five thousand cities.

This extraordinary growth is an example of the power of what economists call "network effects," which can be translated as "the more people use a service, the more people will want to use that service." TripAdvisor's impact has been extraordinary—as evidenced by its importance to a small inn owner in a remote town in Morocco. There are 202 posts about just that one little inn.

Not everyone is happy about TripAdvisor's rise. Hotels regularly complain of amateur reviewers' lack of training, standards, fairness, or balance. In at least one case, a group of more than four hundred hotels and restaurants considered filing a joint lawsuit charging defamation. So the site now gives business owners a chance to respond right next to reviewer criticisms. And with so many reviews, TripAdvisor regulars—and the site claims twenty million members— know how to weigh an outlier against the consensus. But of course, the criticism of TripAdvisor merely reflects its influence—the power of its communications model in driving consumer awareness and business accountability.

TripAdvisor makes a lot of money from advertising and steering users to online travel bookings; others make less money because of the site. Online travel agencies like Expedia, Orbitz, and Travelocity undermined the position of traditional travel agents; now TripAdvisor in turn "disintermediates" the online agencies' own relationships with customers. Many travelers begin their searching with Trip-Advisor and book their reservations only from TripAdvisor referrals. Travel packagers, tour groups, and of course traditional guidebooks have all found their market power diminished by the rise of TripAdvisor.

Who is the TripAdvisor of the health care industry?

If the story of my father's death had appeared not in *The Atlantic* but rather as one of thousands of easily available stories and reviews on, well, let's call it HealthcareAdvisor, it might have been part of a tidal wave of information transforming health care. Can we imagine a hundred thousand preventable hospital deaths, or seventy-five thousand "never events," or one in four Medicare patients victimized by a medical error under the glare of HealthcareAdvisor? What if we all posted our hospital and doctor bills online, our experiences with indifferent physicians, surly nurses, and neglectful staff, our observations of dirty patient rooms or terrible food?

The good news is that there are in fact several candidates capable of performing a TripAdvisor role in health care. Indeed, a number of new trends and ideas are emerging that have the potential to revolutionize health care and transform the relationship between customer and provider. Health care is a huge pie, and venture capital and other investment funds would love to find the transformative idea that nets them a nice slice of it.

But although there are many good new ideas about how to enhance health care—ideas that could reduce costs, drive efficiency, improve results, and expand accountability— none have achieved anything on the scale of the success of "big ideas" in other industries. On the Mainland, no good new idea has it easy, of course; every new business approach must overcome resistance. But in health care, the resistance is across the board, and we, the beneficiaries of new ideas for improvement, are relatively powerless to influence change.

Innovative ideas are hampered by the power of the Surrogates, by the pervasiveness of regulation, and by the opposition of entrenched interests operating in a highly regulated environment.

So, many of the best ideas in health care remain "green shoots"—big enough to suggest promise but not pervasive enough to drive real change. The Island is such a closed world that we can't expect even the best ideas to be transformative, despite similar ideas being wildly successful on the Mainland. New ideas need help to overcome entrenched forces. Unfortunately, the best form of help that government can give to these green shoots is the one most inconsistent with current health care policy: room to experiment. Successful new ideas require an environment that allows innovators to try out new business models, new approaches to pricing, and new definitions and bundles of services. Government policy is a tidal wave in the opposite direction—toward uniformity, defined "minimums," and equal access. Each policy and each rule may sound sensible in a vacuum, but collectively they make it very difficult for the truly transformative ideas to rise to the surface and effect real change.

The kinds of ideas that policymakers consider green shoots in health care are quite different from the ones discussed in this chapter. On the Island, experts look to examples of unusually good care as potential models for the whole system, and one can find truly innovative and promising approaches to care, even in large institutions. Intermountain Healthcare is known for its commitment to information technology; Geisinger for its implementation of coordinated primary and hospital care; Virginia Mason and University of Maryland Medical Centers for patient safety.

While these hospitals and others may have much to teach other providers about techniques of care, their very excellence paradoxically suggests their limits as models.

The best institutions tend to be characterized by extraordinary leadership driving powerful therapeutic cultures. What doesn't differentiate them is a more attractive business model; as a result, the best providers in health care rarely have a way to be more profitable than the average or even the bad. (In fact, an Intermountain executive has written that his hospital's commitment to data-driven accountability reduces profits even while helping patients.) It's tempting to believe that the best practices can be copied from one institution to another, but without an associated economic benefit, this transfer is likely to be resisted at best or, at worst, to be translated into just more paperwork. Until better medicine produces better economic returns—until it either earns a bigger profit or enables the best to drive the worst out of business—it will remain limited to patches of excellence on the Island.

True green shoots in health care are important because they suggest what's possible, what could genuinely change the playing field given appropriate support. Perhaps over time, the impact of these efforts at "revolution from below" might even invade the thinking of our policymakers and serve as a catalyst for a truly comprehensive overhaul of the way we all think about and fund our health care system and of the ways we hold it accountable. But the only real catalyst for transformation will be the shift of decision making in health care from the Surrogates to consumers. Only then will we give green shoots enough access to sunlight and water—also known as profits—to make a real difference.

The crisis of "cost sharing"

Over the long term, it's likely that the best thing that could happen to health care is that which is most painful in the short term: the growth of what's euphemistically called cost sharing.

As insurance premiums have skyrocketed, companies have compensated by choosing policies that force employees to bear a greater share of their health costs. This increased financial burden takes three forms: employers can require their employees to contribute more to the cost of the premium, to bear higher deductibles, or to buy policies that put a greater responsibility on beneficiaries for the price of medical services actually used (co-pays).*

Recently, Becky switched from our PPO to our high-deductible plan. We made it worth her while. To continue in the PPO, with its $250 in-network deductible, Becky would have had to pay $1,931 of the total $7,155 premium. Instead, under the HSA, she'll pay only $708 in premiums; she'll now bear a $1,200 deductible, but we also deposited $750 into her HSA. Many companies are encouraging their employees to switch to high-deductible plans; it's estimated that 13.5 million people took this option in 2012, up almost 20 percent in a year.

For many Americans, this increase in their direct financial burden of health care represents a huge problem; in the

---

* In practice, most of the transfer of the financial burden has occurred in the first two categories: higher premiums and deductibles. On average, employees now pay over 17 percent of the premium cost of single coverage and almost 28 percent of family coverage. Also, over 30 percent of employees have policies that carry a minimum $1,000 deductible, up from only 18 percent just three years ago. Just under 20 percent of employees are now enrolled in high-deductible plans with health savings accounts—an option that originated only six years ago.

past decade, the average share of premiums paid by workers has grown three times as fast as incomes.* The ACA has a number of provisions designed to cap many types of cost sharing, but these reduce just the visible costs of care; none reduce its real costs. As long as health care costs continue to rise faster than income, we'll bear those costs, whether directly through cost sharing or indirectly through reduced wages (or, even more indirectly, through less job creation).

The hardship caused by rising cost sharing does have a positive side: all of us are more conscious of the cost of care. Indeed, one factor behind the rise of high-deductible plans is that employees are attracted to their lower premiums, which can make them a better deal despite the higher deductibles. High-deductible plans also mean that routine health care expenses are paid out of pocket, turning patients into consumers. Even in traditional plans, higher deductibles and co-pays create greater awareness of medical charges, at least in nonemergency situations.

For example, as consumers directly seek discounts, retail markets in pharmaceuticals are quietly transforming. Several big national chains—including nontraditional pharmacies such as those at Costco, Wal-Mart, Kmart, and Target—offer discount drug programs for the most common generics, with economics similar to their bulk-buying models in other goods and services. For more expensive pharmaceuticals, several of the leading drug companies are

---

* Although we've seen consistent increases in co-pays and other cost sharing, direct out-of-pocket payments for medical services at the point of service have stabilized after years of *declining*. In 2010, Americans directly paid only 11 percent of their health care costs. This was the lowest share in our history—a lower share, in fact, than in some single-payer countries. However, let's put this "only 11 percent" in perspective. It represents a full $300 billion a year, meaning we spend more on out-of-pocket care than we spend for clothing, gasoline, or entertainment.

engaging in a subtle form of targeted discounting by offering special coupons covering a qualified customer's cost-sharing requirements.*

Historically, the actual provisioning of health care has been a local business: a person's use of services was limited to her local doctors, hospitals, and clinics. But increasing consumer responsibility for costs has opened up the field of "medical tourism"—traveling, often great distances, to obtain procedures of similar quality at much lower prices. Reliable statistics don't yet exist, but an estimated one million Americans a year now travel abroad for medical treatment. They travel to a variety of locations, including India, Singapore, Mexico, Argentina, and South Africa for procedures as major and diverse as heart valve replacements, transplants, and orthopedic surgery. Prices for these major operations are as low as 5 percent of those in the United States.

As we would expect, medical tourism is concentrated in areas of medicine for which insurance coverage is often limited, such as cosmetic surgery, fertilization treatments, and experimental procedures; patients wanting these services are likely to be paying all of the cost of treatment and so are highly motivated to seek discounts. But even when treatment is covered by insurance, some businesses are apparently encouraging their employees to choose these cheaper options, splitting cost savings as a cash incentive.

* This is an obvious effort to get around the purpose of beneficiary cost sharing, and in any other industry it would be accurately described as a kickback. But it is also a glimpse of how pharmaceutical markets would be price competitive in a non-insurance-driven world (see Andrew Pollack, "Coupons for Patients, but Higher Bills for Insurers," *New York Times,* January 1, 2011). Drug companies have also been accused of offering rebates to doctors—an example of moral hazard in action (see Pollack, "Secret Rebates Offered on Costly Eye Drug," *New York Times,* November 4, 2010).

Medical tourism is possible because so many major procedures are now relatively routine, with short procedure and recovery times, limited use of resources, and very predictable results. Yes, in foreign countries doctors have lower incomes, construction costs are lower, and land costs for hospital facilities may be less. But these doctors are practicing high-tech medicine in new for-profit facilities designed specifically to capture tourist health spending. The travel companies responsible for packaging the travel, treatment, and recovery services often appear more attuned than most established hospitals to consumer perspectives. As Singapore's example demonstrates, high-tech high-quality medicine can be quite cheap in a market where price is an object.

If more consumers are driven by cost sharing to seek out these low-cost options, American institutions will be forced to cut prices to compete—just like in Mainland industries. In fact, some American providers are themselves destinations for medical tourists, offering deep discounts on surgery to Canadians willing to pay to avoid waiting lists at home.

Of course, even the most motivated consumer has difficulty comparison-shopping for domestic health care services today. Many providers and even some clinics refuse to quote prices over the phone. Several Internet sites have attempted to provide competitive price data, but they also have trouble getting the information from providers. Each of these start-up sites faces a common challenge: no provider has an incentive to publish its best prices unless it is ensured a high volume of referrals from the site. And without best prices, it's difficult for the site to attract enough customer-patients to deliver to the provider. There's an additional problem: KonnectMD, an online marketplace in Houston, has found that providers can't post prices low enough to appeal to cash-paying customers because they would be required to retroactively offer Medicaid the same discount.*

The barrier isn't that doctors hesitate to use the Internet for business. The website ZocDoc enables patients to book appointments with a broad range of physicians in a variety of specialties. But rather than post prices, the site merely confirms that your specific insurance plan is accepted by the practice.

Greater consumer consciousness will not in itself create a consumer economy in health care; the Surrogates still dominate the packaging, pricing, and billing of health services. But the greatest obstacle may be our own mentality: we're not used to thinking of ourselves as consumers. Becky told me she didn't schedule a doctor's appointment for a minor problem because of the $300 quoted price; it didn't occur to her to ask for a lower price or shop around for a better deal.

And I suspect Becky sees her new high-deductible plan as an opportunity to have "an extra $50 or $100 a month" rather than to build health independence through savings. When I asked her how high a deductible would cause her to

---

* Castlight Health is a start-up that attempts to bridge this price information gap through its access to actual reimbursement data provided by corporate clients. Castlight provides clients' employees with an aggregated database that compares reimbursed prices received by local physicians, clinics, and hospitals. The start-up has some prominent investors, industry partners, and customers, but its success is likely to hinge on how many employers will be willing to use their leverage with insurers. To date, some insurers have been reluctant to share reimbursement information with a third-party service, even when requested to do so by a corporate client. Yet as greater numbers of employees move into high-deductible or consumer-directed plans, the demand for price information will certainly grow.

ClearHealthCosts, a site founded by a *New York Times* journalist, encourages patients themselves to share price information about their procedures in its quest to build a transparent marketplace in the New York region.

go back to a PPO, she said $2,000. But she's already saving $1,200 a year just in her share of the premiums by accepting a deductible of $1,250; plus, we're putting $750 in her HSA every year. So if she switched back to the PPO policy, Becky would give up $2,000 each year simply to avoid the possibility that she could have to pay an extra $1,750 out of pocket in any year. There may be no more perfect illustration of the absurdity of our low-deductible insurance system—and how our own risk-averse mentality allows its continued inefficiency.

New forms of practice

As Americans' direct responsibility for their health care costs grows, the primary questions faced by the typical family change: What type of care do we choose to pay for? What's worth more to us? What's worth less? This opening—as small as it is in our Surrogate-dominated economy—creates room for some new business models.

Many of these emerging models shift some of the care workload from the most expensive elements of the system (physicians, dedicated medical facilities, specialty care professionals) to lower-cost elements (nurses, shared facilities, primary care physicians) to provide price-sensitive consumers with low-price options for routine care. For example, we now have more than eleven hundred walk-in retail clinics in the United States. Many are led by a single, often salaried physician; others, by nurse-practitioners. The business models vary, but they share some common characteristics. Prices are fixed, transparent, and low. Services are simple and straightforward: flu shots and other vaccinations, cholesterol and pregnancy testing, basic physicals, allergy shots, and sexually transmitted disease treatment. The clinics operate in shopping malls, stores such as Wal-Mart and Target, and CVS (home of the MinuteClinic) and other pharmacies. Many take no insurance, eliminating their need for costly infrastructure to handle complex billing.

According to a recent *Wall Street Journal* article, a "small but growing number of consumers are skipping the time and expense of seeing physicians and are ordering up their own tests, with heart-related assays among the most popular." Many of these tests can be directly ordered from online labs, avoiding state regulations that require physician referral for tests. Some of the more basic tests, such as for total cholesterol or lipids, can even be performed by consumers themselves. Self-administered or self-ordered testing is not the same as self-medicine; most patients-consumers can use the tests to monitor conditions identified by a physician but without paying for an office visit each time they need a test. In addition, some employers are offering on-site testing, reducing costs while ensuring that employees with high deductibles don't skimp on the essential preventive services.

At the opposite end of the price spectrum, so-called concierge medicine has been gaining traction among the very wealthy. The models differ widely, but most concierge services involve membership fees, guaranteed access to the best physicians and hospitals, twenty-four-hour service, and a coordinated approach to care, with the concierge service taking charge of the treatment relationships among primary doctors and specialists.

Concierge care is typically expensive and exclusive. PinnacleCare, which offers a complete personal health record available online, easy scheduling across an extensive network of doctors, and medical travel preparation, has annual membership fees ranging from $2,500 to $30,000 and says it now serves thirty-six hundred customers. Yet concierge care and retail clinics have more in common than a casual observer might think. Both allow consumers to opt out of the complex insurance-based system, and both promise immediate attention and administrative simplicity—"the complex world of healthcare is made simple," to quote Pinnacle's site. With ever greater complexity likely as the ACA is implemented, one suspects that the appeal to consumers of these business models at the income extremes will only grow.

Qliance, for instance, is a new concierge-type service for middle-class consumers, focusing exclusively on primary care. Patients pay a monthly fee of $59 to $169, which covers all of their primary care at a Qliance clinic. Members are guaranteed appointments within one day and "unhurried" consultations with salaried physicians (including phone and e-mail follow-up). How can this possibly work? Qliance doesn't take insurance. According to its marketing materials, administrative costs of insurance eat up 40 percent of revenues in a typical primary care practice, so Qliance can invest some of these real cost savings in better service and better pricing.

The venture-capital-backed One Medical Group also offers membership-based concierge service, for an annual fee of up to $200. Members are guaranteed immediate appointments, responsive doctors, and an integrated approach to care. Operating in three cities, the firm pledges that its physicians will see no more than sixteen patients a day to allow ample time for each consultation.

Stripping out the administrative cost associated with

insurance is the common feature of a range of new models.*
GracePointe Healthcare in Franklin, Tennessee, is a single
practice featuring "self-pay" (that is, no insurance) monthly
plans at $49 or $99. Both plans guarantee $40 consultations,
$10 to $25 basic tests, and house calls. The more expensive
plan offers 24/7 access to a physician. Sprig Health, a network of providers in Portland, Oregon, allows users to book
online appointments with cash-only providers in a variety of
specialties. MediBid encourages cash-only patients to shop
around for low-cost providers as "domestic" medical tourists. Dartmouth College and Iora Health have partnered on
a new primary care model: the college pays a flat annual fee
to Iora for each of its employees to cover all their primary
care services. For an annual family fee of $129, Brighter.com
provides bookings within their network of dentists at published discounted prices.†

United Networks of America has introduced a new business model with a back-to-the-future flavor to it. For a fee, it
will sell to consumers access to a discount network of doctors, dentists, or device providers in health areas not typically covered by insurance. For example, for $90, a patient
can join United's cosmetic surgery network and receive discounts of roughly 20 percent off retail prices on uncovered
cosmetic procedures. Several health insurers have bought
this benefit to distribute to their members—in effect, pro-

---

* ZoomCare offers another concept: its low-cost urgent care clinics are in-
network for most private insurers in the Pacific Northwest, but it doesn't accept
Medicare or Medicaid (again, to keep the cost of paperwork down).

† A *Health Affairs* article notes: "It is surprising how often they [providers for
cash-paying patients] offer the very quality enhancements that critics complain
are missing in traditional medical care. Electronic medical records and electronic
prescribing are standard fare . . . and twenty-four/seven primary care is also a
feature of concierge services and the various telephone and email consultation services" (Goodman et al., "The Economics of Health Care Quality").

viding in-network discounts for services they don't actually cover. The United model is a type of group-buying program, similar to the roots of health insurance itself.

Cost sharing is not the only catalyst for new business models. Roughly three-quarters of insured employees are now enrolled in an HMO or a PPO. Most physicians choose to be part of one or more of these preferred networks, accepting insurers' reimbursement schedules in return for access to this high volume of patients. But not all physicians do. Some are partially opting out of insurance; their patients are directly responsible for paying their own bills and for obtaining whatever reimbursement their insurers will provide. My cardiologist has such a practice. Because many of his patients are making large out-of-pocket payments for his services, they expect more time with him. They're more likely to question charges. Being consumers makes them more demanding patients. So this practice's economic benefit results less from the higher rates he can charge than from the administrative burden he saves. As a result, he believes he can see fewer patients and provide better medicine without suffering economically.

Island experts often criticize new models by pointing out that most people can't afford to pay more out of pocket to see doctors who won't join their insurers' provider networks or to pay the membership fees at even middle-class concierge primary care clinics. But they miss the point: the reason so many Americans can't afford more out-of-pocket payments is that the standard insurance system takes so much of their money for administrative costs. For the "benefit" of having the direct costs of their care hidden through insurance, they bear longer waits for appointments and spend less time with their physicians.

As the burden of health insurance grows, employers are increasingly willing to experiment with more active approaches to reduce their costs. Perhaps the greatest potential is in wellness incentives. Since lifestyle choices are the largest factor in determining health, employers are looking for ways to compensate employees for taking better care of themselves. A recent survey of corporate plans found that more than 70 percent of companies had some type of wellness initiative; nine out of ten large employers did. Many of these companies offered incentives to employees—and in some cases their families—to engage in healthful activities or hit weight or fitness goals. In a few cases, employers were able to offer better terms on insurance—lower deductibles or premium sharing—to employees who didn't smoke or who agreed to maintain exercise or weight control objectives. But in most states, this is discouraged by the regulatory regime; it's considered illegal discrimination. So for the most part, incentives are limited to cash bonuses, gift cards, or loyalty program points. In other cases, employers subsidize positive behavior, such as joining a gym, or invest in altering employee behavior by, say, paying for smoking cessation programs.

It's too early to know which, if any, of these new business models will succeed in American health care. Health care policy is not especially encouraging to experiments outside of the insurance model, and insurance has a poor record of paying more up front—for primary care membership fees, for example—even to achieve total cost savings over time. But questions of value are increasingly affecting the health decisions of ever growing numbers of patients—at the high income level, the low income level, and many points in between—as well as the actions of the providers who serve them.

Too much information?

Health care information has been a staple of the Internet since the medium first became popular, but its growth continues to be staggering. Each month, roughly two-thirds of Americans now seek health information online, mostly on symptoms and conditions. WebMD, the most successful early Internet health information company, serves 18.5 million visitors a month. The National Institutes of Health's site serves 12 million, and the Mayo Clinic's serves another 8 million. Insurers increasingly provide health information online; Aetna's InteliHealth serves 125,000 users a month.

All these sites offer an extraordinary range of information on symptoms, diseases, treatments, risks, and side effects. They are all designed to be clear and comprehensive for patients. And they have all undercut the traditional monopoly that providers had on health information, with effects that are just starting to be felt in the industry.

Patients increasingly have access to websites designed for providers and other health care professionals. The NNT (which stands for "number needed to treat") is a particularly valuable corrective to much medical information, reversing the perspective on treatment efficacy that patients usually get in health care advertisements. For example, the site will translate a pharmaceutical company's technically correct claim that its drug reduces the risk of a specific illness by 40 percent into a more meaningful fact: a hundred patients will have to be treated with the drug before a single patient can expect to benefit.

As good as these health care information websites are, however, their role is being supplemented and increasingly subsumed by online social groups; a recent study suggested that as many as a third of consumers use social media for discussion of health conditions and providers. An example is PatientsLikeMe, which was originally formed to sponsor discussion around the rare disease ALS but now serves over 150,000 users with more than a thousand different conditions. On the site, those suffering from similar diagnoses can compare their experiences and treatments. Users can choose the degree of privacy they want: a few open their health profiles to any visitor to the site, while others restrict access to only registered members of a specific community.

The number of patient-directed online communities seems to grow daily, with a range of missions. Healthetreatment is devoted to patients with chronic conditions, AskaPatient to reviews of medications, Ben's Friends to rare diseases, MDJunction and HealingWell to support groups, Inspire to patient advocacy groups. When you consider all the groups about specific illnesses on Facebook, an estimated seventeen million Americans participate in some sort of online patient group.

Social support groups are essentially different from the health information sites that preceded them. Rather than provide a single expert opinion, these groups offer highly motivated participants a range of insights and experiences from a variety of sources. Most fundamentally, they undercut an assumption underlying much health care regulation: the paramount need for patient confidentiality. Participants in online groups willingly give up at least some—and in some cases most—of their personal information for the benefit of exchanging their experiences and knowledge with others. Indeed, personal information is essential to the financial sustainability of these communities; PatientsLikeMe discloses candidly on its home page that it sells aggregated health profile information of its members—although stripped of individual identifications—to health care providers.

Obviously, many of us prefer to keep at least some of our health information to ourselves. In our employer- and insurance-based health care model, disclosure of personal health care information can hurt our insurability or even employability. But in the age of Facebook and Twitter, our policy obsession with patient confidentiality seems at least a bit misdirected. Since more than 50 percent of the population has been diagnosed with at least one chronic condition, little shame or stigma remains in having a disease; the Beast has ensured that being healthy is a minority status. And health conditions and treatments are a sure conversation starter among my senior citizen friends and relatives.

Yet in supposed service of confidentiality, we sacrifice real potential for transformation in health care. Providers resist disclosing performance records and error rates in deference to patient confidentiality. The adoption of electronic records is slowed by fears of liability from data transfer leaks. Doctors are prohibited from using normal "unsecured" e-mail to communicate with patients.

While online health sites and communities have powered growing patient knowledge, the overall benefit is not yet unambiguous. In a 2009 *Consumer Reports* subscriber survey, 61 percent of patients said they used the Internet to help them with medical care, but only 8 percent of doctors surveyed said such research by their patients had been helpful in treatment. For doctors, knowledgeable patients may be more understanding of the risks of a treatment, but they may be more likely to have treatment preferences based on inadequate understanding. After all, there's a reason many of the health care sites are littered with drug advertisements: "informed" patients may demand procedures or pills that doctors consider inappropriate.

The spread of online information is mismatched with the limits of consumer power. Certainly, some online communities warn against excess treatment, overmedication, and unnecessary procedures. But today these sites live in a Surrogate-led, not a consumer-driven, environment. So their perspective is that of the unempowered consumer: how to get your insurer to pay for the maximum testing and treatment.

Even so, the explosion of online health information undercuts one of the key supports for our Surrogate-dominated system. Recall from chapter 3 the argument originally made by Kenneth Arrow that patients lacked the information necessary to challenge their doctors' recommendations for excess medicine. Now it appears that many patients themselves drive excess treatment from their Internet-fueled demands. Our Surrogates have proved themselves incapable of disciplining these demands; saying no is unacceptable to employers and has made insurers targets of politicians.

The reality is that patients will have the ever greater ability to handle their essential roles as managers of their own health. But unless our system matches patient resources and autonomy to these new tools, the Beast may be the only beneficiary.

Creative destruction

Perhaps the most far-reaching economic innovation of the period between World War II and the birth of the Internet was the standardized shipping container. As described in Marc Levinson's terrific book *The Box*, this simple idea transformed much about how the world economy now operates: "In 1956, the world was full of small manufacturers selling locally; by the end of the twentieth century, purely local markets for goods of any sort were few and far between." The container could be credited with the globalization of manufacturing and supply chains, the democratization of luxury goods, the rise of superstores, and even the creation of whole new cities.

In the strict confines of industry as it then existed, the idea of shipping all goods in boxes of a few standard sizes was grossly inefficient on its face. Since the very beginning of shipping, most of the cost of a voyage was the voyage itself. So packing ships as efficiently as possible was the key to reducing the number of voyages and, therefore, the cost. And putting all goods of an infinite variety of shapes and sizes into a one-size-fits-all box meant that a substantial amount of the space in a ship's hold would now be empty— the empty space in the inefficiently packed boxes.

What does the shipping container tell us about the potential for innovation in health care? Four basic ideas. First, massive transformation of an industry's economics can be generated by very simple ideas. The container was designed only to make shipping more efficient. It also succeeded in reducing damage to goods in transit by 95 percent, but its real impact could not have been foreseen: a four-decade explosion in world trade, enabling manufacturers to build worldwide supply chains, use just-in-time processes, and locate their plants wherever production was most efficient.

Second, true innovation often means questioning an article of faith among experts. The genius of Malcolm McLean, the prime mover behind the rise of shipping containers, was to see that the efficiency unleashed by a standard container would more than offset the inherent space inefficiency within the box. A standard container could be moved from ship to train to truck without needing to be unpacked and reloaded; using them would allow for a much more rapid loading and unloading of a ship, reducing the number of days in port, and for a different design of ship, enabling the construction of truly massive ships. All these factors overwhelmed the obvious "inefficiency" and initial cost of converting to standardized containers.

Third, and interestingly for our metrics-based approach to cost control in health care, greater efficiency may not be measurable in a straightforward manner. Levinson notes that the container so expanded the distances and range of goods shipped that no one has yet calculated a simple number for savings achieved. But he notes that manufacturers' need to keep inventory on hand had declined by as much as $1 trillion by the mid-1980s—an indirect but massive savings.

Fourth, and most immediately relevant, true transformation damages the interests of insiders. By reducing the costs of shipping, containers allowed more production, more hiring, more wages, and more wealth. But many interests were severely hurt, perhaps none more than those of longshoremen; standardized and rapid loading and off-loading led to massive job losses and less leverage in wage negotiations. Entire port cities and shipping companies that were late adopters of the new technology were also disadvantaged, as the larger ships and more modern facilities undercut their markets.

This process is called creative destruction, a term popularized by Joseph Schumpeter, a mid-twentieth-century economist. Schumpeter argued that the reason innovation in capitalism is so powerful is that it is a destructive as well as a creative force. New ideas drive wealth by destroying less efficient business models and transferring resources to better ones. It's a difficult message to hear, especially for politicians and those whose jobs are lost. It's the price we accept for capitalism's dynamism, for its ability to improve lifestyles. Without creative destruction, $750 laptops wouldn't have shrunk the market for $2,000 desktops, which wouldn't have replaced $1,000 word processors, which themselves wouldn't have destroyed the electric typewriter industry.

In his fascinating new book *The Creative Destruction of Medicine,* Eric Topol, the chief academic officer at Scripps Health and a professor of genomics, argues that the technological tools for a revolution in the provision of health care are almost completely available today. He believes that the spread of cheap, noninvasive testing devices covering a wide range of conditions combined with the ubiquity of wireless communications and smart phones could change the very nature of the patient-doctor relationship. New devices would allow patients in their normal lives to continuously—and passively—monitor the key indicators of their health, producing more meaningful data than offered by the snapshot of a physical exam. Wireless communication would ensure that important changes or abnormal readings were instantly communicated directly to physicians—or, more likely, to a service monitoring such data. Topol also believes that even our current progress in genomics allows for much greater use of targeted procedures, especially as it relates to prescription drugs. He argues that "population-based" medicine—where treatments are prescribed based on their average success measured in a large group of people—should soon be replaced by more individually targeted therapies for many conditions.

Topol's book provides an extraordinarily hopeful view of health care in the near future—one in which patients can take advantage of technological innovation and more efficient ways of practicing care to enjoy better health at lower cost and with lower risk of error. But he understands that if we want to enjoy the fruits of revolutionary innovation in health care, we must accept the destruction of existing ways of doing business. We simply cannot hope to achieve such progress without existing interests being hurt. In the years ahead, Topol expects "some 50 to 70 percent of office visits to become redundant, replaced by remote monitoring, digital health records, and virtual house calls." He also believes that "any home can theoretically be transformed into a mobile intensive-care unit. . . . Given that there are 100,000 fatalities in hospitals in the United States each year . . . there are some favorable trade-offs for monitoring people in their home." I don't know if Topol is right about health care's future, but his ideas are a powerful reminder of how there's no reason that the phrases "advanced technology" and "high costs" have to go together in health care.

Does our system allow for creative destruction in health care? Remember that any genuinely transformative idea is likely to initially seem inefficient, ineffective, or too expensive in the context of the existing ways of doing business. Markets allow for creative destruction, but it's difficult for a democratic government to advance the process in the face of opposition from powerful incumbent interests in health care. In most other industries, we recognize business interests as serving their own narrow agenda; in health care, these groups have been transformed by Island language—and the government's expansive role—into "stakeholders" whose interests are worth protecting as public policy. But there can be no real transformation—much less cost control—if the interests of any stakeholders can supersede the interests of patients-consumers. So the more the government's role in health care increases, the less open the system is likely to be to the types of experimentation, new approaches, and new business models that can ultimately produce transformation.

Government policy hasn't encouraged green shoots in the hope that one of them proves to be the shipping container of health care; its greater effect has been to freeze existing arrangements in place. Island experts believe that we can fix the massive dysfunctions of the Beast—cost, waste, error, and service—through thoughtful reform that fits the interests of current stakeholders. In other words, through reform that avoids the "destruction" part of "creative destruction."

For those who believe in the power of experimentation—in encouraging variety for the sake of identifying real improvement—the ACA is a profound disappointment. Drafted on the Island, the ACA treats many of the experiments discussed in this chapter as mistakes, aberrations, and evidence of system failure. The ACA's primary thrust is to complete—rather than reform—our horrifically dysfunctional health care system. By expanding insurance and Medicaid, reducing flexibility, and driving better care through centralized regulation, this is "reform" by stakeholders. It makes genuine transformation only more difficult.

Green shoots will continue to exist in health care: markets will always crop up wherever human needs go unsatisfied. But creative destruction—the transformation of health care to produce truly better medicine at lower cost and risk—will almost certainly have to wait until consumers are in charge.

CHAPTER 11

Transition

Can we get there from here?

For almost eighty years in America, the left and right have been arguing about health care. To the left, it's a fundamental right of all citizens, one the government should guarantee and even fund from our collective resources. To the right, while society might want to aid those most in need, health care is fundamentally best left to the market to maximize innovation, quality, and efficiency.* Most of our health policy can be described as a compromise between these two positions. And what compromise has bequeathed us is an indescribable and complex mess.

I think the extremes of both the left and right offer something essential to a solution to our health care problems. I agree with the left that we need a true cradle-to-grave safety

---

* In today's political terms, leaving matters to the private sector usually means leaving them to private insurance. To be consistent, conservatives should recognize that the insurance model has taken over health care because of the enormous tax and legal advantages afforded it by government. A true free-market reform of health care would be unlikely to feature so prominent a role for insurance.

net for every American—simple, straightforward, and reliable. But the right is correct that we are unlikely to build an innovative, high-quality, accountable system of care at sustainably affordable prices unless we leave most of it to market incentives.

Rather than see these two ideas as being in fundamental, irreconcilable conflict, we need to understand how they can actually be supportive of each other. I've argued that the only way to restore normal functioning and incentives in health care is to regain our status as customers—to eliminate the Surrogates and deal directly with providers. However, in our current reality, such a course appears highly risky to most people; all we've known is soaring prices, incomprehensible complexity, and dismissive service. It may well take a leap of faith to accept that restoration of a consumer role in health care will lead to the same results as in other industries. But if we can ensure that every American has straightforward lifetime protection against the cost of catastrophe, it should give us the confidence to rebuild our health care system.

My answer to those who argue for national health insurance or for a market-based system is to do both. Let's provide national insurance to everyone but not for everything. Then let's run the rest of the enormous resources now running through our insurers, Medicare, and Medicaid through individuals to pay for the health care expenses that aren't true catastrophes—from routine exams, to the management of illnesses and standard chronic conditions, to the predictable infirmities of old age.

Today, most of us seem unalterably dependent on the current system—few have any health savings. So how can we achieve this reform from here? There are two key elements. First is to recognize that it will take time—maybe as long as a generation—to fully transition everyone to the new system. At the start, many people will have to remain in our existing structures or they won't be able to afford care. The second is that as quickly as possible we must divert as much of the resources spent on noncatastrophic care into individual accounts. The faster this happens, the more quickly the health care industry will reorganize itself to serve consumer, rather than Surrogate, needs. And the faster that happens, the more quickly we all will see the benefits of an industry competing on price, quality, and service—just like everyone else does today on the Mainland.

Room for customers

Becky and the rest of us will put $2.5 trillion into health care this year. And we will spend all that $2.5 trillion. So how can we build the health savings necessary to generate a consumer-oriented system?

We have only three possible options: increase the amount we put into health care above $2.5 trillion and save that incremental amount; reduce the amount of health care provided to some people so that others may build savings; or cut our current spending in a way that doesn't affect the quality of care and transfer that amount to savings. I believe only the third course is acceptable. What follows is a conceptual plan—admittedly, something of a thought experiment—for how to make that transition.

What's our goal here? If the widely quoted statement that 25 percent of health care is wasted is true, we're looking at a roughly $625 billion annual opportunity for savings.

We won't achieve all of that, of course: consumer-based care will have its own inefficiencies. So let's use a less ambitious benchmark. The 2011 RAND study of high-deductible plans showed spending savings of roughly 15 percent a year even with only a $1,000 deductible. My approach is likely to have far more impact on people's spending preferences and industry responses, but let's use the RAND number. Let's not apply it to all health care expenditures but "just" to the 30 percent accounted for by the least intense users (that is, 90 percent of the population, recalling the common statistic that 70 percent of health care is used by only 10 percent of the population each year). So that means our base goal is to rely on a consumer-directed approach to save 15 percent on 30 percent of our total spending, which translates into approximately $115 billion a year. We should also be able to achieve very large savings in insurance administration savings— say, two-thirds of its current $150 billion direct cost. So our base goal is $215 billion in savings a year—that's $215 billion transferred from care to savings. In a decade, we'll be sitting on a national health nest egg of more than $2 trillion!

I believe we'll do much better. But let's start with this unambitious goal in building our new system. Here's a test: as you look at the implications for your own family of the new system, ask yourself how much you might expect to save when most of the money you're spending comes out of your own pocket.

Though the following blueprint may seem detailed, it's intended to be more of a conceptual framework. For simplicity of illustration, it freezes our population and spending patterns at current levels. In reality, our population is aging, and our health spending is growing faster than income (or inflation). But the ideas are intended to illustrate that moving to a new system without excessively exposing any part of our population to new risk is possible. And in evaluating this radical approach, please don't compare it to a mythical perfect system. Not only is perfection not an option, but we have a far more relevant comparison at hand: our crumbling system, with all its growing threats to your well-being.

BALANCE

There are three major components of what I'll call the Balanced Health System (BALANCE): health accounts, health loans, and catastrophic insurance with a very high deductible (TruCat). Essentially, all the money that now goes into the insurance system or for out-of-pocket payments (and, as I'll show later, the government money that now runs through Medicare and Medicaid) will run through your individual Health Account. As in Becky's system, that account will be yours over your entire life. The Account will enable you to accumulate funds on a segregated tax-free basis for a health rainy day. And you will use it to pay premiums on your cradle-to-grave TruCat insurance. If you ever run out of money for care expenses, your Health Account can borrow against your future contributions through a Health Loan (discussed in more detail below). TruCat needs to function as a nonunderwritten cradle-to-grave program, so it should be most efficient as a single pool. There may well be a way to structure this with private sector involvement, but for our purposes, let's assume TruCat is managed by a self-supporting nonprofit corporation (let's call it TruCat Corp.) with a strictly limited mandate.*

---

* If TruCat is just a form of catastrophic health insurance, why does it need to be run by the government? Why wouldn't it benefit from the competition of private insurance companies fighting for customers?

    TruCat is insurance, but it is also social insurance—an expression of our society's commitment to help those who suffer health catastrophes. I suspect that for

As discussed above, TruCat doesn't attempt to cover care for every health problem for every person. It will cover everyone, but only for the treatment of truly rare, truly major, and truly unpredictable health problems. TruCat will be low-premium, extremely high deductible insurance. And while I know many Americans hate mandates, I think we do need to require that every citizen maintain a TruCat policy every year of his or her life.

So what will TruCat cover? Let's go back to that Island statistic that 70 percent of health care expenses in any given year are used by only 10 percent of the population. That

---

these types of risks—a child born with cystic fibrosis, a young woman diagnosed with breast cancer, a man left paralyzed after a car accident, a senior suffering a major stroke—any pool smaller than the whole society will be too expensive for those most vulnerable.

One of the many misleading "truisms" in health care today is that group insurance should be cheaper than individual insurance because health risks are pooled. So your company policy should carry a lower premium than your individual policy. Perhaps this was true as a general rule in the recent past, but the growing sophistication of data analysis means that merely establishing a group of people won't reduce risk. Would you charge a lower premium to one healthy, nonsmoking, physically fit young man (i.e., no prospective pregnancy) whose parents lived into their nineties or to a company with a thousand employees with an average smoking and obesity rate?

You can think of the skill of the insurance business as correctly assigning to each type of risk an adequate dollar amount of premium. Or you can think of it as finding the lowest possible risks for each dollar of premium. If we had private insurers compete for TruCat business, they would certainly compete on the basis of their skill in excluding risks from their pools. The most profitable TruCat company would be the one that had most cleverly limited risk. As the ACA demonstrates, many health experts think they can prevent this competition through nondiscrimination rules, but the more likely result is more innovative forms of discrimination.

Powerful data-mining and analytic tools will make discrimination in insurance ever easier. But the greater risk is our increasing knowledge of genetic factors in disease. As the ability to target genetic disposition to specific ailments expands, future diseases will appear as "preexisting conditions" from an insurer's perspective. I suspect the only way to guarantee nondiscrimination in our TruCat pool is by establishing one pool that includes all of us.

would translate to $1.8 trillion being used by thirty-one million people—or roughly $60,000 per person. Let's say our goal is for half of those expenses to be covered by savings (through the high TruCat deductible). That means we need TruCat to fund $900 billion a year. That translates to an annual premium of approximately $3,000 per American per year, assuming we divide up this catastrophic risk equally.

But we shouldn't. An annual premium of $3,000 per person is too big a bill for a family, even assuming we transfer 100 percent of their current insurance premiums to their Health Accounts. So let's say that the annual premium is $750 for people under twenty-one and $2,000 for people under thirty. That would make the annual premium for everyone else approximately $4,000. (I should probably remind readers here—and in every paragraph—that since BALANCE will be running roughly $2 trillion more a year through individuals' own accounts, it's a mistake to put each element in the context of your current financial situation. When the whole system is viewed together, everyone should have roughly similar access to health care services without putting in more money.)

If TruCat is funding half of catastrophic costs, that suggests a deductible of $30,000, obviously very high in today's insurance-driven system.* Practically, it would also make sense for this deductible to rise with age, starting off at $10,000 for younger people and capping somewhere around $50,000 for older people. Because all Americans would be eligible for Health Loans, no one would be unable to pay the

---

* In practice, it would probably make more sense for TruCat to use a lifetime deductible (possibly a lifetime deductible with an ongoing co-pay) rather than an annual one.

deductible; rising deductibles merely reflect the longer time people would have had to accumulate savings.*

Easing into reform

Let's assume that all elements of BALANCE are put into place for everybody immediately. So we all have a Health Account† and a TruCat policy. Obviously, we'd have to make other arrangements for almost all Americans; after all, few today could afford these high deductibles or have savings to start their Health Accounts. So in order to launch TruCat, we'll need to phase in the effective cost of high deductibles. To do so, let's divide the population into three groups.

People in the first group—our existing Medicare beneficiaries and those, let's say, who are fifty-five and up—see no real change in the way they make contributions into the system and the levels of benefits they take out. From the seniors' perspective, Medicare will continue doing exactly what it does now. Behind the scenes, Medicare pays beneficiaries' TruCat premiums and the high deductibles and receives any claim money. To the beneficiaries in this group—who lack the financial resources to participate in a consumer-driven scheme—it's as if TruCat doesn't exist.‡

---

* Just as Singapore has rules governing what can be paid for out of Medisave, there will have to be rules governing what expenses are eligible for payment using these tax-advantaged instruments, as well as some that protect the profligate from themselves.

† There are obviously a variety of ways Health Accounts could be established, invested, and administered. One would assume they would be required to be low risk, with the bulk of their investments maintained in government instruments. Because this discussion is intended to be conceptual, I'm ignoring both the credit risk inherent in any investment and the investment income that would presumably add to availability of health savings.

‡ Again, this transition is intended to be very gradual. But it might not be necessary to allow everyone aged fifty-five to sixty-four to receive full Medicare. Even

At the other end of the spectrum, for people in Becky's age bracket—let's say all people under thirty-five—the full BALANCE is implemented. So Becky's cohorts are required to put some percentage—probably 15 percent up to a maximum figure to start—of their pretax income into their Health Accounts (including the amount necessary to pay their TruCat premium).* They bear the full TruCat deductibles, but they're also entitled to Health Loans—advances on their future Health Account contributions that can cover unanticipated health needs (including a TruCat deductible). This group—and everyone born hereafter—is fully enrolled in BALANCE.

The middle group—let's say people thirty-six to fifty-four—will transition gradually from our existing system to BALANCE. Like everyone else, they will immediately have TruCat insurance. They will also be required to open Health Accounts and, like the younger group, to make annual contributions to them. Because they are replacing existing health insurance with TruCat, lower premiums will allow people in this transitional group to accumulate some

---

encouraging just the better-off to accumulate health savings and opt out of full Medicare would help transform the industry.

* To make BALANCE work in transition will require maintaining some of our existing arrangements and evolving others. For example, health insurance is tax advantaged; most premiums are either tax-free compensation or tax-deductible expense. Tax-advantaging so much of health care has been a key factor in shifting resources from everything else in society to health care, but for a transition, we'll actually have to expand the tax break. Whether money goes to private insurance or Health Accounts, it should be equally tax advantaged.

Similarly, although we're replacing employer-provided insurance over time, maintaining employer funding will be essential in making a transition work. Employers with existing insurance coverage will be required to maintain the amount of funding per employee (again, subject to inflation) as we move from an insurance paradigm to a TruCat/Health Account system.

Over time, if BALANCE succeeds in disciplining health savings, we should be able to phase out the tax advantages and employer mandates; after all, both distort the trade-off between health care and other values.

savings—even if not a lifetime of savings—in their Health Accounts (some of this, of course, they will need for out-of-pocket expenses).

Once the people in the transition group reach Medicare eligibility, they will be expected to bear an increasing share of their health care expenses out of accumulated savings. Expressed differently, Medicare will cover less of their expenses that fall under the TruCat deductible than it does for today's seniors.

I imagine this working on a graduated basis. For example, a fifty-four-year-old today would still receive Medicare at sixty-five but would be required to bear a greater percentage of her costs out-of-pocket. In today's system, that fifty-four-year-old might bear $13,000 in insurance and out-of-pocket costs for a policy covering her and a spouse. TruCat premiums would cost $8,000 a year, leaving $5,000 for out-of-pocket expenses and savings. So if our fifty-four-year-old and spouse spent $3,000 a year on their care, they would each have $11,000 in health savings at sixty-five. For every additional year prior to Medicare eligibility, we could require this transitional generation to contribute an additional amount— probably in the range of $500 to $750—to their cost sharing once Medicare eligible. For thirty-five-year-olds today, it would be reasonable to expect health savings of between $30,000 and $40,000 by the time they reach Medicare age. By the time Becky's peers hit their sixty-fifth birthday— in thirty years—Medicare would add no new beneficiaries.*

---

* Let's look at an average American family at various ages at the beginning of transition to BALANCE. The life experiences in each will be the same in this simplified analysis: married at twenty-seven (and single-earner family), twins at thirty, empty nest at fifty. Let's assume we keep everything about government-supported programs the same so there's no change in any of the contributions made to the

The first decade of the transition will undoubtedly involve a rapid buildup of Health Loans among those who suffer major illness before their Medicare years. In today's insurance system, we transfer the excess premiums paid by the healthy to the sick through insurance claims. In BAL-

---

health care system through taxes. For simplicity, let's also ignore health care cost increases, general inflation, and interest earned on health savings:

		CURRENT SYSTEM		BALANCE		
Age	Status	Insurance Premiums	Out-of-Pocket	TruCat Premium	Annual "excess" available	Accumulated up to age 65 available for health expenses/ savings
22	single	$ 6,000	$ 250	$2,000	$4,250	$ 242,000
30	married, 2 kids	$16,000	$1,000	$9,500	$7,500	$ 214,000
40	married, 2 kids	$16,000	$1,000	$9,500	$7,500	$ 139,000
50	married	$11,000	$1,000	$8,000	$4,000	$ 64,000
60	married	$11,000	$1,000	$8,000	$4,000	$ 24,000

This table shows the immediate impact of the transition to BALANCE. For a twenty-two-year-old, her TruCat premium of $2,000 a year is $4,250 less than her current annual insurance premium and out-of-pocket cost. For a thirty-year-old with kids, this excess is $7,500 per year. For these two, the amount of "excess" cash that BALANCE frees from their expenses under the current system will accumulate to more than $200,000 by the time they reach sixty-five. Some of this excess will be needed to pay their out-of-pocket health costs over that time, and their TruCat deductible should they suffer health catastrophe. But for most people, a substantial share will accumulate as savings.

For our fifty- and sixty-year-olds, there's probably not enough time to accumulate sufficient savings to be fully transitioned to BALANCE. The fifty-year-old will have only $64,000 and the sixty-year-old will have only $24,000 in excess to spend on out-of-pocket; so we would expect that for them Medicare will continue to supplement their noncatastrophic expenses to roughly the same extent as today.

The forty-year-old is in the middle: her $139,000 in accumulated excess under BALANCE is probably enough to hit age sixty-five with substantial health savings (even with an estimated $3,000 per year in annual out-of-pocket expenses, she will reach sixty-five with $64,000 in health savings). We would expect that Medicare would still be available to help with some of her noncatastrophic expenses, but at a lower rate of subsidy than available to the fifty- and sixty-year-olds.

Remember that 40 percent of our spending on health care—the amount spent on Medicare and Medicaid—is unaffected by this simplified analysis. The more money we can run through BALANCE, the more prices are likely to moderate, and then the more likely we'll have even more of our current health care bill available for savings (which is exactly what has happened in Singapore).

ANCE, these excess premiums are now savings in Health Accounts; those whose health needs exceed their savings—likely to be a large number in the early years, declining over time—will take out Health Loans. So the flow of funds remains the same, but the mechanism is different. Most important, this new mechanism puts individuals in charge of their health spending—even with money borrowed from the system—and avoids all the distortions and costs of our current overinsured approach.

This transition takes a full generation. It is intentionally unambitious because I suspect most Americans will be very skeptical of the benefits of a radical transformation such as BALANCE. However, even starting this slow transition will mean a significant percentage of the health industry's patients immediately turning into customers. I expect this effect to be transformative—and I expect the resulting savings will mean that a much faster transition will be not only possible but desirable to most Americans. As health savings accumulate faster—and the industry reforms itself to chase customers—Americans will become more comfortable with taking over their health care resources. And if this transformation leads to real savings—true price competition, waste reduction, and efficiency incentives—BALANCE will become massively overfunded, allowing us to speed up the transition and accelerate the benefits of a consumer-driven system.

Anyone left out in the cold?

Every American won't have equal resources to participate in BALANCE. Though that's true of our current system, the superior economics of BALANCE should enable us to do better.

We'll spend $400 billion this year on Medicaid, and for the sake of this analysis, let's assume that all of that money needs to be spent—that none can be diverted to health savings by a more consumer-oriented industry. Even so, we should establish TruCat coverage and Health Accounts for all Medicaid beneficiaries. To the greatest extent possible, we should run all of their expenses—and their contributions— through the same BALANCE system, enabling these beneficiaries to have the same sense of ownership of their health resources as everyone else.

In fact, when you count all the tax dollars used to subsidize Medicare premiums, the entire Medicaid program, and "uncompensated" care funded by the government, we are now spending over $1 trillion in government funds on helping people pay for health care. That could fund a grant of $10,000 per person per year for fully a third of our population (or cover 40 percent of the population if the grant is limited to our current per capita average spending of $8,500). In the near-term transition, some of these funds will be needed to forgive Health Loans; some who borrow to cover the TruCat deductible will not have enough years (or possibly health) to generate the savings necessary to repay their Health Loans. But over time, as consumer-driven care creates a more efficient health care system, we should be able to transfer a little, then hopefully ever more, from merely paying for needy people's care to helping them fund a meaningful personal safety net by making contributions to their personal Health Accounts.*

* Implementing BALANCE immediately alters the finances of Medicare and Medicaid. Remember that we're going to implement TruCat for all citizens immediately, but no one on Medicare or Medicaid today may notice in terms of benefit levels. However, from the government's bookkeeping perspective, seniors and Medicaid beneficiaries will contribute roughly 35 percent of TruCat premiums but

The ACA calls for increased government spending of roughly $100 billion a year to get people insured. Since the insurance-uninsurance dichotomy goes away in BALANCE, perhaps we can use this money to seed the Health Accounts of Americans who are less well off. Or we can spend all ten years' worth of the bill's cost at once and put $10,000 in the Health Accounts of the lowest-income one hundred million Americans up front. Now that would be transformative.

That's a lot of change, but it leaves us with a far simpler system than we have today. It secures everyone, from the cradle to the grave, against catastrophe. It turns all of us into purchasers of most of our health care and runs the economics of the system through our individual accounts. It protects those dependent on the current system while maximizing the transformative effects of the new system.

But although BALANCE in itself will transform health care, there is an additional opportunity to use the new TruCat itself to change the nature of that care.

A new type of health insurance

Shortly after the publication of my *Atlantic* article, a man attending a public discussion asked me: "I understand why I'd be better off if I could directly spend the $1.6 million I

---

collect—I would estimate—around 60 percent of its benefits. What this means is that TruCat winds up transferring about $225 billion from privately covered people under sixty-five to the Medicare and Medicaid programs. How do we rebalance the numbers and return the money to those under sixty-five?

Today, employed people pay roughly $200 billion a year in Medicare payroll taxes. The TruCat structure allows this tax to be completely eliminated, enabling employees to put additional amounts into their health accounts each year (almost $850 a year for someone with Becky's income). Or we could continue collecting the tax but use the proceeds to equalize Health Account contributions—transferring funds from higher-income earners to the Health Accounts of low-income people.

put into our health care system, but how could I afford it if I contracted a particularly difficult case of cancer that cost $2 million to treat?" I'm embarrassed to admit I responded to this very good question with a less-than-serious quip: "How could anyone afford to charge you $2 million if you only had $1.6 million?" But the more I think about my poorly expressed remark, the more I suspect it suggests the right approach to capping our exposure to unlimited treatment costs.

One of our greatest health fears is that we'll contract an illness so severe, and so complicated to fight, that its cost will outstrip available resources no matter what financial structure we put in place. Even a government system, we know, has some limits (thus the emotions around the fictional "death panels"). Of course, our very efforts to protect ourselves against this eventuality—paying for any open-ended insurance—wind up encouraging the problem. A customer who will pay "whatever it takes" to treat an illness is one who will be charged as much as conceivable; at the upper end of disease treatment prices, we see charges that have no relationship whatsoever to marginal or comparable cost.

If you're from the Island, you believe cost is what cost is, and so it's natural that complex diseases that take a long time to treat will be extraordinarily expensive. If you're from the Mainland, you recognize that the seriousness of the illness—and the desperation of the patient—means treatment is especially valuable, giving providers the ability to charge high prices.

How can we use TruCat to tame this tendency without leaving our sickest most exposed? I propose that TruCat pay out claims on a kind of defined-benefit basis, a new type of hybrid insurance.

Let me explain in terms of Becky. At forty, our friend Becky is diagnosed with cancer. She has a $25,000 deductible on her TruCat policy but more than enough accumulated in her Health Account to cover it.

To find treatment, Becky and her primary physician check the TruCat Corp.'s beneficiary website and enter her diagnosis. She finds that TruCat Corp. will pay a fixed $100,000 treatment benefit (subject to her deductible) to cover her particular stage of cancer. Becky also enters her zip code and finds that five provider groups near her home will accept the benefit as payment for full treatment. Under TruCat Corp.'s rules, all five must accept Becky as a patient at that price if she chooses them.

Each year, the trustees of TruCat Corp. are responsible for matching the total payouts under TruCat policies with the total premiums paid in. On a regular basis, TruCat Corp. updates its diagnosis-benefit schedule to reflect trends in diagnosis and treatment. It will pay benefits only to those providers who can fully treat a disease and who will charge no more than the TruCat benefit. To get more business, providers can offer to treat a disease for less than the benefit (and we could structure TruCat so that patients can share in some or all of this savings, possibly through a decreased deductible), but they cannot charge more than the benefit and still receive TruCat funds.

Now back to my quip. Because TruCat is the dominant payer of major medical, it's hard to see how anyone can make a living charging more than it pays. Of course, some patient cases are more complex than others. But moving the risk of varied complexity of treatment from payers (where it resides today) to providers increases provider interest in efficiency, creating the type of cost-savings incentives that exist in the Mainland.

TruCat will also force providers to coordinate currently disaggregated services to provide catastrophic care; there simply won't be any other way to qualify for payment. But the touch here is lighter than the ACA's approach to forcing integration through complex rules. TruCat will not tell providers how they should be organized; it won't regulate their division of labor. That's up to the providers to figure out; this flexibility—the ability to experiment with different treatment and business models—allows positive incentives to do their work in our health care system.

Let's add another feature to TruCat Corp.'s structure to control costs: premiums will increase each year by no more than inflation. This would lock in our current level of per capita catastrophic spending and force health care to perform for that amount. Like all major industries on the Mainland, health care will have limited ability to raise prices above inflation; its only hope for improved profitability will be improvements in productivity and efficiency.

In the context of our current system, TruCat Corp. is radical. It abandons the cost-plus mentality that underpins most of our assumptions about care. For forty-five years, we have been concentrating paying authority in large Surrogates—believing they have the market power to control costs. They failed because—as discussed in chapter 3—they actually have very little real incentive to control care costs. TruCat Corp.'s structure doesn't just give it an incentive to control costs; its structure gives it no choice but to control costs.

TruCat represents a radical approach to controlling health care costs—something we haven't tried. For the first time ever, a government program will attempt to control health care spending by spending less money on health care.

Health account loans

I must admit that Health Loans are the least popular idea I have ever raised. A cleaned-up version of a typical comment is: "Oh great, as if our existing health care system isn't bad enough, your idea is that I go into debt to pay for health care?" The individual components of BALANCE look unattractive on their own; only together do they produce a better result for all of us. Health Loans are a perfect example. The reason they work is that they transfer money from our future selves to our current selves without the intervention of the insurance system. Since the insurance system takes somewhere around twenty cents out of every dollar every year for its own costs and profit (and then wastes a large amount in medical excess), it's a very expensive alternative to debt. This, of course, is why no one outside of health care uses insurance to transfer money from their future self to their present self.

Let's say Becky has $10,000 in her Health Account and a $25,000 TruCat deductible. Becky has a skating accident and breaks several bones, needing $20,000 in treatment. That's too little for Becky's TruCat to kick in, so she needs another $10,000 to fund treatment. Becky's Health Account borrows that $10,000, and this loan would be paid back from her Health Account over time.*

---

* Health Loans could be a government, a government-guaranteed, or a fully private function. In any case, the government would need to enforce a Health Account contribution mandate. I would imagine these loans would be paid out of 20 percent of future contributions to Becky's health account. So if Becky is depositing $5,000 a year into her health account, the loan would be paid out over ten

Health Loans would be payable only from Health Accounts, not from personal funds. So the availability of these loans allows for the smoothing out of uneven expenditures on care, without affecting a borrower's other choices or priorities. The loans are another reason we need a Health Account contribution mandate; the required contribution allows for the Health Account itself to be collateral for a loan.

Of course, some share of society's subsidy of care for the less well off, or the very ill, will take the form of loan forgiveness. Any American with a loan balance in excess of, say, ten years of expected payback can write the balance down to that amount. And any American who dies with a health loan balance greater than his Health Account balance could have the excess loan forgiven.

Some Americans may have large annual expenditures for their care that don't qualify for TruCat reimbursement. Their need for Health Loans may not be temporary, and so their loan balances will grow. Loan forgiveness has the effect of subsidizing their unique care needs. But as with all elements of BALANCE, the subsidy goes directly to people, rather than to providers, reducing the incentives that have caused even Medicaid spending to balloon while our population got richer and healthier.

All elements of BALANCE are based on the concept that, however imperfect, people in aggregate will prove better stewards for health resources than the Surrogates have been. But for some of our citizens, merely funding their care—and giving them full access to the mainstream health care system—will not be enough. For those citizens whose

---

years (yes, I know I'm ignoring interest—for simplicity's sake). Or if she wanted to, Becky could pay off her loan faster.

physical or mental incapacities prevent them from managing their own health care, we will need a network of health advocates who can act for them in managing their Health Accounts and in applying benefits under TruCat. This problem isn't unique to BALANCE; many citizens have trouble navigating the system today. But health advocates in BALANCE will have one important advantage over our current assistance to the incapacitated: with the government no longer a principal in health care (that is, no longer seeking to directly control the cost of treatment), patient advocates will be much freer—truly unconflicted—in fighting for the best interests of their clients.

Who do you trust?

Though HMOs have been around since at least the 1930s, enrollment only took off beginning in the mid-1970s. As employers began to struggle with health insurance costs, the business model of the HMO—integrating provider care rather than funding fee-for-service medicine—suggested the possibility of cost control. Although experts argue whether the HMO model actually did control costs, the rapid growth of HMOs in the 1990s was coincident with a rare break in U.S. health care inflation. During that decade, enrollment grew from thirty-three million to eighty million. Per capita annual health inflation declined dramatically throughout the first half of the decade, from over 10 percent for the years 1988 to 1990 to just over 4 percent by 1996 before rising again.

However, Americans' general attitudes toward their HMOs is well summarized by the following exchange from the 1997 movie *As Good as It Gets:*

CAROL CONNELLY: Fucking HMO bastard pieces of shit!
BEVERLY CONNELLY: Carol!
CAROL CONNELLY: Sorry.
DR. MARTIN BETTES: It's okay. Actually, I think that's
their technical name.

Americans hated their HMOs despite their seeming success at constraining costs and despite the lack of evidence
that the HMO approach to care had any negative effects
on overall health or treatment. There were plenty of anec-
dotes about the apparently heartless results of the bureaucratic approach of HMOs to managing care; politicians and
regulators threatened all sorts of rules that would undercut
HMOs' ability to save money. The HMO of today is little
more than a preferred provider network.

Americans hated HMOs because they sometimes said
no. Indeed, it's the inability to say no to American citizens
that characterizes our government's health care programs.
The U.S. government will spend just under 10 percent
of GDP on public support of health care this year. That's
roughly comparable to the levels spent by Sweden, the Neth-
erlands, and Canada. But whereas these countries cover their
entire population on that amount, U.S. programs cover only
about a third of our population. And when we look at Medicare, we understand why: U.S. government programs have
little leeway to deny any care—no matter how wasteful or
excessive—to their beneficiaries.

I have discussed the debate over the efficacy of the expensive cancer drug Avastin. When the FDA announced that
it would not allow the drug to be prescribed for treatment
of late-stage breast cancer—because it didn't believe it was
effective—Medicare reassured its beneficiaries with an

announcement the next day that it would continue covering the drug anyway. The ACA's "tough" new Medicare cost control agency has a mandate that prohibits it from even *considering* a reduction in services to achieve required spending cuts!

Critics of consumer-driven health ideas often suggest that the United States should look toward national insurance models in other developed countries. As discussed earlier, I believe these models seem sustainable only in contrast to our own system. But even if we were convinced that, over time, the variety of state-led national insurance models would continue to work in other developed countries, do we really believe they would work in the United States? Is there any real tradition here of a politically insulated bureaucracy that has the authority to make such personal decisions? Can we imagine any discipline imposed by a national health agency surviving the first complaint from a potential Iowa caucus voter to a presidential candidate?

BALANCE may appear radical, but it's not so dissimilar to the health account and catastrophic insurance system in Singapore. It may take a health system collapse and a complete rethinking of our health care assumptions even to consider something like BALANCE. But BALANCE indicates that it is quite possible to keep our health security while transforming our health care system through the normal positive incentives that dominate the production and distribution of normal goods and services. If we ever choose to, it's possible to tow this Island back to the Mainland. And at least then someone with the necessary authority and respect to say no to an American will be in charge—we will.

Mae West Didn't Know Health Care

"When the facts change, I change my mind. What do you do, sir?"

—JOHN MAYNARD KEYNES

My first job after college in the early 1980s was in mortgage finance on Wall Street. In my third year, I was assigned to the team covering Fannie Mae and Freddie Mac, the two big mortgage insurers. These government-sponsored enterprises (GSEs) were lucrative clients, early adopters of financial market innovations that enabled them to raise enormous amounts of capital essential for their operations.

Fannie Mae and Freddie Mac were both created to increase American homeownership by lowering the cost of mortgage loans. They were able to borrow funds at lower interest rates than banks because the markets assumed the government was effectively guaranteeing their debt. In theory, the GSEs could pass these interest savings on to borrowers by making these less costly funds available to mortgage lenders.

I can't say that at the time I gave much thought to the public policy implications of the activities of these two mortgage giants. But I do remember being struck by an irony at the very core of their operations. To ensure that the GSEs were aiding middle-class Americans—and not wealthy homeowners—their lending programs were restricted to loans of a maximum size. When I started work in 1983, this conforming loan limit was $108,300. But to reflect the steady increase in home prices, the conforming limit was raised almost every year for the next twenty-three years. From 1983 through 2006, the conforming loan limit grew to $417,000—a 6 percent annual increase.

Even as an entry-level banker, I couldn't help wondering if Fannie's and Freddie's very success in making mortgages cheaper for borrowers wasn't merely countermanded by causing home prices to rise. When we think of a GSE mortgage—or any government program—we see how it helps us as individuals. The GSEs enabled each of us to borrow money at a low rate. But of course, since all the potential borrowers for a new house could borrow at that same low rate, didn't that merely bid up the price of houses? So we all wound up with a lower interest rate on a bigger loan.

The GSEs were only one component—although a central one—of government efforts to make homeownership more affordable for middle-class Americans. A broad variety of tax and regulatory policies favored the good thing of homeownership. And these programs certainly seemed to be working. The share of American families owning a home grew from a fairly stable 64 percent in the 1960s to a peak just under 70 percent in 2004.

Despite this rise in homeownership, no one declared victory. No one said that we had achieved our goal and could now scale back our support. In fact, the accelerating home prices of the past decade led housing advocates and supportive politicians to ask what more could be done to help make housing affordable for those who still didn't own homes. Or, to borrow a term from health care, how homes could be made affordable for those who still lacked access to the home-buying market. Eventually, regulators, the private sector, and the GSEs came to accept subprime loans as the answer. Essentially, subprime loans were made to people who couldn't afford houses by traditional measures at any interest rate, no matter how low.

The causes of the housing crash that began in the United States in 2007 are complex. Subsequent housing crashes occurred in many parts of the developed world, despite a variety of local conditions. But the result of our crash is unambiguous: roughly eight million American homes were foreclosed, and an additional eleven million people owe mortgages exceeding the value of their homes. An estimated 10 percent of the population lost all liquid savings. The housing crash also destroyed the jobs of millions who had come to depend on the endless stimulus government provided to housing: 1.2 million residential construction workers lost their jobs, as did at least three hundred thousand mortgage brokers and credit officers. With all respect to Mae West, homeownership may be a good thing, but it turns out that too much of a good thing isn't always wonderful.

Helping a person buy his home is a real benefit. Helping everyone buy a home merely places society on an ever faster treadmill. This difference between the effects of aid to a single beneficiary and of aid to everyone seems to be difficult for our political process to understand. People who own homes, finance them, or build them are interested in seeing home prices rise. But those who don't yet own homes— those who care about affordability—really want prices to be as low as possible. Yet the politics of housing grouped these two together. Government programs supported high prices in housing while offering discount loans to help new buyers afford high prices—which, of course, only fueled high prices. As far as I know, no major advocate for the poor or lower middle class ever argued that the key to affordability was to phase out the government programs that propped up home prices.

In housing, we tried to repeal gravity. We pursued the contradictory goals of high home prices and greater affordability. Politics may make strange bedfellows, but the reality is that those pushing for greater affordability were on the wrong side. Broader access to homeownership could not be sustained by policies that pushed up prices. It doesn't matter if these advocates' intentions or motivations were good or noble; our housing policy wound up devastating a large number of middle-class Americans. Yet not even this devastation has caused a true rethinking in housing. No matter how dysfunctional a government policy, its very size can ensure its survival. Home builders, mortgage bankers, and those who already own homes benefit too much from rising prices; they want the treadmill restarted.*

---

* In an almost comical reminder of how difficult it is to change ingrained thinking, Fannie Mae and Freddie Mac still exist! Even after $130 billion in direct taxpayer bailout (with more to come), the two GSEs are still seen as essential to ensuring access to the dream of homeownership for our middle class. And the

So what hope do we really have in health care?

I've already shown how in health care too much of a good thing isn't wonderful, but rather downright dangerous. Our system creates massive incentives for excess care, which is not merely wasteful but—as Medicare data demonstrate—a real threat to the health of beneficiaries. Health care is unaccountable to its real customers, leading to incomprehensible error rates, miserable service, and erratic quality. Low productivity, minimal adoption of even common information technology, and mind-boggling administrative costs mean that even at 18 percent of GDP, the industry often fails to provide needed services to the most vulnerable. And for those in Becky's generation, the cost of health care is already an unsupportable financial burden—the greatest threat to their ability to maintain, much less improve, their real standard of living.

In response, we as a society are still in the "more" stage in health care, just like we were in housing. We believe we can make health care more affordable by spending more on health care. We counter forty-five years of failure by the Surrogates by giving them more control over the health economy. We address the inability of regulators to drive efficiency centrally by mandating that they do more to drive efficiency. And we meet the challenges of staggering industry complexity by passing the ACA, a bill so complicated that many supporters privately admit they don't understand its workings.

Will there be the equivalent of the housing crash in health care? Perhaps it will be the coming unaffordability of Medi-

---

financial reform legislation aimed at preventing a similar crisis in the future bears the names of two legislators who were longtime supporters of the failed system!

care (which not only has no hope of maintaining service levels for future beneficiaries but is increasingly unlikely to meet the perceived needs of current beneficiaries) or of Medicaid (in which the burgeoning demand for services of this bizarrely constructed safety net was already breaking state budgets before the ACA mandated a 40 percent expansion). Perhaps we'll see it in the job market, as companies and their employees figure out how to maintain wage levels while bearing the burden of accelerating insurance premiums—or as more companies drop health insurance altogether. Or perhaps in the medical profession itself, as doctors rebel against suffocating administrative requirements. Or from patients, as the hundred thousand deaths from error each year create an angry class of citizens who understand the destructive power of unaccountable health care.

How our society responds to the coming crisis will depend on whether our perceptions of health care change. This book has proposed a radical restructuring of our health care system. But what's really needed now is a change of philosophy, a new way to think about health care. Today, health care is, essentially, something we expect someone else to take care of. That won't work. Once we recognize the personal nature of health care, we can make a broad range of sensible changes—some quite minor—that can put us on the road to recovery. Imagining a new place for health care will depend on a new public understanding, not on expert opinion.

As in housing, many of the intellectual and emotional justifications for our current approach stem from an admirable desire to help those most vulnerable, least capable, or just plain unlucky. There is also the one reality that does make health care truly special: any of us can be afflicted with a major disease or struck down by an accident, and few of us will have the resources necessary to deal with such catastrophe. So most of us accept that some kind of health safety net is essential to a fair and well-functioning society.

But intentions are not the same as results. Our ability to protect the most vulnerable has been weakened, not strengthened, by our efforts to do so much in their name. And these efforts have paradoxically created even more vulnerable people—as Americans from Becky to her grandparents worry about their access to essential care as the real price of admission to our system goes up. At some point, we will have to decide whether our attachment to the idea of helping people is more important than actually helping them—a decision that will require a rethinking of our assumptions.

Dad's world

My father began his career as an intern at Bellevue Hospital in New York City. He'd gotten to know Bellevue well as a medical student at New York University; he told me that it was a presentation at the hospital on one of the few documented cases of a folie à trois (three people sharing a psychotic delusion) that stimulated his interest in psychiatry. Upon certification, my father looked for a community in the New York area that didn't yet have a practicing psychiatrist. He and my mother settled in a suburb in southern Nassau County. He visited all the other local physicians to introduce himself and seek referrals.

My father maintained a private practice in that town up to his last days. He focused on childhood, marriage, and family issues. Beginning in the mid-1960s, he offered a seminar at the local high school for teenagers who wanted to discuss rapidly changing norms of personal appearance, premarital sexuality, homosexuality, interracial relationships, and drug use. He wrote a column in the local newspaper. Every month, he hosted a dinner for local physicians to discuss emotional issues affecting medicine and their practices. Since he would never discuss the specifics of his practice with us, I learned of my father's successes only when his patients approached me on the street and told me how much he had helped them.

The practice of psychiatry changed massively over the last two decades of my father's life. Traditional talk therapy was squeezed out by the efficacy and economics of psychopharmacology. Managed-care organizations proved more aggressive in limiting the length of therapy and in requiring greater justification to approve any plan of treatment. My father didn't like all the changes in medicine, but he accepted them as the price of being a physician. He loved being a doctor, the sense of service and the intellectual challenge. And he believed that the greatest luxury in life was being able to do what you love for a living; I suspect that if the insurers had insisted, he might have been willing to pay them to see his patients.

My dad was fascinated by technological change but was skeptical of shortcuts. He sometimes prescribed the new drugs but was uncomfortable relying on them as an exclusive treatment. Perhaps he was too much of a traditionalist, but in fairness, what longtime practitioners—in any profession—aren't at least doubtful of the benefits of change? It's one reason that outside pressure (aka customers) are often so essential in driving true progress in any industry.

I sometimes wonder what my father would have thought of the circumstances of his own death. He retained much reverence for the profession of medicine and for its great institutions. Would that have tempered his anger at the carelessness that caused his life to be cut short? On the other hand, I have no doubt that he would have been furious at the mistake that recently caused my mother to be hospitalized. In response to pain, my mother had a CT scan of her abdomen (after a six-hour emergency room wait). The dyes were improperly flushed from her system, leading three days later to kidney failure (from which, fortunately, she quickly recovered).

Put aside the big policy questions in health care; my mother's experience is what we all see in our interactions with the health care system. It's the little picture, if you will.

We may be comforted by the idea that someone else is looking after our health and that clear medical answers exist to our inevitable health problems. From shamans to witch doctors to science-driven modern medicine, we've always been reassured when experts make these emotionally difficult decisions for us. We may now think of our Surrogate-dominated system in these terms. But we maintain this hope for reassurance even in the face of our experience—even though each and every one of us has at least one story about health care that has made us angry, resigned, or afraid.

My first major interaction with our health care system—my dad's death—led me to write this book. I knew my father was aging, and I didn't expect him to live forever. Seeing a loved one's life in the balance is a deeply emotional experience, and not ideal for careful decision making. We all need expert guidance at that moment. But let's stop kidding ourselves: even in our current system, we, the patients and loved ones, make all the important decisions. No one decides for us. And not only is a system that is not responsive to our needs unable to provide us genuine reassurance, it is simply dangerous.

Health care experts want us to believe that health care is too complicated for patients-consumers to serve as an effective disciplinary force. But what's the alternative? With my father, I saw the alternative in action. It is wasteful, expensive, erratic, unresponsive, and often unsafe. We're stuck in a vicious cycle in health care. The more we try to protect ourselves from the realities of care, the more complex and unconnected from us the system becomes. We respond to these problems by seeking greater protection, further distancing this system from our real needs.

Health care will respond to our needs—for true access, reasonable pricing, quality control, respectful customer service, and basic safety—only when we force it to. In towing the Island of Health Care back to the Mainland, we will be confronting our own fears. That won't be easy. But when we think about the "little picture"—the health care story about your wife or about your friend's child or about my father—we have little choice. We need to put ourselves back at the center of health care. It's what's best for our health.

Appendix 1

Unintended Consequences

Could the ACA reduce the number insured?

The essential goal of the ACA is to expand coverage to many of the currently uninsured, and much of the complexity of the legislation is explained by its efforts to achieve this goal without a fundamental break with our existing system. The same is true for ACA's important secondary goal—more insurance coverage per person. No longer will insurers be allowed to exclude preexisting conditions from coverage. Young adults up to age twenty-six are automatically eligible for coverage under their parents' policies. Cost sharing is limited so that the maximum out-of-pocket cost in a year can be no greater than $5,950 for individuals or $11,900 for families. The federal government will also get new power to force insurers to include a defined list of minimum benefits in all their policies.

In short, the bill seeks to reverse the growing burden of out-of-pocket expenses described in chapter 10—to have insurers pick up more of the tab—but without directly increasing the cost of health insurance to beneficiaries. Of course, *someone* must pay higher premiums to cover the costs of the greater benefits "reformed" insurance will provide. To some extent, the ACA merely shifts the immediate impact of these higher costs away from some groups (the insured, the sick uninsured) to others (taxpayers, the healthy, employers, and insurers). But fundamentally, the legislation is based on an assumption that a combination of greater competition among insurers, subsidies to the insured, and mandates will successfully balance four competing goals—expanded coverage, nondiscrimination by health status, lower out-of-pockets, and controlled premiums.

The balance is very delicate, and the sponsors of the ACA may have miscalculated on a number of elements. I suspect they viewed the ACA's complex web of new rules and structures as mostly add-ons to the current system, rather than alterations with the potential to change underlying incentives. Whatever the theory, I worry that structured exchanges are more likely to reduce rather than increase competition among insurers; subsidies, to make consumers less rather than more price sensitive and employers less rather than more likely to offer insurance; and mandates, to cause healthy people to drop rather than buy insurance. None of these effects are intended by the authors of ACA, but it seems to me that the new provisions working together are likely to reduce the value of insurance to the healthy and to employers and to lead to meaningful premium inflation. The dynamic impact could be less coverage at much higher costs to everyone than anticipated. It is even quite conceivable that enough employers could drop coverage and enough unsubsidized people are priced out of the individual insurance market, that the ACA accidentally reduces the total number insured. How is this possible?*

Half of the legislation's anticipated expansion of coverage

* A decline in private market participation (employer and individual policies) of just 6 percent would offset the eleven million additional people covered by Medicaid under the ACA at the Congressional Budget Office's current projections.

was projected to be achieved through the expansion of Medicaid eligibility (as of this writing, it's too early to tell if the Supreme Court's recent decisions will affect this estimate). But the ACA's intervention in the private insurance market is far more complex. Insurance itself will be made more inclusive through regulation. On their own, all the ACA's new goodies discussed above mean that insurers must pay out more in benefits than they do today; this must raise premiums. And all other things being equal, more expensive insurance would cause more companies and individuals to drop health insurance. The ACA addresses this risk through four mechanisms: requiring companies and individuals to buy insurance, establishing exchanges to maximize insurer competition and risk pooling, subsidizing those who can't afford premiums, and penalizing companies that spend too much on insurance for their employees. Each contains the seeds for massive unanticipated consequences.

Should you buy health insurance?

Buying health insurance is expensive, and the more directly exposed individuals are to actual premium costs, the less likely they are to buy insurance. Further, in most states, premiums for insurance for individuals are much higher than for companies.* Yet as fewer employers offer insurance more people will be forced to buy their health insurance in individual markets.

---

* There are a number of theories as to why this is the case. Many Island experts point to what they believe is the inherently higher cost of marketing to and administering insurance for a single policyholder than to a large group. Also blamed is the greater variation in underwriting individual risks. But it's not clear that either of these is the cause: after all, insurers serving other individual consumer markets have no problems pooling risk and administrative responsibilities. One difference may be that an employer-based health insurance grouping offers a fundamentally lower risk: by definition, employees are working, which means someone has vetted their basic productivity (a proxy for health) and is responsible for their honest identification of risks and expenses.

To help them, the ACA provides for newly established state insurance exchanges. The theory is that these exchanges can accomplish two things: they can make sure that all individuals have access to the same type of insurance without discrimination on the basis of their health or risk factors, and they can use competition to keep prices low. Unfortunately, in practice, the two goals are probably mutually exclusive.

Insurers will be allowed to post three types of policies on a state's exchange, each with minimum coverage standards set by the state. The policies—bronze, silver, and gold—are supposed to vary only in the share of the benefits covered by insurance. Seventy percent of benefits are covered by a bronze policy, 80 percent by silver, and 90 percent by gold—each subject to maximum out-of-pocket limits. All policies must be offered on an any-and-all basis, with highly constricted premium adjustments for only certain factors, such as age and smoking. The ACA's supporters envision exchanges as vibrant competitive markets where insurers seeking customers must operate in a transparent environment. Not only should individuals get the benefit of this highly competitive pricing, the any-and-all requirement means that they'll enjoy the benefits of community rating, just as big employers do. Further, since their customers will now come to them, insurers won't need to waste all that money on marketing.

But in practice, insurance exchanges are unlikely to work like commodity exchanges. On a commodity exchange, the identity of the seller, the buyer, and even the product has no impact on price: one corn futures contract is the same as any other. In insurance, the seller—the insurer—always cares a lot about who the customer is (i.e., how healthy that customer is). In fact, health insurers have only two basic tools to drive profitability: designing benefits packages and evaluating customer risk. The exchanges explicitly strip away both of these tools, so why, then, should we expect insurers to compete vigorously on exchanges for new business?

The theory behind these exchanges seems to be that if we prohibit insurers from competing on certain bases (such as health
risk and policy benefits), they will be forced to compete on price.
If you were an insurer and you couldn't know how risky your next
customer is, would you bid aggressively for his business, or would
you price your policies at a level that ensures you'll make money
no matter how sickly he is? Would you bid aggressively for a customer for the gold plan, or would you assume that anyone who
wants so much insurance must be high risk? Would you undercut
the price of a competitor, or would you be content to take your
share of the total business at a high price? Calling something
an exchange doesn't make it a marketplace: the design of these
exchanges seems almost certain to eliminate any reason for true
competition.

But that's not the only problem with the structure of the
exchanges. Any individual with an income up to $44,680 (or a
family with an income no greater than $92,200) can buy a sil-
ver policy on the exchange and have his annual premium capped
at 9.5 percent of income. The federal government picks up the
balance. Perversely, this subsidy for silver policies merely adds
to insurers' incentives to offer only high-price policies on the
exchange.

Think like an insurer instead of like a congressman: the
subsidy means that a significant number of your customers for
individual policies no longer care about price. If the silver level
premium clears 9.5 percent of their income—and for most Americans it will—it could be $1 million a year for all the customer
cares; the government covers the difference. Although insurers
will undoubtedly be politically savvy enough not to raise their
individual premiums to $1 million—at least not immediately—
the structure of the exchange subsidy is a businessperson's dream.

Now remember that the higher premiums incented by the
rules for these exchanges apply to all applicants for individual

insurance—not just to those who are eligible for a subsidy. So if you're forced into the individual insurance market—which is already expensive—you will now bear the additional premium cost resulting from the ACA's new mandated benefits, the exchanges' dampening of insurance competition, and the marketplace dominance of subsidized customers who don't care about price. So, will you still buy insurance if you're not eligible for the subsidy?

In theory, you no longer have a choice, no matter how expensive insurance becomes for the unsubsidized; the ACA includes a mandate that carries a maximum penalty of 2.5 percent of your income. But maybe that's not such a smart idea. Let's say you're earning a good income of $100,000 a year, have a family, and are forced into the individual insurance market. Even at today's rates, that means you're going to spend at least $15,000 on health insurance. If you paid the penalty, you'd save $12,500 a year, probably more than enough for your family's care.

But isn't that irresponsible? What if a member of your family gets seriously ill? In the past, you would have been exposed not only for this year's health cost but for all the future cost of that illness. But under the ACA, you have the automatic right to buy insurance, with your family member's preexisting sickness now covered (this is what's meant by banning the exclusion of preexisting conditions from coverage). There is some risk: depending on when someone gets ill, you may have to wait up to ten months for insurance to kick in. But you're saving $12,500 a year to help pay for that cost. The effect of eliminating preexisting conditions is perverse: it means that the risk of not having insurance is significantly lessened, which makes people less likely to buy it despite the mandate.*

---

* One of the main targets of the individual mandate is healthy young adults, who "underestimate" their chances of getting sick and so "undervalue" health insurance. If Becky didn't work for an employer offering insurance, her $7,800 in total

All this is a huge problem for the theory of how the ACA is supposed to work; the idea is that insurers can handle the burden of the new regulatory goodies because more of the healthy will be forced to buy insurance. But if the real result is that insurance's cost rises dramatically while its benefit for the healthy declines, we run the risk of the dreaded insurance "death spiral"—where only the sick buy insurance.*

The end of employer coverage?

The coming dysfunction in the individual market may not matter much if employers remain the source of most insurance coverage. And while the ACA continues the tax preferences that enabled the rise of employer-based insurance in the first place, its new interventions are likely to make providing insurance simultaneously both more expensive and less valuable for employers.

Under the ACA, almost all companies will be required to offer insurance to their employees, and companies not fulfilling this mandate are subject to a penalty of $2,000 per uncovered employee. But in the real world, this penalty is merely a price—

---

premiums would be subsidized as they exceed 9.5 percent of her income. So her choice would be to pay a capped $3,325 for a policy (plus her deductible for any care she uses) or to pay a penalty of $625 and pocket $2,700 for health expenses and any thing else she wants to spend her money on. Since she can always apply for insurance after she gets sick (because of the ban on preexisting condition exclusion), I'm not sure she opts for insurance, even with the subsidy. Also, if individual premiums continue to rise at double-digit rates, the subsidies may feel like a great deal on a relative basis. But of course, the flip side of that coin is that insurance will seem like an ever worse deal to the unsubsidized.

* Imagine if you were guaranteed the right to buy fire insurance without exclusion of preexisting conditions. A smart homeowner might wait until his house caught fire to apply for fire insurance. As more homeowners did this, premiums would rise to the point where those whose homes weren't on fire couldn't afford insurance. Eventually, the only homes in the insurance pool would be those already on fire. At that point, fire insurance ceases to exist. Since health insurance is already very expensive for the healthy, the possibility that the ban on preexisting conditions could set off such a death spiral in private insurance is a meaningful risk to the system.

the price for not offering insurance. And in many circumstances, it would be smarter for an employer to pay that price.

Let's say most employees earn $60,000 a year or less. If they have families, their insurance is costing their employers on average $13,000 a year and themselves $3,000 a year, both in pretax dollars. But remember that under the ACA, employees can purchase a policy on an exchange for no more than $5,700 (9.5 percent of their income); so instead of offering them insurance, a company can pay the $2,000 penalty and give them each a $10,000 raise—and save $1,000 per employee in compensation cost. Assuming an effective 35 percent tax rate, this company's employees can pay the capped exchange premium and have an extra $2,800 in their pockets. Not only is everyone better off, but the company is rid of the administrative nightmare and unpredictability of health insurance forever!*

Even if the magic of government subsidies didn't make dropping insurance a moneymaking opportunity for employer and employee, the ACA has a few provisions that accidentally undermine the very benefit employers get from offering insurance. For example, although no one talks about it, insurers' current limits on coverage of preexisting conditions were one of the best motivations for employers to offer coverage. Employees were less likely to switch jobs because of these provisions; they created a kind of golden handcuff. So paradoxically, the new preexisting condition rules that may be good for employees make health insurance less beneficial for their employers.

Beginning in 2018, the ACA will also impose a nondeductible

* Interestingly, the ones left out in the cold here are high-income employees. At most businesses, there are probably too few for a company to justify retaining health insurance. But the exchanges are likely to be very expensive for unsubsidized payers. I suspect a new type of insurance—off-exchange insurance—will develop for these high earners. Of course, such a distinction between high earners and everyone else will further undermine the "solidarity" argument often used to justify our insurance-based system.

"Cadillac tax" of 40 percent on employers who pay more than $10,200 for single coverage and $20,750 for family coverage. Only a modest annual increase in premiums is required for the average plan to exceed the Cadillac levels.* The theory is that employers will put pressure on insurers to be more efficient to keep premiums below this level. But that's the last thing an employer wants to do, because an insurer being more efficient means saying no to your own employees. On the Island, only health care matters, but no employer on the Mainland wants to sabotage its relations with employees over health care issues. So the Cadillac tax will force on employers what I suspect is an easy choice: continue to offer health insurance but rigorously control your employees' spending, or write them each a big check and encourage them to get their insurance on an exchange.†

America's biggest, most politically visible companies may not drop health insurance as a result of the exchanges—at least not at the start. But offering health care has always been a competitive need for companies, not a moral obligation; it's a way to attract and retain employees. As some companies find the move away from insurance to be a smart alternative, the effect is likely to cascade. Why offer insurance and lower wages to employees if the competition for their services offers higher wages with no insurance?

So what do we have? A bill that decreases the need for insurance for the healthy while increasing its cost. That allows insurers to compete only on price but gives them a perfect motivation and mechanism to in effect collude. That mandates that individuals

---

* A 4 percent per year increase in my company's premiums would force us to pay the Cadillac tax. I don't remember a year when our premium increase was that small.

† Here's another one: the penalty for noncompliance applies to any employer if any *one* of its employees gets a subsidy on the exchange; so employers in low-wage industries may have to pay the penalty *even if they provide insurance*. Why bother?

and corporations buy insurance but assigns penalties that under-score how terrible a buy health insurance is. That strips from employers some of the major benefits of providing insurance. That enables completely price-insensitive (i.e., subsidized) cus-tomers to drive prices. The designers of the ACA may have been hamstrung by their political requirements, but the complexity of the work-arounds will likely overwhelm their intended effects.

All of the above are merely speculations on the potential unan-ticipated consequences of the ACA. In fairness, I can't predict what will happen. Perhaps hidden or unanticipated incentives will counteract or overwhelm the incentives discussed above. But that's the point: none of us are smart enough to understand how very complex systems will respond to a set of complicated new rules. So in even their most straightforward objective—to increase the number of insured people—the ACA sponsors can-not be confident that their legislation will achieve their desired results. On the Mainland, we use real markets to allocate most resources because the incentives in markets are clear. The results may not be perfect, but at least everyone's underlying incentive fundamentally points in the right direction.

Appendix 2

Déjà Vu

The ACA and the previously failed "new" cost controls

Neither company will disclose the information publicly, but estimates from insurance rates suggest that UPS and FedEx lose no more than one of every two hundred packages they are supposed to deliver. By contrast, estimates suggest as many as one in every twenty patients receives the wrong dosage of a drug—or even the wrong drug—during a hospital stay. Although the shippers' task seems infinitely more complicated, it is no surprise they have lower failure rates. Everything about a modern shipment, from the scheduling of a pickup to the confirmation of delivery, is electronic. Every package is bar-coded and scanned at every transaction point. Conversely, in many hospitals, at least some of the records involved in the process of ordering and delivering drugs are paper, usually the patient information.

Converting our medical system to electronic records is regarded on the Island as a no-brainer reform of care. The 2009 federal stimulus package included $26 billion in grants over the following five years to fund the health care system's conversion to electronic payment records. The ACA supports this initiative with further funding, as well as by establishing penalties for doctor noncompliance.

Bringing an information technology revolution to health care should certainly transform care. From instantaneous availability of patient histories to the tailoring of treatments to avoid mistakes, better IT offers almost unlimited promise in making care more individualized, more flexible, more efficient, and less dangerous. Not to mention cheaper. A RAND study suggested annual savings of more than $40 billion from a total investment in IT estimated at only $50 billion.

If RAND is right, the cost savings alone would represent an 80 percent annual return on investment—unheard of in, well, anything. Fifty billion dollars in needed investment may sound like a lot of money, but it accounts for only 0.2 percent of the health industry's annual revenues. I can't think of any industry that spent as little as 0.2 percent converting to digital records. To summarize: better service, higher quality, fewer mistakes, extraordinary returns, low capital costs, and a path already blazed by every other industry in the country. If this sounds too good to be true, the obvious question is, Why hasn't it happened already? Why didn't the industry put up its own capital to earn that spectacular 80 percent return? But in attempting to force digital conversion, the ACA fails to ask this obvious question.

If you've ever worked in an industry while it was converting to digital records and operations, you know something that the leaders in digitizing health care don't: digitization is an evolution, not a revolution. Electronic records aren't about investing in computers and software; they're about adopting processes that generate and use data electronically. We can buy the industry all the computers it wants, but unless individuals working in health care find ways to use electronic records to improve delivery, pricing, and accounting of services, the computers won't have anywhere near the desired transformative effect. The symptom may be the lack of electronic records, but the real disease is fundamental: no one in health care can capture the financial benefits of better quality, service, and safety. Since no one gets paid for these improvements, no one has made the relatively low-cost investments needed to create such benefits. The slow conversion to electronic records in health care isn't the problem; it's the canary in the coal mine, telling us that something else is terribly wrong. Buying hardware and software doesn't change that fundamental reality.

Achieving the promise of electronic records has little to do with technology. Rather, this promise is far more dependent on how data is used. Companies and industries that use data effectively understand that digitization is a constant process—of trial and error, evolution, and feedback loops. It is bottom up as well as top down, with change and adaptability being key to success. In July 2010, the Department of Health and Human Services issued its final rules for eligibility to qualify for incentive payments to fund digital conversion; the rules fill 276 pages in the *Federal Register*. We may well buy $50 billion of information technology for health care, but nothing in our legislated approach suggests it will transform anything.

At every turn, the ACA is full of ideas—like forcing health care to convert to electronic records—that seem very sensible but are misguided in practice. The cost-control ideas in the ACA aren't particularly new. The Island has long bowed down to them. They reflect the conventional wisdom that centralized authority—using fiat power—can place limits on an otherwise inevitable rise in health care spending. As always, high prices are seen as a consequence of high costs, which are in turn seen—to the extent they're thought tamable—as a consequence of excess, waste, and inefficiency. In this view, if the excess, waste, and inefficiency can be reduced, then—and only then—will the increases in prices begin to level off.

As discussed in chapter 6, this static Island viewpoint is contradicted by the more dynamic relationship between price and cost that exists on the Mainland. The ACA greatly increases the amount of money in health care, so it's highly unlikely to set in motion real economic pressure on costs. The bill satisfies the universally acknowledged need to do something about prices by attacking some of the most visible symptoms of inefficiency. But these policies—like the mandating of digital conversion—merely "correct" the results of poorly structured incentives, leaving the incentives themselves untouched. And the same incentives will ultimately produce the same results.

Accountable bundling

The ACA establishes accountable care organizations (ACOs), cooperative arrangements between primary care doctors, specialists, and hospitals to manage the overall health of a Medicare beneficiary. The theory behind ACOs is similar to that behind HMOs and other earlier efforts to integrate payers and providers: an organization charged with a patient's whole care is more efficient than our current disaggregated approach. And greater efficiency will supposedly drive lower prices.

ACOs are intended to make long-term investments in patients' overall health rather than simply maximizing billable services. Medicare will pay ACOs bonuses (above normal fees for service or diagnosis) based both on annual cost savings and on high-quality performance. Performance bonuses are to be based on thirty-three quality measures, and the rules for measuring savings and bonuses are complicated. As of this writing, ACOs will be able to earn bonuses from savings but will not be penalized if costs turn out to be higher than expected.

In practice, ACOs are unlikely to achieve any real policy goals because these goals are glued to static reality. To simplify (because the real formulas are so complex they deserve their own book), let's say an ACO will earn a bonus if it's able to service a Medicare patient for less than the current annual cost. That bonus will be 25 percent of any savings. The current annual cost of treating a Medicare patient is estimated today to be $10,000, so if an ACO is able to meet a patient's needs for only $9,000, it gets an extra $250 of pure profit presumably.* Proponents believe this provides sufficient incentive for ACOs to control costs. But of course it doesn't. Since in some circumstances, ACOs are not penalized if they exceed $10,000 a year in costs, the incentives are still skewed: for patients who are truly high cost, the ACO would prefer 100 percent of the overage to only 25 percent of any savings. Instead, the ACO formula encourages the organizations to attract as many low-cost patients as possible and claim their naturally lower costs as "savings." These one-way bonus provisions will therefore more likely lead to an increase, not a decrease, in Medicare's total costs.

The benchmark for ACO savings isn't ambitious enough to measure whether they're capable of making a difference. Medicare hopes to save $1.1 billion over five years on the first 900,000 or so patients assigned to ACOs. That may sound like a lot of money, but it translates to $250 per patient per year, which means the "savings" will be smaller than the amount Medicare expects its cost per patient to grow over that same time frame. ACO savings will be like so many previous examples of savings in health care: we are assured they exist, but because the baseline for costs keeps rising, they have no effect. They're like the stores on Fifth Avenue

---

* Assuming the ACO passes the requisite quality benchmarks.

in New York whose permanent signs say SALE! 50% OFF! without specifying exactly what the 50 percent is deducted from.

ACOs will "work" in the way many government programs do: savings will be documented and bonuses will be paid. But will they have any real impact on the efficiency of medical care or on its overall cost? Here's a hint: for the most part, private insurers oppose the concept. Why? They understand that in practice ACOs will be created by merging existing providers—and that this further concentration will give them more leverage in price negotiations with insurers. In this sense, ACOs are potent symbols of how the ACA expands the distance between the Island and the Mainland. On the Island, something that promises greater efficiency of care—more integrated care in this case—is assumed to lead to lower prices. On the Mainland, everyone knows that giving providers more market power leads only to higher prices.

ACOs are a seemingly sensible solution to what everyone on the Island—and I mean everyone—agrees is the fundamental problem with health care delivery: the dominance of the fee-for-service model. According to conventional wisdom, because health care is priced mostly by individual services—instead of by bundled services—providers have an incentive to perform excess services. Since a doctor and hospital can charge for each test, for each procedure, even for each aspirin, they have a financial incentive to provide more care than if they were paid for the patient's overall care.

The fee-for-service model is so universally blamed for the disincentives in health care that it seemingly never occurs to anyone that it is merely a symptom to be understood, not a disease to be cured. After all, the fee-for-service model exists everywhere in the economy, not just in the health care industry. Many lawyers charge by the hour, florists by the number and type of flowers in a bouquet, and carpet installers by the yards of floor covered. But businesses also bundle services everywhere on the Mainland, in an almost infinite variety of combinations—and often side by side with fee-for-service options. Some lawyers charge not by the hour but by the assignment. Some charge only for winning your case. Some florists charge by the arrangement. Carpet installers will quote you a whole-house fee. If you want a new table, you can buy wood and a plan and make it yourself. Alternatively, Ikea will sell you the table manufactured but not assembled. You can order an assembled table from a furniture store and choose your finish. Or you can design your entire table and hire a carpenter to build it for you. In the automobile market, you'll find far more combinations of standard and optional features than you will car models. And different manufacturers of mobile phones and telecom providers offer different packages of bundled services but leave additional features to be provided by third parties in online app stores.

What's unique about health care isn't the dominance of fee-for-service pricing; in fact, there's plenty of bundling in health care (your primary physician doesn't charge you separately for the nurse and usually has an exam fee that includes several services that could be charged for individually). Medicare stopped paying on a fee-for-service basis for most hospital treatments almost thirty years ago. What's truly unique about health care is the lack of diversity among various ways of charging for services. The idea that there *should* be a single business model for providers is what makes health care weird—yet another dysfunctional consequence of a Surrogate-driven economy. On the Mainland, the interplay of fee-for-service and bundled options is constantly in flux, as businesses experiment to find combinations that are most profitable, that attract customers, and that allow the incorporation of new technologies and features. They have to experiment because no one knows in advance what is going to work, what is going to create value as perceived by customers.

I suspect that Island residents are mostly right in their assertion that many customers would like more integration in health care.

I'd like a hospital that had a single fixed fee for surgery—and would even pay a higher fee for a money-back guarantee based on results. By contrast, I wouldn't mind paying my primary care physician by the minute, since the more time he spends with me, the better. What patients would really benefit from is choice. By continuously trying new ways of doing business, providers could identify delivery models—and there may well be many of them—that offer the greatest hope for improving efficiency, service, and value.

Perhaps more integrated care can offer patients advantages in quality, cost, and service. But its proponents have a difficult question to answer: Why isn't the ACO model already dominant in our health care system? After all, Kaiser Permanente has pursued a similar approach, with generally good patient reviews, for more than sixty-five years. Why hasn't the Kaiser model won out?

We all know the answer to this question: the marketplace doesn't pick cost and quality winners in health care because there isn't really a marketplace. And that—not the lack of integrated care—is the true problem. Cost control is the result of a dynamic process—an endless battle among competing models and innovative approaches—not of a single solution being imposed from above. The ACO initiative merely continues a long tradition in health care of static and bureaucratic one-size-fits-all solutions.

Passing the buck

The ACA also establishes a new Independent Payment Advisory Board to make the necessary tough choices in cutting Medicare spending. Like with an earlier commission assembled to cut excess domestic military bases, the theory is that an expert commission without political interference makes the best choices, and those choices become law unless Congress specifically overrules them.

Starting in 2015, IPAB is required to make recommendations

for cutting Medicare if spending exceeds certain targets; the recommendations become law unless Congress acts. To make "tough" choices more palatable politically, IPAB is prohibited from considering recommendations that would raise premiums or any other revenues, change cost-sharing formulas, restrict benefits or care, or alter eligibility. So exactly what subjects can IPAB consider to cut Medicare spending? Reducing Medicare's office supplies budget, perhaps?*

Health care policymakers appear to think like politicians talk when they discuss budget cuts. They always promise to cut the "waste, fraud, and abuse" rather than anything that actually matters to people. Unfortunately, in health care—as in all programs—waste, fraud, and abuse aren't separate budget items; they're woven into our care choices and into the interaction of price and value. We have no easy decisions when cutting health care, which is why unleashing cost-cutting dynamics and incentives will be more effective than relying on central decisions.

If Becky is counting on IPAB to save her money, precedent is not promising. Under a law passed in 1997, whenever Medicare spending exceeds its "sustainable" growth rate—which it has every year since 1997—MedPAC (IPAB's predecessor) is supposed to calculate a reduction in reimbursement levels to doctors to compensate. Doctors, as discussed, are politicians' favorite targets for cuts because their lobbying groups are not as powerful as those of the other players in health care. But even picking on doctors has been too much for Congress. It has overturned the required reimbursement cuts every year. It is difficult to share its faith that IPAB will somehow prove different.

---

* IPAB's very toothlessness allows both political parties low-cost opportunities to show their support for positions that they are not usually associated with. Republicans have called for IPAB's elimination to show their support for Medicare. Democrats have supported it as their solution to exploding Medicare costs.

Better medicine?

Proponents of the ACA believe the law has the potential to improve health care itself—to deliver better results for patients.

One approach is to favor preventive care and wellness. The bill eliminates any insurance cost sharing (deductibles, co-payments) for childhood checkups, for many types of tests, including blood pressure, diabetes, and those for certain cancers, as well as for services such as smoking cessation programs and obesity counseling. Recently, contraception has also been added to the no-cost-sharing list. According to *The New York Times,* the government believes that "Americans use preventive services at about half the rate recommended by doctors and health experts."

Preventive care is the "motherhood and apple pie" of many health care experts: if we could only catch everyone's issues early, we could avoid expensive treatment later. Such experts often make wild claims about the potential savings of an increased focus on wellness and preventive care; my favorite study suggested that since 75 percent of illnesses are "preventable," an emphasis on wellness and preventive care could save 75 percent of our health care spending—$1.9 trillion in savings a year!

As we've seen, this is essentially nonsense. We're already receiving a lot of preventive care in the form of screenings and tests for potentially devastating illnesses. Most of it—thank goodness—is by definition a waste (the results come back negative). Every once in a while, a test catches a serious illness in an asymptomatic person early enough to save his life, but that's rare and limited to only a few conditions. More common is the real health damage caused by preventive care—both in side effects of tests and in excess treatment. In just the time it took to write this book, a government expert panel has found that two fundamental preventive tests—mammograms and PSA screenings—have been shown to have health costs (as opposed to financial costs) greater than their potential health benefits for low-risk people without specific symptoms.

Nor is there anything free about eliminating cost sharing for preventive services. The very intention of eliminating cost sharing is to encourage more consumption of these services without regard to cost. More consumption means more health cost, and more cost means higher insurance premiums. Sure, your preventive care is now free to you, but so is everyone else's: all of that "free" cost will ultimately be added to your premiums. The coming boom in preventive care will be a reminder of how reducing cost sharing for those in the insurance system causes hardship to those out of the system. For example, can you imagine how high a retail price a manufacturer will place on contraception when it knows that almost all customers don't need to pay anything out of their own pockets for it?

Nor is our broadened commitment to wellness consistent or even efficient. Many companies would like to experiment with wellness initiatives that compensate or penalize their insured employees for lifestyle issues that genuinely do affect health: obesity, exercise, smoking, alcohol and drug abuse. These experiments are strictly circumscribed by the ACA, which wants to avoid anything that feels like any kind of discrimination—even if such discrimination can incent behavior leading to better health.*

---

* The ACA also sets up a Patient-Centered Outcomes Research Institute to support "comparative-effectiveness research"—also known as "best practices." The idea is to improve the collection and dissemination of information on what actually works in health care—which treatments are most efficient in managing conditions. As with electronic records, what's really shocking is that this isn't already done in health care, that the larger hospitals and insurers don't already have enough incentive to collect and distribute this information.

In theory, best practices can be enormously helpful to doctors and patients, providing benchmarks for treatments. But translated into bureaucratic realities, they may also become inflexible, harming those patients whose conditions or responses to treatment don't fall neatly into circumscribed procedure. In our Surrogate-dominated system, will best practices become another source of dysfunction, as reimbursement is restricted to qualifying protocols? Or will they

The past forty-five years of health legislation have seen a variety of new ideas for better, cheaper, more efficient treatment imposed through top-down regulation or pilot projects.* Island experts' confidence in this approach is remarkably unaffected by the failure of previous ideas. In just the past year, the GAO criticized Medicare's $8 billion experimental pay-for-quality program as rewarding mediocre results, a *New England Journal of Medicine* study found that mortality rates for hospitals participating in the CMS's Premier Hospital Quality Incentive Demonstration were no different from those of nonparticipating hospitals, and a *Health Affairs* study noted that public reporting of hospital quality measures under Medicare's project Hospital Compare had "modest or no impact" on key results.

How will we evaluate the success of the ACA's initiatives? If each is as effective as proponents contend, the overall consequences should be meaningful. Shouldn't we see the total cost of health care decline as preventive care makes expensive treatments unnecessary, electronic records make delivery more efficient, and best practices squeeze out unneeded care? Or will each initiative be regarded as a success just for "showing up"? Will the availabil-

---

serve as a source of knowledge, guiding improved provision and consumption of care?

Pamela Hartzband and Jerome Groopman have written that "a lucrative industry has grown up to generate ever more medical metrics, to give report cards to doctors and hospitals, and to base payments on compliance with 'best practices.' Yet beyond safety protocols, there is scant evidence that such measures improve our health" ("Rise of the Medical Expertocracy," *Wall Street Journal*, March 31, 2012).

* According to a MedPAC report submitted to Congress, "The process of initiating, designing, implementing, and evaluating a Medicare demonstration is highly complex, involving multiple stakeholders within the legislative and executive branches of the federal government, providers, beneficiaries, and research institutions (both private and academic). In many ways, each Medicare demonstration is a microcosm of the policy and implementation complexities of the larger Medicare program" (*Aligning Incentives in Medicare*, June 2010). Of course, if we didn't have a single-payer system for seniors, this torturous pilot program process would be replaced by businesses experimenting with new care and payment models.

ity of more preventive care, the very existence of digital record keeping, and the mere publication of lots of documents on best practices suffice? Will the latest flavor-of-the-year top-down ideas for transforming the industry genuinely transform health care in ways we can notice or measure? And if not—if centralized reforms "succeed" without a clear impact on the overall picture—will we look for new rules or will we instead consider that dynamic incentives may work better?

Appendix 3

Shifting the Government's Focus to Better Health

In 1958, Congress restructured the Civil Aeronautics Board, shifting its responsibilities for managing the nation's air-traffic control system and regulating air carriers for safety to the newly established Federal Aviation Administration. The CAB was left primarily with the power to regulate the economics of the airline industry. For the next twenty years, the CAB exerted tight control over all the major business issues of the airlines: the airports they could serve, the routes they could fly, the prices they could charge. Airlines competed on everything except for the things that really mattered.

In 1978, the government began deregulating the airline industry by phasing out—and ultimately abolishing—the CAB. Thirty years of competition have taught airlines that the single most important selling point for consumers is the lowest possible price. Consumers bear some trade-offs for this priority: more crowded planes, fewer amenities, more restrictive tickets. We all complain about these trade-offs, but no major airline has been successful by offering a premium price for premium service (other than to a small group of business travelers).

Similar to other expensive equipment-based services, airlines find it very difficult to make money consistently. They need to invest a significant amount of money up front to buy the airplanes. Labor is highly trained and expensive, and safety requirements demand continuous maintenance. Since competitors can always add one more passenger to already scheduled flights at minimal cost, airlines struggle to maintain ticket prices at levels that cover overhead. So it's understandable that from early on many experts believed government control was essential to maintaining a stable airline industry.

Airline deregulation has been an unqualified economic success—but not by making the industry more stable. In fact, all the recognized structural issues of the business model continue to plague the companies. Most of the nation's major carriers have been in receivership for some period over the past decade. Many famous names from the regulated era—Pan Am, TWA, Eastern, Northwest Orient—have disappeared. From the perspective of the industry, the regulated age was a golden age, when a return on capital was practically guaranteed. The financial troubles of the industry have also affected its workforce; unions for pilots, mechanics, and flight attendants have all been required to negotiate givebacks of previously won wages and benefits.

So why do I call this an economic success? Airline deregulation is a success solely because of the value it has created for consumers. In deregulating airlines, our government was changing its focus; policy would no longer serve all stakeholders but rather the best interests of consumers. Supporters of transportation deregulation in the 1970s embraced change, believing that competition was necessary to bring down prices and enable innovation. They abolished the CAB because they knew every regulator eventually suffers from "industry capture"—the warping of the original regulatory mission into the protection of industry incumbents and existing ways of doing business. (My favorite example of this is the Interstate Commerce Commission, which, created to protect consumers against railroad monopolies, would go on to back such absurdities as requiring trucks on certain routes to make return trips empty to protect railroads from "unfair" competition. The ICC was also ultimately abolished.) Deregulation was almost certain to proceed in ways that hurt the existing powers in the airline business. But by clearly defining their objective—enabling competition—the deregulators achieved extraordinary results, not just with airlines but with trucking, railroads, and shipping.

In health care, by contrast, the government is on everyone's side. Doctors, nurses, insurers, hospitals, drug companies, device manufacturers, Medicare beneficiaries, you name it—our government's philosophy is to weigh everyone's interests when designing policy. Look under the hood of the ACA and you find a complex web of gifts, favors, preferences, and protections given to the various interest groups. Not surprisingly, these groups paid for their goodies. Here are amounts spent on lobbying and campaign contributions at the federal level by various health care stakeholders in 2010, the year the ACA was enacted:

	Lobbying	*Campaign contributions*
Pharmaceutical and device companies	$244 million	$32 million
Hospitals and nursing homes	$108 million	$21 million
Health professionals	$ 86 million	$76 million
Health plans	$ 74 million	$14 million

You might suspect that voices of patients are hard to hear under this pile of money. And although some groups claimed to speak for consumers, they usually had other ties. As a group, patients contributed zero dollars to congressional and presidential campaigns. We did no lobbying. And unfortunately, just like other stakeholders, we got our money's worth in the ACA.

Of course, health care is a huge business, and so it has extensive interests in government policy. But our expectation that government will take care of everything in health care—that government should and will solve every problem—creates an enormous opening for these stakeholders to craft legislation and regulation that serve their own needs. In health care, industry capture is especially pernicious because the unlimited scope of the government's role allows for an unlimited use of government to serve the interests of groups other than patients. As with the airline industry thirty-five years ago, the status quo makes it legitimate for legislators to argue for policies that protect doctors, nurses, hospitals, insurers, drug companies, and on and on.

Legitimate, but disastrous. The health care crisis is a crisis for patients, not for the industry; no industry is in crisis when its revenues grow from $75 billion to $2.5 trillion in two generations. I've met a lot of committed and ethical professionals in all areas of health care. Organized as interest groups, however, each of the industry actors has interests opposed to ours as patients and consumers.

High prices, excess treatment, lack of accountability, constrained competition, weak safety oversight, and limited transparency are in everyone's interest in health care—except patients'. Our interest is in seeing the various players in health care compete for our business on price, access, quality, service, and safety; their interest is in avoiding such competition. As long as we passively accept that it is legitimate for our government to seek compromise among industry interests, our interests will be outvoted.

I have argued that redirecting back to us as much as possible of the enormous amount spent on health care will bring essential consumer discipline to the industry. But to complement that effort, we also need to rethink the government's role. I saw this most personally with my father's death. No consumer would have paid my father's hospital a penny, and no hospital would have dared to even try to collect from an actual person. Yet Medicare, at most, subtracted a small penalty from the reimbursement. As the biggest customer of the hospital system, Medicare is a partner in hospital care; any penalty it charges a hospital will have to be made up somewhere else. Why essentially penalize yourself for terrible treatment?

Reducing government's role in paying for health care—and simplifying that role—will also allow government to redefine its overall mission. Government's objective in health care should be to improve our health, not to maximize our use of care. And government's role in achieving this goal should be to support the interests of consumer-patients. This means encouraging competition and transparency, tearing down barriers to innovation, and protecting consumers against unsafe practices. If any or all of those goals hurt the economic interests of doctors or hospitals, drug companies or device manufacturers, so be it. They can take care of themselves.

Some people believe government is inherently incompetent. I don't. The hospital system run by the Department of Veterans Affairs, which directly serves a large population on a limited budget, has been a consistent leader in using electronic records to coordinate patient care and in reducing hospital-acquired infections. The VA has its flaws, but it has built a distinctive business model to serve its patients. By contrast, CMS, which runs the absurdly complex Medicare and Medicaid programs (on unlimited entitlement budgets), is incapable of effectively regulating even the one program for which it is the sole customer: treatment for end-stage kidney disease.

The government will become more effective in health care if it plants itself squarely on the side of protecting the interests of consumer-patients. Airlines weren't necessarily happy that the government no longer proactively worked to help them achieve stable profitability, but the legacy of deregulation is that asking for government price-fixing is now viewed as illegitimate for the airline business. We need a similar revolution in our thinking about health care.

We won't be able to stop the many large interests in health care from lobbying Congress and regulators for preferred treatment. But we can begin to expose the arguments they currently use to demand such intervention—their need for "adequate" returns on investments, for protection against "unfair" competition, for confidentiality, for "stable" (aka fixed) prices—as illegitimate. A more focused government will be a more effective government.

When the government embarked on airline deregulation, some critics argued that safety would suffer: competitive pressures might lead airlines to scrimp on needed maintenance. But in fact, airline accidents have consistently declined since deregulation. In 2012, we marked the third consecutive year without a major air crash in the United States. For 2009, the fatal accident rate in U.S. commercial aviation was one person for every two hundred thousand flights (compare that with the greater than 1 percent chance that an admission of a senior to a hospital will involve a death due to error). As it relates to airline safety, a more defined government role has proved to be more effective.

The point is that government can achieve social goals by unleashing proper incentives rather than by administering from the top. Many health care experts—including the sponsors of the ACA—think that's exactly what our current policy does. But they confuse the endless microscopic and overly detailed rules straitjacketing the industry with true incentives, which are both big and simple and thereby encouraging of variation. In the last two chapters, I called for massive new government-sponsored programs—cradle-to-grave catastrophic insurance, mandatory health accounts, and health loans—to replace our current system of financing care. To work, they must remain simple and straightforward.

But government has an additional role to play if a truly reformed health care system is to thrive. In public health, safety regulation, and information standards, government investments can seed true and effective innovation. Policies favoring transparency, consumer interests, and openness of data can have enormous positive impact even within our current dysfunctional system. But all of this requires a simple reexpression of government's role: the job of government in health care is to protect the interests of consumers-patients. This won't in itself stop lobbyists from seeking special treatment, but it will limit the boundaries of what's legitimate to request.

Saving lives through transparency

The U.S. government will spend roughly $32 billion this year on research aimed at combating some of our biggest killers: cancer, heart disease, kidney failure, and Alzheimer's. Yet it is just sitting on knowledge that could immediately reduce a danger of roughly equal size: the harm done by excess medicine and medical errors.

Medicare maintains a database of claims that is a true gold mine of health information. And it has made that database partially accessible for research—although often for high fees. Some commercial organizations merely sort and resell the mined information to clients in the health care industry. But Medicare has drawn the line at allowing the identities of doctors to be used by researchers, even though it's clear that public availability would "out" physicians who perform an unusually large number of risky or useless treatments. While it's true that a 1979 U.S. District Court decision held that Medicare needed to keep the earnings of individual doctors under the program a secret, CMS has interpreted this single judicial decision as broadly as possible, disallowing the use of physician data in almost all circumstances. CMS appears to believe that since it uses the database to conduct its own fraud investigations, there couldn't be much benefit from greater disclosure.

In 2010, *The Wall Street Journal* used information from the database in a series of articles on unnamed physicians who were clearly abusing Medicare to the detriment of their patients. The paper reported on a New York physical therapist whose $2.5 million in billings exceeded the amount of care he could have possibly provided during the period involved. Another doctor billed for $2 million of sophisticated tests outside her specialty. The paper also found that Medicare continued paying large claims even to doctors whose billing patterns had already been flagged by its antifraud unit.

As a follow-up to the investigation, *The Wall Street Journal*'s parent company sued CMS for broader access to the database, including the right to disclose the identities of individual physicians. But after passage of the ACA, CMS has decided it finally has the legal basis to give certain types of researchers access to physician names. Even now, however, CMS is dragging its feet on opening up its invaluable database. It is considering restricting its use to organizations expert in claims data (presumably excluding the press) and has proposed absurdly high charges—in effect, granting access only to commercial organizations that serve the industry. CMS is just seeking to balance the interests of patients and doctors. But this is a mistake: CMS should be on the side of patients, period.

CMS's attitude is a classic example of the industry capture that is plaguing government health care agencies. Just imagine how much good could come from giving patients open access to the data generated by their visits to doctors—visits paid for by their taxes. Or how much more comfortable with your doctor's recommendation for a bypass you would be if you knew that he recommended bypasses at an industry-average rate, rather than at an abusive rate. Shouldn't we be encouraging the TripAdvisors and the Zagats of health care to use the Medicare database to generate a usable picture of our doctors? Wouldn't that be more likely to drive accountability than CMS's own work?

The American Medical Association has consistently opposed the release of physician data from the Medicare database and was the party that filed the successful 1979 lawsuit. The organization has argued that the database contains errors and that the data could be misinterpreted, unfairly besmirching doctors' reputations. But this confidentiality extends even to those doctors who have been sanctioned for malpractice or other disciplinary issues. The Department of Health and Human Services' National Practitioner Data Bank, which allows hospitals to check the disciplinary records of doctors, prevents the public from seeing the names of even those doctors with long histories of infractions!

Two years ago, I joined the board of the Leapfrog Group, which is dedicated to transparency in hospital safety issues. Leapfrog was founded by Lucian Leape, author of the report that first uncovered the high rate of deaths from hospital errors. The organization uses the leverage of major employers to encourage hospitals to disclose data on their safety practices and results. The annual Leapfrog survey is the gold standard in the field, and more than twelve hundred of the nation's fifty-four hundred hospitals participate. Many of the country's safest hospitals proudly display their Leapfrog results on their website or in marketing materials. But I've been struck by how many of our best-known hospitals seem to view any hint of transparency as somehow a violation of their right to practice medicine without accountability.*

Information could be transformative in health care, but trans-

---

* In June 2012, Leapfrog announced the release of its Hospital Safety Score, which assigns hospitals letter grades based on their safety records and practices.

formation won't be the result of hardware or software. It will occur when we patients get access to information, which in turn will encourage innovative uses of it. Unfortunately, our government is not committed to the widespread availability of information that could force accountability. The government can save lives immediately—and drive better care—by switching sides today.

National health database

My company runs a series of online game sites. Like any digital business, we know which site you left to come to us, which part of our site you clicked on first, which games you played and for how long, and where you went after you finished a game. Analyzing this data is our business, because it tells us how to optimize the experience for each visitor. Before we make any significant changes to a site, we conduct a test: some of our visitors receive the proposed change; the rest don't. The results help us understand what impact the change will have on our customers' experiences. We continuously look for patterns that will tell us what's working and what isn't for each cohort: young men or middle-aged women, night owls or early risers, "whales" or "minnows," you name it. These patterns drive what games we design, what prizes we offer, what advertisements we sell.

Most businesses today run on this type of data mining, using extraordinarily large numbers of data points to find patterns that enable more precise tailoring of a product or service. And I do mean large numbers: for the biggest digital businesses, their visitors are almost certainly registering hundreds of billions of clicks each year.

By contrast, health care is an anecdote-mining business. Depending on her specialty, your physician may have seen only ten or a hundred or at most a thousand cases like yours. And she knows that many of them aren't relevant to your situation—some patients were much younger or older, and others had complicating conditions or different tolerances to discomfort or specific medications. For most issues in health care, we simply don't have enough data to discover that a certain implant is more likely to fail in men in their forties with a body mass index above 28 or that a certain drug is more likely to cause severe side effects in a woman who had previously taken a certain other drug. If we're not looking for a specific pattern to analyze in health care, we won't find it.

With all the resources going into the research of new treatments in health care, we'd benefit most from removing the roadblocks to understanding what we could know. Each patient's interactions with the health care system could be the equivalent of a click online—if only we had the ability to collect the information and make it available for analysis. I have argued that our lack of electronic records is a failure of incentives—despite all the supposed benefits from such records, no one in the system has been able to make the investment in them pay off. A health database faces a similar problem, with a major complication: no one party could collect enough data to make analyzing it meaningful. The value of a database improves with its size and scale, and no one in health care has enough scale—and enough motivation—to invest in such a project. Except society as a whole.

While it may be possible to imagine electronic patient records being efficiently sorted out by the marketplace, a national health database is more like an infrastructure project. So I would propose that the government at least sponsor the building of the database—as well as set the standards for data entry, ensure compliance, police confidentiality, and enable open access.

Current data collection is hampered by confidentiality laws; many of us are uncomfortable with our health data being made available to anyone else for any purpose, even if the data doesn't include our names, addresses, or other identifying elements. Some of those fears are well founded, given our current insurance-based system: a leak of our private medical records can genuinely reduce our access to insurance coverage or even employment opportunities. In a guaranteed national system like the one proposed in this book, those fears would be groundless. Even so, many of us would prefer strict confidentiality. However, I believe we have a public health issue here similar to that of vaccinations. The maximum benefit to us all comes only if all of us participate; opting out creates a danger to those opting in. I believe it's a fair trade: if we want society to provide us with a health safety net, then we have an obligation to society to participate in the database.

The purpose of the national health database is to allow as many minds as possible to innovatively attack the issue of what works and what doesn't. The ACA has a similar objective but a needlessly old-fashioned approach: data is for experts, for insiders. In this, the ACA reflects a common bias against commercialization in health—a bias, of course, that merely protects the economic interests of incumbents. We should want the database to be used for commercial purposes because we want people and companies to be financially incented to find better approaches, avoid treatment errors, and develop new products and services. The database needs to be a national resource for innovation, and innovation often comes from the least expected sources. Transformation rarely comes from asking the "smart" questions but rather from asking the question no one else knew was smart.

To allow for truly open access, the government must make sure that the database records are available only in a confidential no-names form. And it must make a crime any private effort to identify patient names by comparing the national health database with any other database. The government may well need to accredit database users to ensure compliance. Charging researchers a usage fee to support the cost of the database might be appropriate. But the overriding objective must be to use our health care information as a national asset, enabling in health care the type of transformation that a previous government investment in the Internet enabled in communication and information.

Real-world regulation

Government has an essential, irreplaceable role in regulating the safety of medical devices and drugs. Moving away from our insurance-based system could enable a greater focus on safety, a more realistic approach to effectiveness, and, ultimately, enhanced medical innovation. Today, the Food and Drug Administration is responsible for approving new medical devices and drugs. Requiring proof of a new product's safety and efficacy, the FDA approval process is both expensive and time consuming. Current estimates are that it takes roughly ten years and $1 billion for a new drug to achieve approval. A new device requires on average three years and $30 million.

In balancing our concern for safety with our desire for new treatments, the FDA faces criticism from all sides; industry claims that it acts too slowly, while some consumer groups say it acts too precipitously. Desperate patients for whom other treatments have failed clamor for limited approval of only partially tested or even untested drugs. Economists note that the lengthy and expensive regulatory process favors large companies, as smaller competitors lack the sophistication and resources to navigate it.

Some of these conflicts are inevitable in a regulatory process that involves such emotional issues. But I suspect we can make the FDA's job more manageable—and better reflect the realities of contemporary health care—by moving away from the thumbs-up-or-thumbs-down approval model to one based on grades. Right now, our approval process follows the insurance model: a drug or device is either approved to treat a condition or it isn't. Perhaps we can develop a system that recognizes that both safety and efficacy have gradations and that identifying these gradations is more useful than approval.

How would this work? All new drugs and devices would first have to meet the FDA's minimum standards for safety, but then the manufacturer would need to apply for safety and efficacy grades based on testing data. For example, let's say we graded all drugs on a scale from A to D. For safety, an A rating would mean a drug had minor side effects in almost all patients; a D would signify dangerous side effects in many patients. For efficacy, an A would mean that the drug was effective for the indicated condition in almost all patients; a D would mean it was effective in only a small percentage. For this grading system to have maximum benefit, we would have to transform one of the underlying assumptions about regulation. Rather than grades being the result of the regulatory process, they would signal the beginning of a regulatory process. We would expect the safety and efficacy grades to be under constant review, rather than decided at the end of a regulatory process.

But wouldn't this make for an impossible regulatory burden? Doesn't the FDA already have enough trouble keeping up with its obligations? Here's where the availability of real-life results from the national health care database could be especially transformative. The database would allow the FDA access to real-world information on regulated devices and drugs after they've been put into use. Most important, it would allow third parties the same access, permitting groups to push for better grades for more effective and safe drugs and lower grades for less effective and more dangerous ones. The database would allow us to take regulation from the somewhat unreal world of manufacturer-sponsored testing into a more relevant one enabled by the transparency of the database.

This new approach would align our expectations of regulation with the realities of measuring treatment effectiveness. For all the scientific rigor of double-blind testing—the current gold standard employed in regulatory review—we have evidence that it remains subject to subtle biases (not the least in the decision as to which trials to continue to completion). We also know that the limited duration of current testing fails to measure long-term effectiveness and identify delayed side effects or dangers. Currently, a drug is either approved or not; only overwhelming later evidence of its danger is likely to cause an approval to be overturned. Physicians on their own are expected to determine which approved drugs and devices fail to live up to their tested promise, despite the limited number of patients in any practice.

Perhaps testing can prove that an innovation is essentially unsafe and ineffective, but that doesn't mean that we can confidently rely on testing to consider a treatment essentially safe and effective. At best, our knowledge is about degrees of safety and effectiveness; a regulatory system that recognizes that reality would be of greater value to patients and practitioners. Such a regulatory system would also realign the government's goal with its health-driving potential in our information age. Government can use its powers to help consumer-patients make better decisions within a framework that capitalizes on the additional information created by each treatment on each patient.

Procompetitive

By its nature, most government regulation tends to be anticompetitive; compliance favors those companies with the resources necessary to devote to the task. So it's hard for small companies to enter highly regulated industries; they often have difficulty funding both a competitive product or service and the cost of compliance.

In health care, government regulation and the burden of administration imposed by insurance, Medicare, and Medicaid have themselves created meaningful economies of scale that favor large institutions. Even the traditional model of a physician's office providing most services and feeding patients to hospitals has come under enormous pressure. The growing cost of being in private practice has led to a tenfold increase in doctors' debt in the past ten years; hospitals now own over half of doctor's practices, up from barely 25 percent as recently as 2005.

Hospitals themselves have been combining into ever bigger groups. Roughly four hundred hospitals have merged over the past decade, with nonprofits also feeling the need to do so. The extraordinary cost of launching a new medication has led to concentration: the top ten drug companies account for more than half of pharmaceutical revenues.

Of course, there's nothing inherently wrong—and often much right—with bigness in industry. Big companies have the capital and scale necessary to drive cost efficiencies, innovation, and quality control. Unfortunately, in health care, consolidation seems driven more by factors relating to the unique structure we've imposed on the industry than by opportunities to serve customers better. The insurance model places a premium on leverage in negotiations, so hospitals merge to better wrestle rates from insurers. The regulatory process imposes enormous testing costs—and often long waiting periods—on new products. The price of the emergency room safety net disproportionately hits hospitals in poor neighborhoods, forcing them to find partners with more affluent patients. In many states, the realities of Medicaid administration lead to resources being channeled to those organizations with political connections. Medicare's massive size means that obtaining its approval for reimbursement for new products is a matter of corporate life and death. And everyone in the system looks for economies of scale to handle the mountain of billing and administrative requirements generated by our insurance model.

I can't pretend to know how big a doctor's practice, hospital, drug company, or device manufacturer should be—or if an optimal size even exists. But I do know that serving us better is not the reason for most of the consolidation today. And I suspect that the extraordinary cost of compliance is excluding from the health care marketplace innovative business models and lower-level technological and treatment ideas.*

A more consumer-oriented system will in itself counter the incentives to merge. The push for efficiency, customer service, marketing, and other commercial considerations should trump the compliance issues in determining the best size for industry players. But a new government philosophy, one that actively encourages competition, can help this along—even without changing the other elements of our system.

The government can use its buying power through Medicare and Medicaid to drive greater transparency, aiding those consumers who need better information. For example, Medicare can require hospitals to publish the range of prices they have actually charged for each procedure (the reporting of list prices, as required by some states, is useless). The government can mandate public disclosure of safety data through Leapfrog or other accredited organizations. It can prohibit device companies from insisting that hospitals keep the prices they pay for equipment confidential (an obviously anticompetitive arrangement that illustrates how weak insurers are as consumers in our current system).

A separate book could be devoted to the many ways govern-

---

* For example, authorities often take the interests of local hospitals into account when deciding whether to license competitive facilities. That's anticompetitive. They limit purchases of some high-tech equipment to those demonstrating "need." That's anticompetitive. State and local authorities restrict many types of routine care—such as certain drug-prescribing and equipment-ordering privileges—to doctors, despite evidence that nurse-practitioners can easily and safely perform these procedures. That's anticompetitive. And a broad range of government provisions on billing, confidentiality, and patient access that may seem sensible on their face but actually have the effect of discouraging experimental business approaches are also anticompetitive.

ment could make our health system more competitive. But first it has to want to. This means rejecting one of the key elements of Island philosophy: that the most efficient, least costly, safest, and most effective way of doing everything in health care can be discovered or invented by a central authority. The idea of letting variety bloom in health care—that diversity itself can help drive better results—is anathema to this view. One problem is that new business models—by, for example, charging for some services or products that are currently bundled or hidden—often seem to cost more than existing ones. While a true marketplace sorts this out over short periods of time, centrally administered reimbursement may focus only on the higher short-term cost. By making competition an explicit goal of government policy—right now—we increase the chances that some innovator somewhere is going to build the Wal-Mart, the Apple, or the FedEx of health care, even if not ordered to do so by a government rule.

Acknowledgments

This book is about the damage done by unquestioned assumptions and conventional wisdom in health care, yet many of the purveyors of both are also essential sources for any understanding of the field. It's only possible for an outsider to write a book such as this because of the extensive data collection, detailed research, and extraordinary range of published work by the very people I perhaps unfairly refer to as "Island experts." Their individual names and credits may be too extensive to be listed here, but, at best, this work stands on their shoulders.

I had the opportunity to write this book only because my favorite magazine, *The Atlantic*, made the courageous (or reckless, depending on your point of view) decision to give an unknown, nonexpert writer the cover for an unorthodox take on the day's most contentious policy issue. Many thanks to James Bennet for taking that risk, to Don Peck for editing my essay into an article (and for his thoughts on this book as well), and to Kurt Andersen for bringing us together. Thanks also to Dale Hopkins and Jenny Snegaroff for handling the unanticipated press requests that the article generated, and to Michael Sheehan for preparing me for interviews.

Over the past four years, I have enjoyed innumerable conversations with experts in various aspects of health care and public policy, but I have especially benefited from the generosity of Dr. Jeffrey Flier, Dr. Ashish Jha, Dr. Barbara McNeal, Michael Cannon, and Jim Marshall. After writing the *Atlantic* piece, I was asked to join the board of the Leapfrog Group, the nation's foremost hospital safety and transparency organization, where I've had the opportunity to learn about the pervasiveness of medical errors and the efforts of our best institutions to address these issues (and be a part of the development of the Hospital Safety Score, Leapfrog's safety rating now available to all consumers). Special thanks to Leapfrog's executive director, Leah Binder, our current chair Keith Reissaus, and his predecessor, David Knowlton.

Michael Botta assisted me in the research for this book, helped by Laura McDaniel and Hannah Neprash; all three are Ph.D. candidates in health policy at Harvard University. For the purpose of salvaging their careers, they have asked me to mention that they fought vigorously against many (in reality, only some) of the ideas in this book. Thanks also to Ann Marie Healy and Alice LaPlante for early editing assistance.

I would have been unable to pursue my health care "hobby" without my superb colleagues at GSN, who ensure that the regular distraction of our company's CEO is irrelevant. I am very fortunate to work with such a talented team across all facets of our business.

A number of friends, family, and colleagues have been strongly supportive of each step in the development of these ideas, meaning they've devoted unusual amounts of their precious time to discussing health care with me (without, of course, necessarily agreeing with my conclusions). Thanks to Al Puchala, Roy Oppenheim, Len Baxt, Larry Graham, Sylvia Berg, Chris Binkley, Peter Blacklow, Steve Brunell, Gifford Combs, Jon Darnell, Roy and Carol Doumani, Mark Feldman, Jason Fish, Julius Genachowski, Richard Goldberg, Wendy Hoffman, Steve and Bobbie Jellinek, Joe Keene, Dr. Tyler Krohn, Joanne Lipman, Jamie Lynton, Greg Maffei, Duby McDowell, Navid Mahmoodzadegan, Dan Marks, Ken Mendez, Christian Meyer, Pam Meyer, Susan Morrison, Adam Press, Jeff Raich, Chip Robie, James Rubin, Dr. Bernie Saks, Ralph Schlosstein, Andy Tobias, and Dr. Hooman Yaghoobzadeh.

Two good friends played an especially large role in this work. Michael Lynton encouraged me, just short of actually ordering me, to write this book (which he could do as the boss of my parent company); I have benefited enormously from his expertise as a former publishing CEO. My ex-boss at Universal, Michael Jackson, must have read every word of every draft, each and every time with patience and wise commentary.

Andrew Miller, my editor at Knopf, not only demonstrated unusual faith in the oxymoronic concept of a health policy book intended for a general audience, but worked tirelessly to make it possible. Andrew somehow tightened up a meandering first draft (and each subsequent effort) without undermining the confidence of this inexperienced author. Thanks also to Mark Chiusano and Maria Massey.

My agent, Zoe Pagnamenta, believed in this project from our first meeting. I am very grateful for her calm counsel, and her boundless tolerance for naïve questions and demands.

My interest in health care began with a family tragedy, and I am enormously appreciative of the courage of my mother, Elaine Goldhill, in letting me share this very personal experience with a broader audience. In my sister, Vicki, I have a daily reminder of the reason so many doctors choose the profession—an almost obsessive desire to be of service to others.

And, of course, this work would have been truly impossible without the loving support of my wife, Natasha, and the occasional cooperation of our perfect sons, Aleksei and Vasily.

Notes

INTRODUCTION *How American Health Care Killed My Father*

4   **If Becky's hoping:** "National Health Expenditures," Centers for Medicare and Medicaid Services.

CHAPTER 1 *Island-Speak*

21   **polls showed that 71 percent:** Gallup poll quoted in *USA Today,* May 9, 2008.

24   **The Centers for Disease Control and Prevention shows:** Donna Hoyert, "75 Years of Mortality in the United States, 1935–2010," NCHS Data Brief, March 2012.

24   **A 2007 study published:** Earl S. Ford et al., "Explaining the Decrease in U.S. Deaths from Coronary Disease, 1980–2000," *New England Journal of Medicine* (June 7, 2007).

25   **The factors that most predict:** Sabrina Tavernise, "Longevity Up in U.S., but Education Creates Disparity, Study Says," *New York Times,* April 3, 2012.

27   **a third of Americans:** In 1966–67, 31.9 percent of Americans reported that they had not seen a doctor in the past year (http://www .cdc.gov/nchs/data/series/sr_10/sr10_049.pdf).

31   **U.S. health insurance companies employ:** America's Health Insurance Plans, *2011 Health Insurance: Overview and Economic Impact in the States* (September 2011).

33   **That's one geriatrician:** More precisely, in March 2011 there were 7,162 board-certified geriatricians serving 38.6 million seniors.

34   **yet another article explaining that technology:** For example, the Congressional Budget Office's 2008 paper *Technological Change and the Growth of Health Care Spending* quotes three academic studies that attribute between 38 and 65 percent of the growth in real health care spending per capita from 1940 to 1990 to "technology-related changes in medical practice."

43   **Christi Turnage of Madison:** Associated Press, "FDA: Avastin Should Not Be Used for Breast Cancer," *USA Today,* December 16, 2010; Jason Millman, "Following Avastin Decision, Republicans Say FDA Rationing Care," *The Hill,* December 16, 2010.

46   **a book about the powerful place of health care:** William Cutter, ed., *Healing and the Jewish Imagination: Spiritual and Practical Perspectives on Judaism and Health* (Woodstock, Vt.: Jewish Lights Publishing, 2007).

47   **a very good scholarly analysis:** Joseph P. Newhouse, "Assessing Health Reform's Impact on Four Key Groups of Americans," *Health Affairs* (September 2010).

CHAPTER 3   *The Disconnect*

67   **In the words of the great historian:** Paul Starr, *Remedy and Reaction: The Peculiar American Struggle over Health Care Reform* (New Haven, Conn.: Yale University Press, 2011).

68   **Only 11 percent of American households:** These calculations are based on 12.8 million light vehicle sales a year (2011 figure), 9.4 million domestic refrigerator shipments (2010), and a divorce rate of 3.4 per every thousand people (2009).

70   **a highly influential article:** Kenneth J. Arrow, "Uncertainty and the Welfare Economics of Medical Care," *American Economic Review* 53, no. 5 (December 1963): 941–73.

72   **In May 2012, the *Los Angeles Times* wrote:** Chad Terhune, "Many Hospitals, Doctors Offer Cash Discount for Medical Bills," *Los Angeles Times,* May 27, 2012.

76   **Medicaid pays for more than 40 percent of all deliveries:** Kaiser Family Foundation, *State Medicaid Coverage of Perinatal Services: Summary of State Survey Findings* (November 2009).

76   **Medicaid began helping low-income seniors:** Families USA, *Cutting Medicaid: Harming Seniors and People with Disabilities Who Need Long-Term Care* (March 2011).

79   **Medicare spends almost twice as much:** Elliott S. Fisher et al., "Slowing the Growth of Health Care Costs—Lessons from Regional

Variation," *The New England Journal of Medicine* (February 26, 2009).

80   **when Medicare cut reimbursements**: Alex Berenson, "Incentives Limit Any Savings in Treating Cancer," *New York Times,* June 12, 2007.

80   **the average insured American**: Study by George Mason University and the Urban Institute, cited in the *Wall Street Journal,* August 25, 2008.

82   **Twenty-five years after deregulation**: Government Accountability Office, *Airline Deregulation: Regulating the Airline Industry Would Likely Reverse Consumer Benefits and Not Save Airline Pensions* (June 2006).

87   **Hospitals have begun building**: Anemona Hartocollis, "For the Elderly, Emergency Rooms of Their Own," *New York Times,* April 9, 2012.

87   **A recent *Health Affairs* study**: Paper by the Center for Studying Health System Change, quoted in the Kaiser Health News blog, April 9, 2012.

88   **A recent survey in Nashville**: Change Healthcare, Survey, March 29, 2012.

88   **Studies of hospital mortality**: John Birkmeyer et al., "Hospital Volume and Surgical Mortality in the United States," *New England Journal of Medicine* (April 11, 2002).

88   **Seventy percent of hospitals**: Wolf et al., "Hospitals Ineligible for Federal Meaningful-Use Incentives Have Dismally Low Rates of Adoption of Electronic Health Records," *Health Affairs* (March 2012).

91   **Paul Starr has written**: Starr, *Remedy and Reaction.*

CHAPTER 4   *The Fallacy*

101   **In the past twenty years**: *Health, United States, 2010: With Special Feature on Death and Dying* (Hyattsville, Md.: National Center for Health Statistics, 2010).

102   **nearly a third of American adults**: *Health, United States, 2008: With Special Feature on the Health of Young Adults* (Hyattsville, Md.: National Center for Health Statistics, 2008), table 71.

102   **According to a recent article**: Laura Landro, "Hidden Heart Disease," *Wall Street Journal,* November 9, 2010.

102   **"four modifiable health risk behaviors"**: See http://www.cdc.gov /chronicdisease/overview/index.htm.

103   **Like an estimated one in four Americans**: See http://www.health .harvard.edu/blog/statin-use-is-up-cholesterol-levels-are-down -are-americans-hearts-benefiting-201104151518.

105   **Pharmaceuticals are the primary treatment:** Bill Hendrick, "Prescription Drug Use on the Rise in US," WebMD Health News, September 2, 2010; Anna Mathews, "So Young and So Many Pills," *Wall Street Journal,* December 28, 2010.

105   **generics sell at an average discount:** See http://www.insurance quotes.com/health-insurance-generic-drugs/.

106   **In 2010, drug companies spent:** See http://www.pharma-mkting .com/news/pmn1016-article03.htm.

106   **A 2004 estimate suggested:** See http://www.plosmedicine.org /article/slideshow.action?uri=info:doi/10.1371/journal.pmed .0050001&imageURI=info:doi/10.1371/journal.pmed.0050001 .t001.

108   **The industry's trade association notes:** PhRMA, *2009 Pharmaceutical Industry Profile;* PhRMA, *What Goes into the Cost of Prescription Drugs?*

108   **In 2009, the revenue:** The figures in this paragraph were calculated by the author using data from "Pharmaceutical Sales 2009" on the website Drugs.com.

110   **Last year, a study:** Reza Fazel et al., "Exposure to Low-Dose Ionizing Radiation from Medical Imaging Procedures," *New England Journal of Medicine* 361, no. 9 (August 27, 2009): 849–57.

111   **As Shannon Brownlee points out:** Shannon Brownlee, *Overtreated: Why Too Much Medicine Is Making Us Sicker and Poorer* (New York: Bloomsbury, 2007).

111   **to use Dr. H. Gilbert Welch's term:** H. Gilbert Welch, Lisa M. Schwartz, and Steven Woloshin, *Overdiagnosed: Making People Sick in the Pursuit of Health* (Boston: Beacon Press, 2011).

112   **As a recent *BMJ* article:** Ray Moynihan, Jenny Doust, and David Henry, "Preventing Overdiagnosis: How to Stop Harming the Healthy," *BMJ* 344 (May 29, 2012): e3502.

113   **Karen Young-Levi:** Roni Caryn Rabin, "New Guidelines on Breast Cancer Draw Opposition," *New York Times,* November 16, 2009.

115   **Fortunately, two clever economists:** Richard B. McKenzie and Dwight R. Lee, *Ending the Free Airplane Rides of Infants: A Myopic Method of Saving Lives,* Cato Institute briefing paper no. 11, August 30, 1990.

117   **Some recent studies suggest:** Michael Bartholow, "Top 200 Prescription Drugs of 2009," *Pharmacy Times,* May 11, 2010; Jay C. Fournier et al., "Antidepressant Drug Effects and Depression Severity," *Journal of the American Medical Association* 303, no. 1 (January 2010).

117   **over 70 percent of which:** Ramin Mojabai and Mark Olfson, "Proportion of Antidepressants Prescribed Without a Psychiatric Diagnosis Is Growing," *Health Affairs* (August 2011).

120   **Ten states require coverage:** Victoria Craig Bunce and J. P. Wieske, *Health Insurance Mandates in the States 2008* (Alexandria, Va.: Council for Affordable Health Insurance).

121   **Deepak Chopra has said:** Deborah Solomon, "Questions for Deepak Chopra," *New York Times Magazine,* September 3, 2010.

CHAPTER 5   *The Seduction*

124   **an analysis of all Medicare patients:** Alvin C. Kwok et al., "The Intensity and Variation of Surgical Care at the End of Life: A Retrospective Cohort Study," *The Lancet* 378, no. 9800 (October 15, 2011): 1408–13.

129   **My mom's sister once told me:** The figures in this paragraph come from *Health, United States, 2010: With Special Feature on Death and Dying* (Hyattsville, Md.: National Center for Health Statistics, 2010), table 91; Donald Cherry, Christine Lucas, and Sandra Decker, *Population Aging and the Use of Office-Based Physician Services,* National Center for Health Statistics, August 2010; MedPAC, Report to the Congress: Medicare and the Health Delivery System, June 2011, p. 35.

129   **According to the most recent data:** *A Data Book: Health Care Spending and the Medicare Program* (Washington, D.C.: MedPAC, June 2011), chart 2.3.

130   **many die-hard supporters:** Pelosi quoted in http://www.washingtonpost.com/blogs/plum-line/post/nancy-pelosi-we-have-a-plan-its-called-medicare/2011/03/03/AFO4WE7G_blog.html;McCaininhttp://nymag.com/news/politics/powergrid/62668/; the *New York Times*/CBS News poll in http://www.scribd.com/cbsnews/d/53582911-CBS-News-Poll-Budget-042111; the *Washington Post* poll in http://www.washingtonpost.com/politics/poll-shows-americans-oppose-entitlement-cuts-to-deal-with-debt-problem/2011/04/19/AFoiAH9D_story.html; and the AFL-CIO in http://www.aflcio.org/Issues/Health-Care/Controlling-Health-Care-Costs.

132   **in 2011 the FBI arrested:** Michael Rothfeld, "Medicare Scheme Netted $35 Million, Officials Say," *Wall Street Journal,* October 14, 2010; Robert Fear, "Report on Medicare Cites Prescription Drug Abuse," *New York Times,* October 4, 2011.

132   **Office of Management and Budget said:** OMB data discussed in www.healthcarefinancenews.com/blog/feds-review-medicare-and-medicaid-error-rate-data. In 2011, Medicare reported that its error rate had declined to 8.6 percent of claims (ModernHealthcare.com, November 15, 2011).

133   *The Dartmouth Atlas of Health Care*: *The Dartmouth Atlas of Health Care* is a publication of the Dartmouth Institute for Health Policy and Clinical Practice.

133   **What is spent on a patient in some areas**: Fisher et al., "Slowing the Growth of Health Care Costs," *NEJM*.

135   **Unbelievably, Medicare even pays**: Rochelle Sharpe and Elizabeth Lucas, "Forty Percent of Medicare Spending on Common Cancer Screenings Unnecessary, Probe Suggests," *iWatch News*, October 7, 2011; Rita Redberg, "Squandering Medicare's Money," *New York Times*, May 26, 2011.

136   **more than 5 percent of Medicare patients**: Jordan Rau, "Double Chest CT Scans Persist, New Data Show," *Capsules* (blog), Kaiser Health News, August 8, 2011.

136   **According to a 2010 study**: Department of Health and Human Services Office of Inspector General, *Adverse Events in Hospitals: National Incidence Among Medicare Beneficiaries* (November 2010).

138   **At today's levels**: Calculation is based on Medicare's 2007 spending and deaths that year of 1.75 million Americans sixty-five or older.

139   **Approximately 33 percent of our seniors**: "32 percent of all deaths in the U.S. in 2007 occurred in the hospital. . . . Among the elderly, 31 percent of deaths occurred in the hospital, while 34 percent of nonelderly deaths took place in the hospital" (http://www.nlm.nih.gov/medlineplus/news/fullstory_91474.html).

146   **essentially every government projection**: "Health Costs and History," *Wall Street Journal*, October 20, 2009.

147   **Yet the average person joining Medicare**: C. Eugene Steuerle and Stephanie Rennane, *Social Security and Medicare Taxes and Benefits Over a Lifetime* (Washington, D.C.: Urban Institute, 2011).

148   **the number of Americans suffering from Alzheimer's**: Alzheimer's Association, *Fact Sheet* (March 2012).

148   **In 2010, 2.3 million Medicare beneficiaries**: Statistical supplement, *Medicare and Medicaid Research Review* (2011): table 4.4.

149   **In 1970, Medicare premiums**: "Family Health Expenses, July–December 1962," from the Department of Health, Education, and Welfare's *National Health Survey*, reported that individuals sixty-five and older had an average of $189 in health expenses (including dentistry) in 1962 but had no breakdown of payment sources for that expense (such as employer-based insurance). That year, the *Statistical Abstract* gave the median income for households headed by a senior as $1,910 for men and $920 for women. In *The Politics of Medicare*, Theodore Marmor quotes data showing seniors' out-of-pocket expenses around 15 percent in 1966 and declining to under

12 percent by 1977 before rising again to pre-Medicare equivalence in 1984 (figure 7.4).

151 **a story about a more effective blood-clotting treatment:** Donald McNeil Jr., "A Cheap Drug Is Found to Save Bleeding Victims," *New York Times,* March 21, 2012.

CHAPTER 6 *The Mirage of Efficiency*

153 **This fundamental change in reimbursement:** Most of the data regarding hospitals in this paragraph is from CMS, 2011 Data Compendium, chapter 5, Utilization table 5.1.

154 **an influential 2009 study:** Joseph Antos et al., "Bending the Curve: Effective Steps to Address Long-Term Health Care Spending Growth," The Brookings Institution, September 2009.

155 **outpatients accounted for:** CMS, 2011 Data Compendium, table 5.18; American Hospital Association, "National Community Hospital Utilization 1973–2009."

155 **When the DRGs were enacted:** Statistical supplement, *Medicare and Medicaid Research Review* (2011): table 5.1.

156 **a recent study showing that doctors:** McCormick et al., "Giving Office-Based Physicians Electronic Access to Patient's Prior Imaging and Lab Results Did Not Deter Ordering of Tests," *Health Affairs* (March 2012).

159 **A recent *Economist* article:** "The Dialysis Business: Stakes in Kidneys," *The Economist* (April 17, 2010).

165 **Writing in *The New York Times*:** Ezekiel Emanuel, "Cancer Drugs, Effective but Scarce," *New York Times,* August 7, 2011.

168 **America's pharmaceutical companies spent:** PhRMA, *2011 Pharmaceutical Industry Profile.*

169 **finding a pill:** Andrew Pollack, "Looking for a Superbug Killer," *New York Times,* November 6, 2010.

CHAPTER 7 *The Tyranny of Rules*

177 **In America, there are approximately:** American Hospital Association, Survey 2010; FDA, Orange Book; CMS ICD-9 version 29.

179 **In some states:** "Rural Health Care: Country Doc, City Doc," *The Economist* (January 8, 2011); *Health, United States, 2010: With Special Feature on Death and Dying* (Hyattsville, Md.: National Center for Health Statistics, 2010): table 111.

179 **There are only 7,160 geriatricians:** American Geriatrics Society, *Documenting the Development of Geriatric Medicine: Frequently*

Asked Questions (Cincinnati, Ohio: University of Cincinnati, 2012).

180 **A recent survey showed**: American Medical Group Association, *Physician Compensation Survey, 2011.*

180 **Not only has this pay gap**: Christopher Weaver and Anna Wilde Mathews, "An Rx? Pay More to Family Doctors," *Wall Street Journal,* January 27, 2012.

180 **Medicare bases its reimbursement rates**: MedPAC, Report to the Congress: Medicare and the Health Delivery System, June 2012, p. 76.

181 **So the reimbursement for a procedure**: MedPAC, *Hospital Inpatient and Outpatient Services,* Report to the Congress: Medicare and the Health Delivery System, June 2012, table 3.9.

182 **Spending on Medicare and Medicaid**: Karen E. Lasser, Steffie Woolhandler, and David U. Himmelstein, "Sources of U.S. Physician Income: The Contribution of Government Payments to the Specialist-Generalist Income Gap," *Journal of General Internal Medicine* 23, no. 9 (September 2008).

182 **A 2006 report estimated**: Ha Tu and Paul Ginsburg, *Losing Ground: Physician Income, 1995–2003* (Washington, D.C.: Center for Studying Health System Change, 2006).

182 **As recently as 2005**: Accenture study quoted in "Doctors Struggle to Make Ends Meet," *Wall Street Journal,* March 15, 2012.

184 **Two years ago, CMS reported**: The margin had improved to −5.2 percent in 2009. *A Data Book: Health Care Spending and the Medicare Program* (Washington, D.C.: MedPAC, June 2011), chart 6.15.

185 **more hospitals have opened**: MedPAC, Report to the Congress: Medicare and the Health Delivery System, June 2012, figure 3.1.

187 **"Most Medicaid programs stipulate"**: Clayton M. Christensen, *The Innovator's Prescription: A Disruptive Solution for Health Care* (New York: McGraw-Hill, 2009), xliv.

192 **The average supermarket**: "You Choose," *The Economist* (December 18, 2010).

CHAPTER 8 *Last Gasp*

195 **Senator Tom Harkin expressed**: Quoted in "Senate Democrats Lead Historic Passage of the Patient Protection and Affordable Care Act," United States Senate Democrats, December 24, 2009.

196 **the president remarked**: "Speeches and Remarks," White House, Office of the Press Secretary, March 23, 2010.

198 **In 1999, the Institute of Medicine published**: Linda T. Kohn, Janet

M. Corrigan, and Molla S. Donaldson, eds. *To Err Is Human: Building a Safer Health System* (Washington, D.C.: National Academy Press, 2000).

201 **Nothing better illustrates the flaw:** Estimates used in this section come from the Congressional Budget Office and Joint Committee on Taxation's *Estimates of the Effects of the Affordable Care Act on the Number of People Obtaining Employment-Based Health Insurance* (March 2012) and from the CBO's March 20, 2010, letter to Nancy Pelosi.

201 **Less than 10 percent:** CMS, 2011 Data Compendium, tables 7.9 and 7.2.

202 **As recently as 2009:** *Statistical Abstract of the United States* (2012) table 151.

205 **Several analysts have argued:** See Scott Gottlieb, "Medicaid Is Worse Than No Coverage at All," *Wall Street Journal*, March 10, 2011; Jonathan Cohen, "Are You Better Off with Medicaid Than No Insurance? A Landmark Study Says Yes," Kaiser Health News, July 7, 2011.

206 **As one journalist wrote:** Timothy Noah, "Hillarycare: The Sequel," review of *Remedy and Reaction*, by Paul Starr, *New York Times*, November 20, 2011, Sunday Book Review.

207 **The most recent estimate:** See http://www.whitehouse.gov/blog/2010/09/16/affordable-care-act-helps-america-s-uninsured.

207 **Almost 20 percent of our population:** All data on the structure of the uninsured population is from CDC, *Health Insurance Coverage: Early Release of Estimates from the National Health Interview Survey, January–March 2011;* U.S. Census Bureau, *Income, Poverty and Health Insurance Coverage in the United States: 2010* (September 2011); Kaiser Family Foundation, *The Uninsured: A Primer* (October 2011).

208 **Roughly half of the uninsured:** Sources for data on the uninsured are Kaiser Family Foundation, *The Uninsured: A Primer* (October 2011); U.S. Census Bureau, *Income, Poverty and Health Insurance Coverage in the United States: 2010* (September 2011); CDC, *Health Insurance Coverage: Early Release of Estimates from the National Health Interview Survey, January–March 2011.*

209 **A 2008 study:** Jack Hadley, John Holahan, Teresa Coughlin, and Dawn Miller, "Covering the Uninsured in 2008: Current Costs, Sources of Payment, and Incremental Costs," *Health Affairs* 27, no. 5 (September 2008).

209 **For example, 48 percent:** *Health, United States, 2011: With Special Feature on Socioeconomic Status and Health* (Hyattsville, Md.: National Center for Health Statistics, 2011), table 83.

209   **A recent study of low-income uninsured people:** Rachel L. Garfield and Anthony Damico, "Medicaid Expansion Under Health Reform May Increase Service Use and Improve Access for Low-Income Adults with Diabetes," *Health Affairs* 31, no. 1 (January 2012): 159–67.

209   **A study now under way:** The Oregon Health Study Group, "The Oregon Health Insurance Experiment: Evidence from the First Year," National Bureau of Economic Research Working Paper Series 2011; also discussed in Jonathan Cohen, "Are You Better Off With Medicaid Than No Insurance? A Landmark Study Says Yes," Kaiser Health News, July 7, 2011.

214   **the latter providing major financial support:** See http://abcnews .go.com/blogs/politics/2012/06/memos-unveil-how-white-house -worked-with-phrma-to-sell-obamacare/.

215   **A recent Citigroup research report:** Citigroup Global Markets, *Health Care Facilities 2012 Outlook* (January 3, 2012), p. 37.

217   **To build support:** http://stories.barackobama.com/healthcare.

217   **An *Archives of Internal Medicine* study:** Quoted in Drew Armstrong, "Doctors in U.S. Turning Away Insured Patients on Low Payments, Study Finds," Bloomberg News, June 27, 2011.

217   **A 2011 report from the Medicare Payment Advisory Commission:** MedPAC, *A Data Book: Health Care Spending and the Medicare Program* (Washington, D.C.: MedPAC, June 2011), table 4.1.

217   **In California, 25 percent of Medi-Cal beneficiaries:** Anna Gorman, "Medi-Cal Works for Most Enrollees, Survey Finds," *Los Angeles Times,* May 31, 2012.

218   **roughly 98 percent of residents:** Massachusetts Division of Health Care Finance and Policy, *2010 Household Insurance Survey.*

218   **So which is the better measure:** Annie Lowrey and Robert Pear, "Doctor Shortage Likely to Worsen with Health Law," *New York Times,* July 29, 2012.

219   **the words of an Arkansas hospital CEO:** Darren Caldwell, quoted in Robert Pear, "In Health Care Ruling, Vast Implications for Medicaid," *New York Times,* June 16, 2012.

CHAPTER 9   *In Search of Balance*

231   **its population of 5.2 million:** See http://www.singstat.gov.sg/stats /themes/people/popnindicators.pdf.

232   **Singapore's system has five:** See http://www.moh.gov.sg/content /moh_web/home/our_healthcare_system.html.

232   **A 2003 study:** Meng-Kin Lim, "Shifting the Burden of Health Care Finance: A Case Study of Public-Private Partnership in Singapore," *Health Policy* 69 (2004): 83–92.

233   **Singapore's Ministry of Health claims:** See http://www.health
       xchange.com.sg/healthyliving/SpecialFocus/Pages/Understanding
       -Medisave-MediShield-Medifund.aspx.
234   **"Singaporeans are a pragmatic lot":** Lim, "Shifting the Burden," 89.

CHAPTER 10   *Green Shoots*

255   **Can we imagine:** "Never events" figure derived from the Octo-
       ber 2008 figure in Department of Health and Human Services
       Office of Inspector General, *Adverse Events in Hospitals: National
       Incidence Among Medicare Beneficiaries* (November 2010).
257   **an Intermountain executive has written:** Brent James and Lucy
       Savitz, "How Intermountain Trimmed Health Care Costs Through
       Robust Quality Improvement Efforts," *Health Affairs* (June 2011).
       "Unfortunately health care providers today are paid for precisely
       those care delivery episodes that quality improvement seeks to
       reduce. As Intermountain teams implemented clinical manage-
       ment, clinical outcomes improved and costs fell. However, our
       payments also fell—often even further than our operating costs.
       For example, although improvement in Intermountain's appropri-
       ate elective induction rates saved the citizens of Utah more than
       $50 million per year through reduced payments, Intermountain's
       costs fell by only about $41 million. Intermountain thus lost more
       than $9 million per year in operating margins."
258   **it's estimated that 13.5 million people:** Melanie Evans, "HSA,
       High Deductible Plans Growing: AHIP," ModernHealthcare.com,
       May 30, 2012.
261   **The travel companies responsible:** James Surowiecki, "Club Med,"
       The New Yorker (April 16, 2012).
261   **some American providers are themselves:** John Goodman, "An
       Online Market for Medical Care," *Health Alerts*, February 29, 2012.
264   **PinnacleCare:** See http://www.pinnaclecare.com/about and Eliza-
       beth Ody, "Wealthy Families Skip Waiting Rooms with Concierge
       Medical Plans," Bloomberg News, March 16, 2012.
269   **Roughly two-thirds of Americans:** Pew Internet Survey Project,
       February 2012.
269   **WebMD, the most successful:** Figures on site traffic in this para-
       graph are from Compete.com.
269   **a recent study suggested:** PwC Health Research Institute report,
       quoted in LATimes.com, April 17, 2012.
270   **an estimated seventeen million Americans:** Laura Landro, "The
       Growing Clout of Online Patient Groups," *Wall Street Journal*,
       June 13, 2007.

273 **"In 1956, the world was full"**: Marc Levinson, *The Box: How the Shipping Container Made the World Smaller and the World Economy Bigger* (Princeton, N.J.: Princeton University Press, 2006), 3.

276 **Topol's book provides:** Eric Topol, *The Creative Destruction of Medicine: How the Digital Revolution Will Create Better Health Care* (New York: Basic Books, 2012).

CHAPTER 11 *Transition*

282 **The 2011 RAND study:** Melinda Beeuwkes Buntin, Amelia M. Haviland, Roland McDevitt, and Neeraj Sood, "Healthcare Spending and Preventive Care in High-Deductible and Consumer-Directed Health Plans," *American Journal of Managed Care* 17, no. 3 (March 2011): 222–30. Note this study is of beneficiary behavior in 2004 and 2005. See also Amelia M. Haviland, Neeraj Sood, Roland McDevitt, and M. Susan Marquis, "How Do Consumer-Directed Health Plans Affect Vulnerable Populations?" *Forum for Health Economics and Policy* 14, no. 2 (April 2011): 1–23.

298 **During that decade:** See http://www.rand.org/pubs/rgs_dissertations /RGSD172/RGSD172.ch1.pdf.

299 **The U.S. government will spend:** See http://www.kff.org/insurance /snapshot/oecd042111.cfm.

AFTERWORD *Mae West Didn't Know Health Care*

303 **roughly eight million:** See www.realtytrac.com; Les Christie, "Nearly 25% of All Mortgages Are Underwater," CNNMoney, February 24, 2010.

303 **1.2 million residential construction workers:** Kathryn J. Byun, "The U.S. Housing Bubble and Bust: Impacts on Employment," *Monthly Labor Review* (December 2010).

APPENDIX 2 *Déjà Vu*

321 **one in every twenty patients:** Surveys showing a wide variation are presented in Institute of Medicine, *Preventing Medication Errors* (2007).

330 **"Americans use preventive services":** Robert Pear, "Health Plans Must Provide Some Tests at No Cost," *New York Times,* July 14, 2010.

332 **In just the past year:** Robert Pear, "G.A.O. Calls Test Project by Medicare Costly Waste," *New York Times,* April 23, 2012; Jordan Rau, "Effort to Pay Hospitals Based on Quality Didn't Cut Death Rates, Study Finds," Kaiser Health News, March 28, 2012; A. M.

Ryan, B. K. Nallamothu, and J. B. Dimick, "Medicare's Public Reporting Initiative on Hospital Quality Had Modest or No Impact on Mortality from Three Key Conditions," *Health Affairs* 31, no. 3 (March 2012): 585–92.

APPENDIX 3 *Shifting the Government's Focus to Better Health*

336 **Here are amounts spent:** See opensecrets.org, a service of the Center for Responsive Politics.

339 **For 2009, the fatal accident rate:** See http://www.bts.gov /publications/national_transportation_statistics/html/table_02 _09.html.

340 **The U.S. government will spend:** See http://www.nih.gov/about /director/budgetrequest/NIH_BIB_020911.pdf.

346 **Current estimates are that it takes:** Christopher Paul Adams and Van Vu Brantner, "Spending on New Drug Development," *Health Economics* 19, no. 2 (February 2010): 130–41.

348 **it's hard for small companies:** "As recently as 2005, more than two-thirds of medical practices were physician-owned—a share that had been relatively constant for many years, the Medical Group Management Association says. But within three years, that share dropped below 50 percent, and analysts say the slide has continued" (Gardiner Harris, "More Doctors Giving Up Private Practices," *New York Times,* March 25, 2010).

349 **The growing cost of being in private practice:** See http://money.cnn .com/2012/01/20/smallbusiness/doctor_loans/index.htm.

349 **Roughly four hundred hospitals have merged:** Thomas C. Brown Jr., Krist A. Werling, Barton C. Walker, Rex J. Burgdorfer, and J. Jordan Shields, "Current Trends in Hospital Mergers and Acquisitions," *Healthcare Financial Management* (March 2012); American Hospital Association, *TrendWatch Chartbook 2012.*

A NOTE ABOUT THE AUTHOR

David Goldhill is president and chief executive officer of GSN, which operates a U.S. cable television network seen in more than 75 million homes and is one of the world's largest digital games companies. He is a member of the board of directors of The Leapfrog Group, an employer-sponsored organization dedicated to hospital safety and transparency. Goldhill graduated from Harvard University with a BA in history and holds an MA in history from New York University.

A NOTE ON THE TYPE

This book was set in Minion, a typeface produced by the Adobe Corporation specifically for the Macintosh personal computer, and released in 1990. Designed by Robert Slimbach, Minion combines the classic characteristics of old-style faces with the full complement of weights required for modern typesetting.

Typeset by Scribe,
Philadelphia, Pennsylvania

Printed and bound by Berryville Graphics,
Berryville, Virginia

Designed by Cassandra J. Pappas